RESEARCH BOARD
THE INSTITUTE OF
CHARTERED
ACCOUNTANTS
IN ENGLAND & WALES

NEW WORKS IN ACCOUNTING HISTORY

Richard P. Brief, *Series Editor*

Leonard N. Stern School of Business
New York University

RESEARCH BOARD
THE INSTITUTE OF
CHARTERED
ACCOUNTANTS
IN ENGLAND & WALES

Accounting Innovation

Municipal Corporations 1835–1935

Hugh M. Coombs
and
John Richard Edwards

Garland Publishing, Inc.
New York and London 1996

Library of Congress Cataloging-in-Publication Data

Coombs, Hugh M. (Hugh Malcolm)
Accounting innovation : municipal corporations 1835–1935 / Hugh M. Coombs and John Richard Edwards.
p. cm. — (New works in accounting history)
Includes bibliographical references and index.
ISBN 0-8153-2244-5
1. Municipal corporations—Great Britain—Accounting—History. 2. Municipal corporations—Great Britain—Auditing—History. 3. Municipal finance—Great Britain—Accounting—History.
I. Edwards, J.R. II. Title. III. Series.
HJ9779.G7C66 1995 95–33793
CIP

All volumes printed on acid-free, 250-year-life paper.
Manufactured in the United States of America.

Design by Marisel Tavarez

CONTENTS

TABLES AND FIGURES

ABBREVIATIONS

BPP	British Parliamentary Papers
CTAI	The Corporate Treasurers' and Accountants' Institute
DEB	Double entry bookkeeping
IMTA	The Institute of Municipal Treasurers and Accountants
ICAEW	The Institute of Chartered Accountants in England and Wales
LGA	The Local Government Act
LGB	The Local Government Board
MCA	The Municipal Corporations Act
PHA	Public Health Act
Proceedings	Proceedings of the Annual Meeting of the Corporate Treasurers' and Accountants' Institute, 1886-1900 Proceedings of the Annual Meeting of the Institute of Municipal Treasurers and Accountants, 1901 onwards

PREFACE

The Municipal Corporations Act 1835 created the modern municipal corporation out of the ancient borough and, as part of the endeavour to ensure proper regulation, it introduced requirements for statutory accountability. During the remainder of the nineteenth century, municipal corporations grew from small-scale organisations administering a limited range of services through the borough fund to massive entities responsible not only for the health and well-being of local inhabitants but also, in many cases, the management of significant water, gas, electricity and tramway undertakings. At a time when many industries continued to be dominated by the unincorporated enterprise, municipal corporations were major employers within local communities through which were channelled substantial financial and physical resources.

This book examines the previously neglected accounting implications of these developments and places them within the social and organisational contexts in which the events took place. We chart the major changes that occurred in the range of financial reports published, as they were expanded from single sheets of paper to bound documents comprising hundreds of pages. The content of these accounts are examined in terms of the financial data reported and the valuation procedures employed. The struggle which took place between various groups keen to obtain appointment as borough auditor is discussed in depth, and comparisons are made, where appropriate, between accountability within the private and local government sectors.

We identify the changes that took place and also why they occurred, and find much to commend Sowerby's colourful assessment that 'Their practices outran their theory and later theory developed out of practice' (1985: 4). We also identify the individuals and organisations responsible for implementing accounting change, and give particular emphasis to the respective roles of regulation and market forces in the transition from one method of financial reporting to another.

The period 1835-1935 merits particular attention in view of the fact that it saw the development of the structure of local government which remains broadly intact today and also the growth of modern financial reporting procedures. The late nineteenth century is generally acknowledged as the period when modern financial reporting practices became firmly established - that is, the 'British contribution' to accounting development. The part played by private sector-based companies in this process is widely recognised, if under-researched, but the role of local authorities has previously been overlooked, save for the work of Rowan Jones who pioneered research in this area.

The heavy involvement of municipal corporations in 'trading' activities meant that they had to face similar problems to those encountered by public sector-based companies. An investigation of the affairs of municipal corporations can therefore be expected to throw light on developments in other organisational entities, and chapter 9 compares and contrasts the way in which companies and corporations handled problems of accountability.

The research is based on the contents of government reports, the substantial contemporary literature which dates from the mid-1870s and the archival records of five municipal corporations - Birmingham, Bradford, Bristol, Cardiff and Manchester. References is also made to the accounting practices of other municipal corporations, based on our examination of the existing literature, in order to give this study greater depth and coverage. We were fortunate, for the purpose of this study, to discover the vast range of data which has been preserved for municipal corporations; a situation which is in sharp contrast to that relating to most private sector-based companies.

We have benefited from the generous access allowed to the records of the five corporations, and particularly wish to acknowledge the co-operation of Mr John Williams, City Archivist, Bristol, Mr D. James, District Archivist and Rebecca Beswick, Archives Assistant, West Yorkshire Archive Service, Bradford, Mr N. Kingsley, City Archivist, Birmingham, Jill Taylor, City Hall, Cardiff, and Lynne Burrows, City Hall, Manchester. We are also grateful to the Research Board of the Institute of Chartered Accountants in England and Wales for the financial support which made this research possible and to Sandra Edwards and Lesley Ingram for typing the manuscript.

University of Glamorgan — Hugh M. Coombs
Cardiff Business School — John Richard Edwards

Acknowledgements

'Capital Accounting in Municipal Corporations 1884-1914. Theory and Practice' by Hugh M. Coombs and John Richard Edwards: Financial Accountability and Management, Autumn 1992, is reproduced with amendment as chapter 6.

'Companies, Corporations and Accounting Change, 1835-1933. A Comparative Study', by John Richard Edwards: Accounting and Business Research, Winter 1992, is re-printed with amendment as chapter 9.

'Record Keeping in Municipal Corporations: A Triumph for Double-entry Book-keeping', by Hugh M. Coombs and John Richard Edwards: Accounting, Business and Financial History, March 1994, copyright 1994, Routledge, is reprinted with permission and amendment as chapter 4.

'The Accountability of Municipal Corporations', by Hugh M. Coombs and John Richard Edwards: Abacus, March 1993, is re-printed, in part, in chapters 2 & 3.

'The financial reporting practices of British municipal corporations 1835-1933: A study in accounting innovation', by Hugh M. Coombs and John Richard Edwards: Accounting and Business Research, Winter 1992, is re-printed with amendment as chapter 5.

INTRODUCTION

The nature of accountability

According to Bird, the accountability of an agent to his principal involves two fundamental features: the need for the agent to 'render an "account" of his dealings with the stewardship resources, and [to] submit to an examination (usually known as an "audit") of that account by or on behalf of the person or body to whom he is accountable' (1973: 2).

It is possible, of course, for an agent to serve more than one principal, at the same time, and a good example is a local authority which is accountable to central government for its use of government grants, local inhabitants for the application of council tax proceeds and creditors for loans raised. This has given rise to the development of a framework of accountability and control which comprises the following five main elements: the duty to make returns to central government; central control over the levels of capital and revenue expenditure; statutory control over the management of local authority debt and its repayment; the duty to provide annual reports to elected members, council tax payers and local electors; and the external audit. The first three provisions are principally concerned with enabling central government to monitor and control local operations, while the last two are directed, first and foremost, towards protecting the interests of local inhabitants.[1] It is the last two aspects of accountability that are the subject of this investigation, which is undertaken in relation to the activities of municipal corporations covering the period 1835-1935.

The organisational entity

Our choice of the municipal corporation as the basis for this study has been motivated by our conviction that these economic entities are of particular relevance to our understanding of the development of accounting practice but, to date, have received little attention. The municipal corporations were the subject of radical reform in 1835 and, over the next 60-70 years, grew into enormous 'trading undertakings' which, in addition to providing a wide range of civic amenities, became responsible for the supply of water, gas and electricity and the provision of transport. The leading municipal corporations rivalled in size the largest limited liability companies of their day, and undertook activities which gave rise to comparable accounting problems during a period - the late nineteenth century - when the fundamental features of modern day financial reporting concepts and practices were developed (Yamey, 1960).

The lack of interest shown by the recent literature[2] in their accountability is unfortunate in view of the significant role played by the municipal corporation in the economic development of Britain, particularly from about 1870 onwards. Some figures might help to underline this point. In 1905 there were 10 municipal corporations with loans outstanding in respect of tramways, water, gas and electricity of over £4 million: Birmingham, Bradford, Bristol, Leeds, Liverpool, Manchester, Nottingham, Sheffield, Cardiff and Leicester (BPP 1906, ci: 607-11). Treating loans outstanding as the broad equivalent of the paid up capital (shares and loans) of registered companies, two municipal corporations in the provinces (Manchester, £20.1 million and Liverpool, £17.6 million) were larger than the Imperial Tobacco Co. Ltd, £17.5 million - the top company in Payne's (1967) list of the 52 largest British manufacturing companies in 1905. Indeed, if we take only the loans outstanding in respect of municipal corporations' 'trading services', three boroughs (Birmingham, Manchester and Liverpool) would feature in the top six of a revised list of largest British 'companies'. On a broader basis, the total expenditure of municipal corporations in 1904/5 was £95.1 million, which is roughly equivalent to about £5 billion at 1995 prices.[3]

The period selected for study is one representing 'what historians recognise to be the formative period of continuous progress in developing the United Kingdom's system of local government' (Jones, 1991: 81). It was also a period which saw the development of a financial reporting framework for local authorities which remains in place today, despite the abolition of the municipal corporation in 1974. The particular importance of these institutions is referred to by Carson Roberts, then probably the leading authority on local authority financial affairs, writing towards the end of the period covered by this study: 'It is only right and fitting that the municipal system should in all respects give us a lead as to how accounts should be kept; and undoubtedly it is rapidly advancing to this position' (1930: 445).

Research sources

The research is based on the substantial body of contemporary literature which includes the following main sources.

* Professional journals. *The Accountant* and *Financial Circular* debated a wide range of accounting matters in great depth.
* Government reports. These have been used extensively, but particular mention may be made of two items. The first decade of the twentieth century saw the appointment of two important government investigations, motivated by a determination to ensure the security and effective use of public money: the Joint Select Committee of the House of Lords and House of Commons on Municipal Trading, which reported in 1900 and 1903 (referred to in this report as the 1900 Select Committee and the 1903 Select Committee) and the Departmental Committee appointed to inquire into the Accounts of Local Authorities (1907 Departmental Committee).
* Municipal archives. The archival material available in respect of the following five municipal corporations: Birmingham, Bradford, Bristol, Cardiff and Manchester.[4]

The municipalities dealt with in this study comprise a reasonable sample in terms of: longevity (Bristol and Cardiff are both ancient boroughs, whereas the remainder reflect growing industrialisation during the nineteenth century); geographical spread (two northern boroughs, one from the midlands and two from the south); industrial specialisation (Burdett, 1890, lists the following: Birmingham, hardware; Bradford, wool; Bristol, shipping and manufacturing; Cardiff, shipping, coal and iron; Manchester, cotton); and range of trading services supplied (Birmingham, Bradford and Manchester purchased or established works to provide all four major services - water, gas, electricity and tramways; Cardiff supplied all except gas, while Bristol supplied only electricity). In addition, Bristol had responsibility for its docks from 1848 and Manchester built its ambitious ship canal in the 1890's.

Accounting change

The most effective mechanism for achieving accounting change - regulation or market forces - is a topic of contemporary importance and interest, and we hope to be able to contribute to this debate in view of the growing tendency to cite historical evidence to support a favoured stance. For example, Watts (1977) argues that voluntary disclosure and audit of financial information occurred in nineteenth-century Britain before the re-introduction of regulations by the Companies Act 1900. On the basis of this and similar work (Leftwich, 1983; Watts and Zimmerman, 1979; Watts and Zimmerman, 1986), there has been developed a literature which sees market forces as the most efficient mechanism for ensuring that directors (the agents) keep shareholders and creditors (the principals) well informed. Regulations are the subject of criticism on a number of grounds, e.g. they are not cost effective, and are seen to create a demand for accounting theories (excuses) designed to justify the self-interest of a particular pressure group.

In a recent paper Parker has argued, correctly in our view, that this is an unduly restrictive view of nineteenth-century accounting developments. He sees certain economically significant categories of company - railways, public utilities and financial institutions - as subject to regulation for a variety of inter-related reasons which include: the desire to control monopoly power; the price to be paid for privileges granted by the state; and the general need to ensure financial stability in the case of such institutions (1990: 54-8). This study therefore focuses on the process of accounting change within a further, unexplored, class of organisational entity.

The relative importance of these two mechanisms - regulation and market forces - as a means of explaining changes in the accountability of municipal corporations is a central theme of this study, although we question whether these factors, either individually or in combination, provide an adequate explanation. Another (closely related) theme is that the development of accountability is a gradual process which has occurred in response to changing social and environmental conditions. Until quite recently, the range and level of services provided by local authorities had risen both continuously and dramatically, and this had increased the need for reliable accounting information as a means of monitoring progress and change. In our efforts to identify and evaluate these events, we find little support for the historical theory of 'discontinuities' in relation to accounting development; we are more attracted to the 'gradualist' school of thought which argues that even dramatic events which, at first sight, appear totally unrelated to what has gone before, when examined more closely turn out to be no more than major landmarks in the transition from one state of affairs to another.

The idea that change can be identified with a single causal factor has obvious appeal - if it were true, the chance of the researcher finding answers to questions which puzzle them would be significantly increased - but this is not, perhaps, the way things happen within a social science such as accountancy. We therefore have much sympathy with the view that

> accounting cannot function in isolation from the social context in which it operates. [For example] In the past, the rise of a political

> interest in institutional accountability provided the context for a vast expansion of the audit function in both the public and private sector (Hopwood et al, 1990: 51)

Even where the influence of societal factors is recognised, there remain diametrically opposed views concerning the motivations of those associated with the process of accounting change. Accounting practices can be seen as 'pragmatically derived from the needs of accountable organisations or individuals' (Funnell, 1990: 319), and thus portray accounting as a value-free and neutral function (for example Chua, 1986; Peasnell, 1978). A competing view is that accounting is value-laden and dominated by self-interest (for example, Tinker et al, 1982), with the accounting process 'a captive of dominant power groups who see it as a means by which they can not only consolidate their position of influence but also extend their power base to augment their wealth and power' (Funnell, 1990: 319).

Each of the above theories, and others, undoubtedly possess explanatory potential and, at particular points in time, one set of ideas may better describe the process of accounting change than the other. In this study, however, we will show that, in the long run, change is brought about by a combination of the above factors; with at the one extreme an altruistic desire to inform ratepayers about the disposition of their 'investment', and at the other a determination to obtain a monopoly of well-paid work irrespective of the relative merits of the services available. This study will also show that there are a myriad of influences responsible for observed changes, some competing and others complimentary - and it is quite possible that the contribution of certain factors is insufficiently prominent to permit identification. We will also show that even those factors which can be identified are numerous, and it is an enormously difficult task to assess their relative importance.

Agents of change

This brings us to the question of precisely how change is brought about. The list of principal 'change agents' will be seen to include, of course, the regulatory bodies, but also the accountants, auditors, local authority members and officers, and the professional literature. A few introductory remarks will help to set the scene.

The rapid development of economic activity, within both government and the private sector, during the nineteenth century, gave rise to the need for financial record keeping, reporting and control on an unprecedented scale. The nineteenth-century accountant was equal to the challenge and, eager for new work, probably saw no boundaries between private and public sector-based organisations. The career of David Chadwick illustrates their willingness to become heavily involved in business and politics. He was treasurer of the Corporation of Salford 1844-60 and then went into private practice where he was extremely active as both a company promoter and auditor of companies and municipal corporations. As a liberal MP between 1868-80 he campaigned for company law reform and, in particular, favoured the introduction of a requirement for companies to prepare accounts conforming to a standardised format (Parker, 1980b: 208-9; Cottrell, 1984).

Chadwick's political career was certainly not typical, for an accountant, but the few entries[5] for accountants in the *Dictionary of Business Biography* (Jeremy, 1984-6) do show that Edwin Guthrie (Bywater, 1984) and Sir John Sutherland Harmood-Banner (Davenport-Hines, 1985) were also actively involved in local politics during the nineteenth century and beyond. The *Dictionary* sheds rather more light on the extent to which industrialists moved into the public limelight to achieve greater influence and social esteem. The first volume (A-C) contains upwards of 200 entries for subjects whose business careers occurred, in the main, during the period covered by this study. The entries, which are good but not comprehensive, show seventy-four businessmen as having a significant involvement in local and/or central government, including thirty-seven MP's, twenty-eight mayors (seven of whom also became MP's) and sixteen other council members. We suspect that some of these individuals, although principally concerned with more weighty matters, were well equipped to help the transfer of accounting practices from one sector to the other.

The professionalisation of accountancy, during the nineteenth century, might be expected to have helped bring about improvements in the general standard of accounting and auditing, and members of the newly formed bodies were in a good position to disseminate innovations among the organisations they served. Provincial societies were established in certain Scottish towns in the 1850's, and this process spread to England in the 1870's with a number of the newly formed local societies soon merging to form the first national body - the Institute of Chartered Accountants in England and Wales (ICAEW) - in 1880. A little later (1885) the Corporate Treasurers' and Accountants' Institute (CTAI) was established (renamed the Institute of Municipal Treasurers and Accountants in 1901 - IMTA - and the Chartered Institute of Public Finance and Accountancy in 1973).

A number of the leading professional bodies published their own accounting journals to act as a focal point for debate and as a vehicle for official pronouncements; the notable private sector journals were *The Accountant* (first published 1874 for chartered accountants) the *Incorporated Accountants Journal* (1889, for the Society of Accountants and Auditors (Incorporated)), and The *Accountant's Magazine* (1897, in Scotland). The official organ for local authority accountants, *Financial Circular*, was first issued in 1896 (renamed *Local Government Finance* 1924). These publications were important media for the criticism of prevailing accounting practices, and for bringing together accountants from different backgrounds to discuss various ways of improving general standards.

The determination of private sector-based professional accounting bodies to obtain a share of local government work for their members is first illustrated by the ICAEW's attempt, in 1888, to get written into the Local Government Bill a provision confining appointments to the position of local government auditor to members of the ICAEW. This naturally provoked opposition from the other senior contemporary accounting body, the Incorporated Society of Accountants and Auditors, and the complete failure of this initiative might be partly attributable to the public squabble which ensued (Stacey, 1954: 25-6). We will see that the professional accountant's determination to obtain a share of local authority work remained strong throughout the period covered by this study.

Objectives of study

Against this background, the purposes of this study may be summarised as follows:

* To examine developments (between 1835 and 1935) in the form and content of financial reports published by municipal corporations in a stewardship environment, and the auditing requirements attaching to those reports.
* To understand the accounting practices presently followed by local authorities.
* To examine, in depth, both the general forces at work within society leading to accounting change, and the specific factors which proved crucial at various corporations at particular points in time.
* To explore differences between the accounting practices of municipal corporations and limited companies.

Pioneering research into the development of UK local authority accounting, in general, has been undertaken by Rowan Jones (1985a; 1985b; 1986; 1989; 1992), who believes that the purpose of these techniques 'is to impose a financial control on elected authorities, by government, through statute law' (Jones, 1992: 42). This is a plausible explanation, and we would certainly agree with Friedman's related conclusion that, in order to understand the form and limitations of regulations, 'we have to understand our own legal culture'

(1985: 113). Moreover, the sheer volume of legislation and statutory instruments examined during the course of this study is impressive, and we have found much evidence to support the idea that accounting regulations were an essential component in the develoment of local authority financial reporting

Important differences between this study and the work of Jones are that we demonstrate how the experience of municipal corporations led to the general advancement of financial reporting practices within local government, and we explore a wider range of societal forces as having played their part in the process of accounting change. This is achieved by examining the practices employed by individual municipal corporations, and considering the influence exerted by particular individuals - municipal officers, elected council members, amateur auditors, professional accountants, etc. - and the profession in general. Importantly, this shows that, almost always, statute or statutory regulation followed actions taken by the profession, while new innovations were, in turn, first adopted by one or another corporation in response to personal initiative, drive and determination.[6]

Undeniably statutory regulation provided a framework which initially, for example, established the fund as the cornerstone of the accounting process, but this study shows that authorities pushed forward the boundaries of accounting development from this base. While it can be argued that the accounting practices of some categories of local authority (notably those involved with the administration of the Poor Law) were significantly affected by central government regulation, the power-houses for accounting development were the major municipal corporations which do not fit the simple model of statutory control dominating accounting developments.[7]

Structure of text

Municipal corporations were just one of a number of types of local authority which were established to supply essential local services. Chapters 2 and 3 therefore place municipal corporations in the wider context by examining, first, the nature of, and reasons for, the development of different categories of local authorities and, second, the regulatory framework which applied to them. Chapter 4 briefly reviews methods of accounting and record keeping employed by boroughs pre-1835 and then moves on to chronicle the transition from charge\discharge accounting to double entry bookkeeping after that date. Chapters 5-8 explore, in depth, the preparation and audit of the financial statements prepared and published by municipal corporations. The practices employed at particular points in time are described, changes identified and explanations sought. We will see that a prominent, and recurring, feature is the struggle which took place between various pressure groups keen to ensure that developments followed their preferred pattern. In chapter 9 we contrast the development of accountability within municipal corporations and the private sector-based limited companies, again seeking causes for differential rates of progress. In the final chapter we review our findings and present our conclusions.

NOTES

1 We recognise that the district audit was also an instrument of central control, being extended to various sectors of local government when central government grants reached a significant level.

2 The work of Rowan Jones is a notable exception.

3 The 1993 equivalent of the 1905 figure taken from 'Statistical Abstracts for the UK' (BPP 1909, c: 1) is obtained using indices contained in 'Back to an Age of Falling Prices', *The Economist*, 13 July 1974: 62, for the period up to 1974 and, afterwards, figures published monthly in *Accountancy*.

4 The archives for the five municipal corporations are located respectively at: Birmingham Central Library; West Yorkshire Archive Service, Bradford; City of Bristol Record Office; Cardiff City Hall; Manchester Public Library and Manchester City Hall.

5 A more extensive coverage of 'early' professional accountants, though in some cases the entries are necessarily short, can be found in Parker, 1980a.

6 Some initiatives, such as the standard form of accounting adopted by local authorities, are non statutory requirements even today.

7 Even the authorities regarded by Jones as being more directly controlled by central government (the District Councils) (1992: 123) were referred to by *The Accountant* as follows: 'the Accounts Order of 1880 ... has been more honoured in the breach than in the observance by many authorities which keep their accounts well' (1909: 857).

2

STRUCTURE OF LOCAL AUTHORITIES

Early administrative developments

In Britain during the Dark Ages, a limited range of community services were provided locally. With the emergence of a united England, beginning in the reign of Alfred (871-99), the separation of functions between central and local government gradually began to develop. In medieval times the sheriff acted as the local representative of the King in a particular county, and he possessed considerable powers. An important contribution made by the office of sheriff, from the King's viewpoint, was that it helped limit the power of the barons. The sheriff presided over the shire (county) courts. He also had responsibility for: collecting taxes and paying the proceeds over to the Exchequer; military organisation in times of war; administering a rudimentary policing system; and bringing prisoners to justice.

Successive monarchs became increasingly uneasy about the extent of the sheriff's powers and, from the thirteenth century, they began to transfer some of his powers to justices of the peace (JPs). The first JPs were Knights given responsibility for maintaining law and order and, over the years, they became responsible for what might be described as county-based government. Their judicial duties extended to the petty sessions, special sessions and quarter sessions, while their administrative duties covered such matters as the granting of licenses for public houses, controlling the administration of the poor law, the building of bridges and roads, and the management of prisons and houses of correction. Independently of these 'county' based developments, services were provided at the level of the town and parish.

It was in the twelfth century the Crown started to issue Royal Charters to certain towns, usually in recognition of financial or military assistance. This gave the town a 'borough' status and contained arrangements, which varied from one charter to another, for its local government. The powers of government were placed in the hands of a council, which might be elected by the freemen or might be self-perpetuating, initially based on the membership of a guild, a group of merchants, or simply a special court of favoured individuals. The leader of the borough was the Mayor, and all boroughs had the right to return members to Parliament. The first boroughs included Southampton and London. Their number increased slowly whilst in other areas the sheriff retained his authority.

Following the dissolution of the monasteries, in the 1530's, the parish (an ecclesiastical unit whose boundaries usually coincided with those of the feudal manor) gradually achieved recognition as the focal point for making provision for the relief of the poor. The most prominent parish officers were the churchwarden (whose duties in the main part were ecclesiastic rather than administrative), the overseer of the poor and the surveyor of the highways. Money was raised mainly on a voluntary basis from wealthy local residents, though it sometimes proved necessary to elicit statutory support for a degree of compulsion. By 1597 the cost of poor relief was sufficiently great to justify the introduction of the system of local rating. The Poor Relief Act gave clear statutory support for the idea of the parish as the area to be used for the purpose of levying the rate.

In the middle of the eighteenth century England and Wales still consisted mainly of numerous small rural communities, with a rudimentary system of local government - at the level of the county, town and parish - continuing to cope in a broadly satisfactorily manner with the provision of local requirements. During the industrial revolution (1760-1830) the system was placed under intolerable pressure by the rapid development of urbanised areas. Large numbers of houses were built quickly, producing sanitation and health problems. Some of the more progressive boroughs obtained private Acts of Parliament to enable them to supply essential services; in certain other areas applications were made to Parliament for the appointment of commissioners and trustees to do a similar job. In Birmingham, for example, the provision of local services dates from 1769 when commissioners were appointed to improve, clean and light the 'street, ways, lanes, and passages' of the town (Bunce, 1878: 75).

A number of disparate groups began to emphasise the need to provide improved services during the second quarter of the nineteenth century. Their motives differed. Socialist thinkers argued that the equality of man demanded an improvement in the working and living conditions of the low paid; while right wing politicians believed that conditions should be improved, but in this case mainly because the social order was otherwise likely to come under threat. Reform was resisted by industrialists who believed that a significant increase in public expenditure would damage the economy by placing additional burdens on business.

Development of the local authority structure, 1834-1935

The present structure of local and central government is considered to be mainly a product of the thinking of Jeremy Bentham (1748-1832), although the process of its creation was not completed until 62 years after his death. His philosophy was that government action should be designed to produce the greatest good for the greatest number. He believed this objective could be achieved by putting local affairs under the control of an elected body responsible for an identified geographical area. These local authorities were in turn required to be answerable to a central authority in order to ensure that they did not take actions which were detrimental to the interests of people in the country as a whole.

An important event which focussed attention on the need to develop a broader and more coherent network of local services was the cholera epidemic of 1831. This disaster underlined, in particular, the dangers of uncontrolled and unregulated urban development. One difficulty faced by the House of Lords Committee (1831) set up to examine the problem was how to obtain accurate accounts of the vast annual sums raised for the support of the poor. It reported that wide variations in the schedules prescribed by Parliament made it difficult to frame the accounts and also to make a 'just comparison' between the different items of expenditure, or any estimate of the extent of its misapplication in different periods. There was also an observed delay in the submission of accounts to Parliament and the committee issued directions for a Bill to be prepared containing a prescribed form of accounts for the purpose of parish returns. Further investigation was considered desirable and, in 1833, a Royal Commission was appointed.

The commission's work was largely conducted by Edwin Chadwick who was a pupil and friend of Jeremy Bentham, and, latterly, one of his secretaries. Just 32 when Bentham died, Chadwick devoted his working life to giving practical effect to Bentham's ideas on the organisation and operation of local authorities. Chadwick was appointed an assistant commissioner of the inquiry into the working of the poor laws in 1832. Promoted to commissioner in 1833, he made a substantial contribution towards drafting the 1834 report.

The Commission's Report identified the following checks against bias or fraud on the part of churchwardens and overseers: the fact that they were ratepayers themselves; the requirement to submit accounts annually to the vestry and have them allowed by JPs. The effectiveness of these checks was criticised as was the way that the overseers carried out their duties. The accounts were dismissed as 'a mere daybook of receipt and expenditure' (BPP 1834, xxvii: 179), and receiving only 'a cursory examination' (BPP 1834, xxvii: 180). To deal with these matters the commissioners recommended the establishment of a central board with power to 'take measures for the general adoption of a complete, clear, and, as far as may be practicable, uniform systems of accounts' (BPP 1834, xxvii: 184).

The report's main proposals were implemented by the Poor Law Amendment Act 1834 passed roughly at the end of an era (1689-1835) during which, according to Sidney and Beatrice Webb, 'the country possessed the largest measure of self government, when its local administrators were most effectively free from superior control, either of the National Executive, Parliament or the law courts' (quoted in Burdon, 1986: 2). The main objective of the new measure was to bring under control expenditure on poor relief[1] and counter growing fears among landowners that, otherwise, consequential increases in rates would erode the farmers' profits and the landlords' rents. An important practical reason for transferring the responsibility for poor relief from JPs to an anonymous administrative unit - the Poor Law Commission - was to dissociate personalities from what were likely to prove unpopular policies. As Nassau Senior put it, so that the reform might be enforced by 'those who had no stacks to burn' (quoted in Hammond, 1935: 44).

To help control expenditure the following strict principles were laid down: 'no relief except for destitution' which meant that relief should be granted, not to alleviate poverty, but only where immediate assistance was required to prevent either a complete breakdown of health or death; and 'less eligibility', which dictated that relief granted should leave the recipient in a condition less desirable than that of the worst paid workers.[2] Modern features of the new organisational structure were: a centralised department with executive control; and a network of local boards of guardians to administer the poor law for specified geographical areas in accordance with regulations laid down by statute.

The fifty years following the passage of the Poor Law Amendment Act 1834 saw the development of a range of local government services, including public health, sanitation, highways, education, lighting and a wide range of other amenities. A feature of this period was the establishment of separate institutions, sometimes called 'boards' to provide the services deemed desirable.

An important development, in this context, was the establishment of the General Board of Health (1848-58), to deal with unhealthy living conditions. Its origin may be found in the work of the Poor Law Board which, although principally concerned with the administration of Poor Law, began, with government encouragement, to examine the 'causes of destitution and death' (Newman, 1935: 158). The inadequacy of sanitary conditions is vividly illustrated in Chadwick's famous *Report on the Sanitary Condition of the Labouring Population of Great Britain* which concluded that 'the annual loss of life from filth and bad ventilation are greater than the loss from death or wounds in any wars in which this country has been engaged in modern times' (quoted in Newman, 1935: 160). The need for government action was brought to the attention of the cabinet by the home secretary, Sir James Graham. This led to the appointment of a Royal Commission (1845), which investigated a sample of fifty large towns, and made recommendations which led to the passage of the Public Health Act (PHA) 1848. According to Jennings, the Act 'provided for the greatest measure of central control since the Poor Law Amendment Act of 1834' (1935a: 438).

Under the central General Board of Health, local boards were established in certain areas - when located in the borough the town council served as the Board of Health - and made responsible for water, drainage, management of the streets, burial grounds, and the regulation of offensive trades. To finance their activities, they were authorised to levy a number of additional rates based on the poor law assessment. Because the Act depended on local initiative rather than centralised control, it was not particularly successful. The Local Government Act (LGA) 1858 disbanded the general board, whose responsibilities were split between the Privy Council and the Home Office. The powers to be exercised by local boards of health were at the same time amended and extended.[3]

A further separate development, beginning in the 1840's, was the passage of legislation designed to remove nuisances and prevent diseases. It indicates the piecemeal, experimental and *ad hoc* nature of contemporary legislation that these matters were treated separately from the public health legislation designed to tackle more general sanitary problems.

Many writers have been extremely critical of the creation of *ad hoc* bodies in what appears to have been a fairly haphazard manner. Others have pointed out, perhaps more fairly, that new and substantial problems were being faced for the first time - e. g. hazards caused by crowded and dirty living conditions in urban areas - in the absence of any real understanding of the causes of disease or the means by which they could be controlled. It is therefore possible to argue that a process which, with the benefit of hindsight, can be dismissed as a clumsy effort characterised by administrative chaos, should more generously be categorised as a necessary period of experimentation.

An important obstacle hindering the development of an improved scheme of local government is considered, by some, to be the fact that the topic never became one of burning interest to the public in general, nor the preoccupation of a major statesman. As Hammond puts it 'the men who were pushing for the reform of local government [between 1830-1880], men like Chadwick, Ashly, Normanby, Hume, Toynbee, Dickens, and Delane were pushing against a dead weight of apathy just because local government was not a party question or a question over which church fought chapel or landlord fought manufacturer' (Hammond, 1935: 40). However, the practice of appointing government committees or commissions to enquire into particular problems, a tradition began in the eighteenth century, aroused some concern in Parliament and in the press. It also enabled the views and ideas of contemporary experts to be canvassed. A possible drawback of this approach, however, was that it contributed towards the consideration of problems, in isolation, and helped produce the above patchwork of different solutions.

It was the Royal Sanitary Commission's Report (1871) that contained the first comprehensive survey of the state of English local government. The picture it presented was summarised by Goschen as follows: 'the truth is that we have a chaos as regards authorities, a chaos as regards rates, and a worse chaos than all as regards areas' (quoted in Hammond, 1935: 48). Acting on the recommendations of this and other committees, steps were taken, in the last quarter of the nineteenth century, to give full effect to the Bentham idea of the 'general purpose' authority. Acts of 1875, 1882, 1888, and 1894 established a coherent structure of councils, at district (rural and urban), borough, county borough and county level (see figure 2.1).

These Acts together set up what might be described as the 'dual system of local government'. Within each borough, the council of the borough or county borough was the sole general authority; elsewhere local government powers were shared between county councils, urban district councils and rural district councils. This 'dual system' imposed on counties or boroughs the obligation to provide services appropriate for larger geographically areas, while the duty to provide services appropriate for smaller geographical areas was imposed on the district councils. Finally, poor relief continued to be provided, on a local basis, by unions controlled by guardians of the poor.

Central government agencies

The provision of services, particularly at the level of county and parish, was monitored by a series of government agencies, starting in 1834 when the Poor Law Amendment Act made provision for the appointment of three fit persons to act as a Poor Law Commission to put into effect the provisions of the Act. Chadwick was naturally appointed secretary of this body, which was given the power to summon and examine witnesses and call for the production, on oath, of 'books, contracts, agreements, accounts, and writings' (s. 2). The Poor Law Commission was required to issue rules, orders and regulations for the relief of the poor, the government of workhouses, the education of children therein, for the apprenticing of children of poor persons, and for the guidance and control 'of all guardians, vestries, and parish officers, so far as relates to the management or the relief of the poor, and the keeping, examining, auditing, and allowing of accounts' (s. 15). It could also direct the overseers or

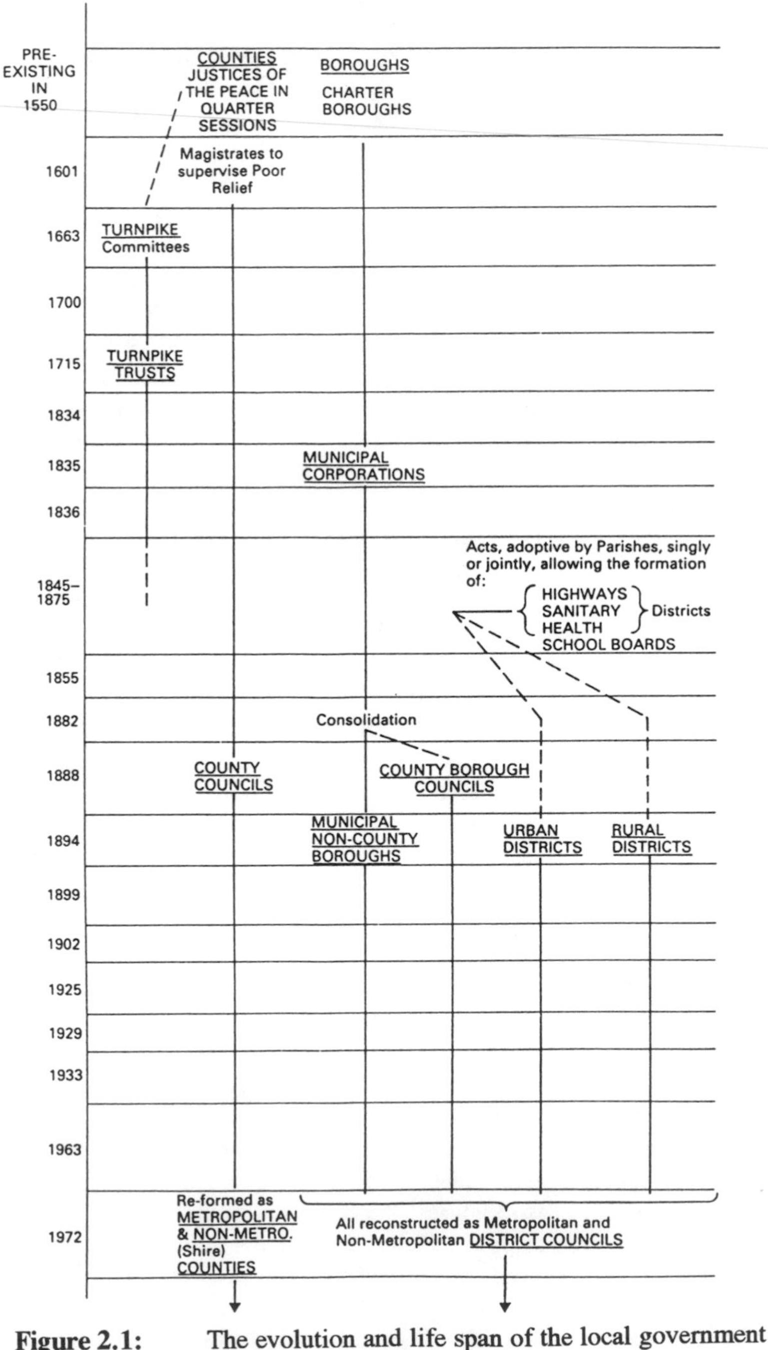

Figure 2.1: The evolution and life span of the local government authorities in England and Wales

Structure of Local Authorities

PARISHES			RELEVANT MAJOR STATUTES	PURPOSES
ECCLESIASTICAL PARISHES				
Care of Poor: Overseers to collect Rate			Relief of the Poor 1601	Consolidation of earlier provisions for Poor Relief and Rating: Decline of ancient HUNDREDS
			An Act for Repairing the Highways etc. 1663	The first TOLL ROAD – Wadesmill – under a Committee of Magistrates
Start of Parish Poor Law Incorporations			Various	Incorporations beginning with London and Bristol: Development of Turnpike Committees
			Various	Advent of Turnpikes under Trusts, independent of Magistrates
	POOR LAW UNIONS BOARDS OF GUARDIANS		Poor Law (Amendment) Act 1834	National system of locally elected *ad hoc* bodies
			Municipal Corporations Act 1835	First step in rationalisation of boroughs
	REGISTRATION DISTRICTS		Act for the Registration of Births, Marriages and Deaths 1836	An extension of the Guardians' duties, though not strictly a Poor Relief function
			Various Acts, especially Public Health Act 1875	The era of 'chaos of areas'
			Elementary Education Act 1870	Period of decline of Turnpike Trusts
		METROPOLITAN BOARD OF WORKS	Metropolis Management Act 1855	First of three major attempts to establish 'county type' structure for metropolis
			Municipal Corporations Act 1882	Consolidation in anticipation of forthcoming reforms
		LONDON COUNTY COUNCIL	Local Government Act 1888	Elective County Councils – end of administration by Magistrates: Creation of all-purpose County Boroughs
Administrative (RURAL) Parishes			Local Government Act 1894	Elective County District system (UDC's, RDC's, and N–CB's) established
		LONDON METROPOLITAN BOROUGHS	London Metropolitan Boroughs Act 1899	Creation of Metropolitan Boroughs
School Boards abolished			Education Act 1902	School Board duties transferred to local authorities
Overseers abolished			Rating and Valuation Act 1925	County Boroughs and County Districts created Rating Authorities
	Guardians abolished		Local Government Act 1929	County Councils and County Boroughs made Poor Law Auths.
			Local Government Act 1933	Consolidation of system of Counties, County Boroughs, County Districts, Parishes
		GREATER LONDON COUNCIL & LONDON BOROUGHS	London Government Act 1963	Material expansion and area re-organisation under GLC
Parishes retained			Local Government Act 1972	Drastic re-construction: Non-County and (All-purpose) County Boroughs abolished.

Source: Page (1985: 32-3)

guardians to appoint paid officers, including auditors, with such qualifications as it considered proper. The Poor Law Commission was not represented in Parliament and, therefore, not subject to its control, except in the sense that its initial mandate was for only five years and any general orders had to be laid before Parliament.

An order had the force of law, and was binding on all unions to which it was issued. If it was issued to only one union it was called a special order; if to two or more unions a general order. The new system came into operation piecemeal, with the Poor Law Commission issuing special orders to the overseers and boards of guardians of individual unions. Books and detailed forms of accounts, the form of the audit certificate, and the duties of the auditor were all prescribed. By 1842 nearly the whole of England had been brought under the operation of the Act, and the Poor Law Commission then recinded the separate orders and replaced them with general orders. These were first consolidated in 1847. Circulars issued by the Poor Law Commission were more in the nature of declarations of policy or exhortations which could not be enforced. However, they were generally complied with and to all intents and purposes had the same impact as a general order. The Poor Law Commission was required to submit to the Secretary of State, once a year, a report of its proceedings which was then laid before Parliament.

The powers (and responsibilities) of the Poor Law Commission were renewed at various intervals until, in 1847, they were transferred to a newly constituted Poor Law Board (Poor Laws Administration Act 1847, s. 10). The Poor Law Board consisted of a paid president (s. 8) and, as ex-officio members, the Lord President of the Council, the Lord Privy Seal, Her Majesty's Principal Secretary of State for the Home Department, and the Chancellor of the Exchequer (s. 2). Section 9 made it permissible for the president to be elected an MP. These changes automatically ensured representation in Parliament. They increased the possible influence of party politics, and also the degree of public accountability by giving MPs the opportunity to question one or more of the persons responsible for the administration of the poor law.

The Local Government Board (LGB) was established in 1871 to take over the activities of the Poor Law Board together with certain functions performed by the Secretary of State and the Privy Council concerning public health and local government (Local Government Board Act 1871, s. 2). The prescribed composition of the LGB was similar to that of the Poor Law Board (s. 3). Again the president was the only paid official. On establishment of the Ministry of Health in 1919 (Ministry of Health Act 1919), the new government department took over all the powers and duties of the LGB (s. 3), as well as that of various other bodies including the Board of Education.

Municipal corporations

Within the general framework of local authorities, described above, municipal corporations may be considered *sui generis*, deriving from the fact that these 'little republics' were self financing and its 'management' democratically elected. This had not always been the case. By the early nineteenth century there were about 180 boroughs which ranged from large cities such as Leeds, Nottingham, Bristol and Norwich to remote villages. It was at about this time that the description municipal corporation first began to be used although, up to 1835, the 'corporation' consisted simply of the freemen who numbered in some cases as many as 5,000 but in others as few as a dozen.

The Municipal Corporations Act (MCA) 1835 gave official recognition to 178 municipalities,[4] and tackled financial and other abuses by transferring control of the corporation's property to elected councils: three-quarters of which were to be elected by household franchise; the other quarter (the aldermen) by the council itself. A degree of democracy was therefore introduced, for the first time, into local government, but the new measure was less radical than it appeared; in Liverpool, for example, there were only 6,000 eligible voters out of a population of 200,000. A relatively narrow range of powers (mainly relating to aspects of policing, lighting, street improvement and sanitation) was made available to the re-constituted municipalities, partly because the Government was afraid they would be political, and partly because existing vested interests (water, gas, railway and burial companies) feared possible competition or takeover (Hammond, 1935: 41).

The initial range of services provided was administered through the borough fund. From 1848 onwards town councils, functioning as local boards of health, supplied the range of additional facilities designed to raise general standards of health through the district fund account. This did not define the full extent of their potential because, as Falkus has pointed out, municipal corporations, run by elected town councils, were bodies both reasonably equipped and, arguably, with a popular mandate to undertake any activities deemed suitable (Falkus, 1977). Possible areas for the expansion of operations included the provision of public utilities which were already well established within the private sector by the mid-nineteenth century. For example, just ten out of approximately 190 municipal corporations owned their own water supply, in 1846, at which time gas supply also remained almost entirely in the hands of private enterprise.

The desire to expand the services supplied by municipal corporations first had to overcome central government's conviction that each of these services would be more efficiently supplied in an atmosphere of private enterprise and competitive market conditions. A number of factors gradually led the government to reconsider its attitude: recognition of the appalling state of the existing supply of water and its impact on public health; the need to ensure that water and gas were made available to everyone including the poorer classes; the wasteful costs associated with competition in activities where a single supplier was most suitable; and the need to ensure that the profits accruing to natural monopolies went to the state. There was also a growing public demand for the provision of improved local amenities, particularly as the result of unfavourable comparisons being made, by ratepayers, between their own towns and services provided elsewhere.

In an atmosphere of 'civic consciousness', this resulted in at first a steady and then more rapid increase in municipal activity. LGA 1858 gave the directors of water companies power to sell out to local authorities where the action was approved by 3/5ths of the shareholders, while PHA 1875 placed an obligation on urban authorities to ensure satisfactory water supplies, empowering them to construct, purchase, lease or hire any waterworks subject to the consent of the LGB. In the main, however, the move towards municipalisation, in the case of gas as well as water, was almost entirely the result of corporations acquiring existing companies.[5]

After 1870 two further major trading undertakings were developed - tramways and electricity supply. Their growth and municipalisation were facilitated by the Tramways Act 1870 and the Electric Lighting Act 1882, which authorised municipal authorities to initiate undertakings. The Tramways Act also gave local authorities the right of compulsory purchase at any time after the expiration of 21 years from the date of the company's initial formation (s. 43); in other cases acquisition could proceed by mutual consent. MCA 1882 removed any remaining restrictions on the services which municipal corporations could provide and, in the larger boroughs, 'municipal socialism preceded national socialism, in practice by nearly half a century' (Poynton, 1960: 18). John Bright encouraged the Birmingham authority to be 'more expensive' (*ibid*), and many of the larger industrial boroughs followed this advice, so that most public utility provision was in the hands of local authorities by the beginning of the twentieth century.

Review

Hammond painted a bleak picture of local administration in England at the beginning of the nineteenth century: 'the country districts and those districts that were country one day and town the next were under the control of squires, men often of character and courage but not as a rule men of large views or wide imagination; the towns were under the rule of little oligarchies, seldom public spirited and often corrupt' (1935: 38). By way of broad comparison, the state of the towns and the general infrastructure in the country were immeasurably improved by 1935, producing the further observation that 'the creation of our modern system of local government is the greatest British achievement in the last 100 years' (Hammond, 1935: 37). This transition was achieved as the result of an enormous investment of public and private money, and the broad scheme of regulations designed to ensure adequate accountability for these resources is next examined in chapter 3.

NOTES

1 It has alternatively been argued that the main reason for the new Act was not really that the amount of relief distributed was totally unreasonable (it represented 3% of estimated national income), but that it was unfairly distributed; nearly half of the total was spent on agricultural labourers in the South of England (Smellie, 1968: 25-6).

2 This philosophy underpinned Poor Law policy from 1834 to 1929 when new concepts of social security and social justice were introduced (Smellie, 1968: 28).

3 As an example of the progress which could be made using powers to raise a rate under the 1848 Act and loans from the government, *The Times* observed (1869) that in the following 20 years Bristol had been transformed 'from nearly the most unhealthy to the nearly most healthy town in Britain' (quoted in Ralph, 1973: 36).

4 The Act authorised the Crown to extend its provisions to municipal corporations subsequently granted a Royal Charter.

5 It should be pointed out that trading activities were also operated by urban district councils and, even in some cases, rural district councils.

3

REGULATORY FRAMEWORK

This chapter has two aims. First, the essential features of accountability, which we concentrate on in subsequent chapters, are shown to have their origin well before the start date (1835) for our main study. Second, we describe the regulations in force between 1835-1935 in order to provide a framework for our analysis of developments within municipal corporations during that time period.

Accountability - medieval times to 1835

The earliest known reference in English legal records to a form of 'local government audit' is dated approximately 1430. It seems that money was collected to repair and improve the walls of a town, and it was suspected that certain individuals had converted some of the proceeds to their own use. Commissioners were appointed and charged with the responsibility for examining the accounts, and the individuals involved, under oath, and if 'there remains in their possession any money so collected, to charge that sum on the same collectors' (Jones, 1981: 1).[1] A power was therefore granted to recover amounts improperly remaining in their possession. According to Jones, the investigation 'was an adoption, evolved by the courts, of the writ of account which from the thirteenth century had been available against bailiffs, factors and receivers' (*ibid*).

Following the introduction of the rating system, in 1597, the Poor Law Act 1601 provided for a degree of accountability from churchwardens and overseers who had the job of levying and collecting the rate. The specific requirement was that they should 'within four days after the end of their year ... make and yield up to two such justices of the peace ... a true and perfect account of all sums of money by them received, or rated and sessed, and not received, and also of such stock as shall be in their hands' (s. 2). There was no requirement, however, for the account to be in writing, and it may well be that the presentation was often made orally. The fact that the new regulations placed squarely on the shoulders of JPs the ultimate responsibility for raising and spending local monies is demonstrated by the requirement for them to nominate churchwardens and overseers (s. 1) and to imprison any of those who failed to make a true account (s. 4).

The poor law rate increased steadily to about £1 million over the next 150 years and, during this time, there was growing criticism of the lack of control over the power of churchwardens and overseers to spend ratepayers' money, sometimes for private ends. An early report which drew attention to the inadequacy of the accounting system of parishes was completed in 1715 (BPP 1715, xviii). This focussed on the affairs of St. Martins-in-the-Field, apparently chosen as the basis for the inquiry on the grounds that it was the parish considered to be most free from financial abuse. The accounts for 1712-14 were studied and judged to be unsatisfactory, however, on the grounds of incompleteness and their failure to distinguish between different types of expenditure. The report also pointed to the need for better controls to ensure collection of the poor rate and the elimination of improper expenditure.

In an attempt to impose a more effective system of control, the Poor (Overseer's Accounts) Act 1744 stiffened the duties and responsibilities of overseers and churchwardens by requiring from them a greater degree of accountability. More specifically, annual provision was made for: the draft accounts to be entered in books; the books to be signed by the churchwarden and overseers; the delivery of accounts to their successors within fourteen days of the new appointment being made; any money or other goods in their possession to be handed over to their successors; the account to be *in writing* and verified on oath before one or more JPs; the JPs to sign the account; the overseers and churchwardens to make the books available for inspection by ratepayers, and give copies of the same at a rate of 6d. per 300 words (s. 1). These apparently stringent regulations were often ineffective, however, because, provided the overseers swore to the accuracy of the accounts, there was no effective way of checking or controlling them. According to Robson 'the administration of the oath by the justices was a mere formality and was in no sense an audit' (1930: 1).

Regulations which imposed an obligation for someone to check the poor law accounts were first contained in Gilbert's Act 1782, named after the MP who introduced the Act into Parliament. A degree of accounting control was provided by the requirement for guardians to nominate three persons 'respectable in character and fortune', of whom one was to be appointed 'visitor' by two local JPs. The visitor was empowered to 'settle and adjust the accounts between the guardians and the treasurer, if any question of dispute shall arise respecting the same ... and by every prudent means in his power enforce and promote the rules and regulations enacted under this Act for preventing all unnecessary expenses and burdens on the said parishes' (s. 10).

However, this in no way constituted a general system of audit; it applied only to the Gilbert unions, the visitor could intervene only where there was a dispute, he had no power to approve or disapprove the nature of the expenditure, and was entitled only 'to check the accuracy of the items and see that they corresponded with the [guardian's] orders (Robson, 1930: 2).

The cost of poor relief continued to spiral because of the need to provide support for large numbers of unemployed factory workers when slump followed boom (an obligation impossible to envisage in 1601). A further upsurge in poor law expenditure resulted from the decision of the Berkshire judges of Speenhamland (1795), allowing poor relief to be given in supplementation of wages. This led very soon to the subsidisation of employers and huge increases in the rates in certain areas. At Cholesbury in Buckinghamshire, for example, the rate rose from £10 in 1801 to £150 in 1831.

In an attempt to control expenditure, an Act was passed (1810) conferring on JPs wide powers. They were empowered to examine churchwardens and overseers under oath concerning 'the truth of such account, and to disallow and strike out of every such account all such charges and payments as they shall deem to be unfounded,[2] and to reduce such as they shall deem exorbitant' (s. 1). The reason for the disallowance or reduction was to be stated on the account. The practical effect of a disallowance was the same as raising a charge, in the sense that 'A debt was created from those responsible and restitution made to the ratepayers' (Helmore, 1961: 127). The Act is therefore notable for the fact that, for the first time, emphasis was given to disallowance as well as allowance. Features recognisable in today's legislation therefore came on to the statute book, and the development of the district auditor's powers of 'disallowance and surcharge' were foreshadowed.

A further early regulation of interest and relevance to the development of local authorities in the period covered by this study was 'Hobhouse's Act' 1831.[3] This contained an elaborate scheme for electing auditors and setting out their powers to audit the accounts at least twice a year and call for any person, books or information that they required (ss. 34-5). The Act could be adopted only by parishes with more than 800 ratepayers, and was put into force only by certain large parishes in the metropolis (Robson, 1930: 3). However, it was an adoptive Act which, like others, appears to have achieved very little (Helmore, 1961: 14), but it did point the way towards regulations which were eventually introduced for general application.

The need for Parliament to be informed of the application of public monies was also recognised in a series of statutes, commencing with the Poor Law (Returns) Act 1776 which required overseers to make a return of the sums raised and spent on poor relief.

Table 3.1: Significant events in the history of municipal corporations

Date	General Developments	Specific Provisions
Pre-1835	Boroughs run as clubs for the benefit of local officials - characterised by mismanagement and corruption	Accounting provisions contained in some charters
1835	MCA 1835 established a democratic structure and a broad framework of accountability based on the borough fund	Treasurer to prepare account of receipts and disbursements Hold elective audit Make abstract available to rate payers
1836/7	Requirement for annual returns to Parliament	Statements to show receipts and expenditure
1848-75	PHA's 1848-75 designated the town council a board of health/ sanitary authority providing services through the district fund	Audited by borough auditor Annual report to Secretary of State and published in local newspaper Auditor to be paid at least 2 guineas for work on district fund account
from 1858	Development of trading activities	
from 1874	Audit requirements under scrutiny Voluntary adoption of professional audit Application of district audit to certain borough activities	
1882	MCA 1882 - consolidating statute	
1885	Establishment of CTAI	
1888	LGA 1888 established county boroughs	Usual municipal corporation accounting provisions apply
from 1889	Accounts requirements under scrutiny	
	1889 - CTAI's 1st attempt at standardisation	Recommended use of double account system for each fund plus publication of aggregate balance sheet
	1903, 1907 - Government investigations	
	1913 - IMTA's first attempt to achieve standardisation	Revised standard forms for eleven of the main non-trading organisations
	General move towards accruals accounting	
1930	Government issues accounting regulations for boroughs	Main principles established, including formalised use of the double account system
1933	Municipal Corporations (Audit) Act 1933	Permits municipal corporations to choose a professional or district audit instead of the elective audit
	LGA 1933 - consolidating statute	
1937	IMTA's second attempt at standardisation	
1940s	Gas and electricity nationalised	
1955	IMTA issues 'The Standard form of Accounts of Local Authorities'	Detailed standard analysis of income and expenditure issued for individual services
1961	IMTA issues 'The Standardisation of Accounts: General Principle'	
1974	Municipal Corporations abolished	Elective audit lapses

Table 3.2: **Selected comments of the Commissioners (1835) investigating municipal corporations on the matters of accounts, audit and neglect of account keeping**

Borough	Comment
Accounts of Corporation Funds[1]	
Aberavon	No regular accounts.
Andover	Ill-kept. Produced only to self elect council, seldom examined.
Bedford	A detailed account of the receipts and expenditure is published annually and circulated amongst the inhabitants.
Berwick	Kept by town treasurer and rendered to bailiffs. Annual audit by self elect council. Non publication.
Bristol	Audit Committee of whole house. Admirable method of keeping of accounts.
Chester	Funds received annually by the clerk who keeps the accounts. The treasurer audits, examines and signs the Audit committee appointed by the council, examine the bills go through each item and sign the book. All members of the select body permitted to inspect but no instance of an application being received. Nor woul any freeman or stranger be permitted to inspect. The duty of treasurer was attached to the office of coroner under the charter granted by Henry VIII and was chosen by the mayor.
Congleton	Town clerk is treasurer. Quarterly audit by self elect council. No right of freemen to examine books.
Conway	The accounts are all laid before the burgesses at the public meeting. The items are read aloud. A burgess takes the vouchers and compares them.
Grantham	Accounts of the chamberlain and cashier audited by a court of alderman. Treasurer of the 'soke' audited by magistrates with abstract published in a newspaper.
Liverpool	Excellent account keeping. Mode discussed by council, report on. Balance ledger annually. Printed and published. Audit committee. The accounts of the corporation are kept with a punctuality, clearness and regularity worthy of their magnitude and importance: a little more minuteness of detail might be desirable in the printed statements. Office of treasurer established in 1716. Salary fixed in 1820 at £1,000 p. a. with tw securities to be given of £5,000 by the treasurer. The father of the treasurer at the time of the report was an alderman with other relatives on the council.
Llanelli	Irregularly kept and unbalanced for six years.
Ludlow	Earliest book of account kept from October 1722 and since that date on a regular basis.
Northampton	Regularly kept and audited. Discontinued publication since political contests commenced.
Owestry	There is no publication of the corporation's accounts nor indeed any other statement of them, otherwise tha by casual entry in the books.
Romney	Accounts kept by Chamberlain and published March, yearly.
Tiverton	One small book only.

Wigan	All the burgesses have notice to appear at a common hall and the accounts are read publicly. All the burgesses may see the accounts.
York	Kept by Chamberlain. Audited by small committee and shown to all.
Auditors of Corporation Accounts[1]	
Beceles	Ancient law of the town:- 'Item, that an audit shal be kepte once everye years, upon the day of changing the new portreeve and surveyors'. On the day after the audit the accounts were open for inspection of all the inhabitants and the bellman was sent out to remind residents of this privilege.
Cambridge	Auditors were tradesmen who were present when their own accounts were audited. No evidence that they withdrew.
Dorchester	Annual audit by council.
Grimsby	Six elected by lect jury.
Kingston	18 Auditors annual appointment by bench. Two upon Hull Chamberlains always included. Family relationship.
Lincoln	If a tradesman on the council, and has bills with council, not disqualified from acting as auditor.
Ludlow	6 auditors. Annually appointed by council.
Rye	Never audited between 1818-1833 though committee appointed for that purpose yearly. In the greatest confusion, bills outstanding from 1825, ground rents unconnected for ten years.
Southampton	Auditors functions nominal, account kept by treasurer, examination by council, no publication.
Worcester	4 auditors. Election by self elect council.
Neglect[1]	
Aberystwyth	Irregularities in accounting for finance on leases, usurpation of an estate allowed.
Axbridge	Sale of corporation property on terms of 1000 yrs. Little left. Application not clear by accounts.
Huntingdon	Debt without hope of liquidation.
Newark	Neglect of charity revenues, long continued. Misappropriation of revenues. Immoderate expenditure on festivities.
Saltash	Imputed misappropriation of revenues.
Totnes	Reckless contraction of debt.
Note 1	These titles are taken from the report. Minor amendments have been made to wording of 'Comment' to help make clear their meaning.
Source:	Appendix (Parts IV, V) to the First Report of the Commissioners on the Municipal Corporations of England and Wales: 2103-939.

The boroughs, not being responsible for the provision of poor relief, remained almost free from regulation, despite their long history. However, by the 1830's, they were responsible for supplying a significant range of other services in some areas. Significant events in the development of boroughs are set out in table 3.1.

Government investigation of the ancient boroughs

Earl Grey's Whig Government (1830-4) harboured suspicions of maladministration within the 'unaccountable boroughs' (see chapter 4) and set up a Select Committee in 1833 to investigate their affairs. The committee observed defects in their organisation and administration, and found evidence of corruption and undue privileges enjoyed by those in control. It attributed these weaknesses partly to the fact that 'publicity has been rarely given to the amount and application of the funds belonging to the different Corporations' (BPP 1833, xiii: 4). These matters called for further investigation and the Royal Commission was instructed 'to proceed with the utmost despatch to inquire as to the existing state of Municipal Corporations in England and Wales and to collect information respecting the defects in their constitution ... and into the nature and management of the income, revenues and funds of the said Corporations' (BPP 1835, xxiii: 5).

The Commission's report was highly critical: corporation property was used as if it belonged to the council members rather than held in trust for the benefit of the corporation's inhabitants. Properties belonging to the corporation were sometimes let to members at very low rents and often for a large number of years; corporate revenue was frequently spent on feasting members of the common council and their friends; while many corporate officers were paid substantial salaries for doing little or nothing by way of public duties. At Berwick-upon-Tweed money was even borrowed in order to divide it among the freemen (Jennings, 1935b: 58-59). A relatively modest proportion of the corporate property appears to have been expended for eligible purposes such as the prosecution of offenders, the maintenance of prisons, policing, and public improvements. Many of the corporations owed a great deal of money on which the interest absorbed a very large proportion of the revenue. Some corporations were completely insolvent.

The Commission specifically inquired into the method of keeping and auditing the accounts. The key financial official was the borough Chamberlain or Treasurer, usually chosen by the common council and in the majority of cases one of its members. His duties were to receive revenues, to make necessary payments, to keep accounts and generally to superintend the property of the corporation. In some cases the Mayor acted as treasurer. Accounts were maintained in an irregular manner so it was difficult to establish expenditure, debts and assets. In some places no accounts were kept; in very few were regular and efficient audits held, and in still fewer were accounts published (BPP 1835, xxiii: 32). Where audits were held, the work was usually undertaken by the common council, with the result that the Treasurer was often a member of the body which audited his accounts. In certain large towns, such as Bath, Bristol and London, however, care was taken to ensure that this situation did not arise.

The appendices to the Commissioners' report contain detailed returns from each borough which are, to a large extent, consistent with the Commissioners' conclusions. Comments such as 'inextricable confusion of accounts' (Haverfordwest, BPP 1839, xviii: 458), 'immoderate expenditure of charity funds for festivity' (Newark, BPP 1839, xviii: 459), 'no right in freemen to examine accounts' (Congleton, BPP 1839, xviii: 15) and 'non-publication' (Beaumaris, BPP 1839, xviii: 14) are commonplace (See also table 3.2). At Ipswich:

> The practical working of the Municipal System may be summed up in bribery, invasions of personal liberty, and the destruction of industrious habits among the freemen; the election of local functionaries, by whom official power is abused and official duty neglected; the administration of justice by magistrates, whose authority, acquired by violations of the law, is unsupported by the respect of the inhabitants ... mismanagement and waste of the town property; misapplication of revenues obtained at the expense of the comfort and security of the inhabitants, alienations for objects unknown, or for the avowed purpose of thwarting an useful body of local commissioners; hospitals perverted to party purposes; charity funds converted into election funds. (BPP 1835, xxvi: 262)

It has been suggested, however, that the Commissioners were expected to reach conclusions which justified the Whig Government's desire to impose stricter control over municipal corporations (Jennings, 1935b: 60), and a careful examination of borough returns reveals no shortage of favourable comments, of which the following is a small selection. The accounts of Ludlow had 'been regularly kept [from 1722], down to the present day' and were 'submitted once a year to the inspection of the auditors, who make a report thereon at a chamber meeting' (BPP 1835, xxvi: 727), those of Liverpool were prepared 'with a punctuality, clearness and regularity worthy of their magnitude and importance' (BPP 1835, xxvi: 654), while Bristol operated an 'admirable method of keeping the accounts' (BPP 1839, xviii: 15). Conway's accounts were read aloud before the burgesses at the annual public meeting (BPP 1839, xviii: 15), similarly at Wigan where all the burgesses were entitled to see the accounts (BPP 1837/8, xxxv: 385). At Bedford a detailed account of receipts and expenditure was published annually and circulated among the inhabitants (BPP 1835, xxvi: 39), while at Chester, the accounts were kept by a clerk, examined and signed by the treasurer, and submitted to an audit committee appointed by council which went through each item, examined each bill, and signed the account book (BPP 1835, xxvi: 557).

Regulations, 1835-1935

The Government was determined to make boroughs more democratic and accountable, however, and a Bill was presented to Parliament within one month of the date of the Commission's report. We will see that the accountability of boroughs, as in the case of other local authorities, was based squarely on a system of fund accounting; that is, a self-balancing set of accounts, established for a specific purpose, and segregated from all other funds.

Fund accounting

The new accounting requirements contained in MCA 1835 covered the responsibilities of the borough treasurer, and the financial reporting and audit obligations attached to the borough accounts. Jones has pointed out that the new system of fund accounting served two purposes:

> it required the assets and liabilities of the corporation to be distinguished from the individuals who belonged to it. Equally important [s. 71], what it also did was to separate those monies which belonged to the corporation from those which were held in trust. (1992: 134)

The treasurer was obliged to keep 'true accounts of all the sums of money by him received and paid' (s. 93), and the Act detailed the receipts and payments which might be entered in the borough fund account (s. 92). Where the borough fund was insufficient to finance the corporation's statutory obligations, the council had power to levy a rate.[4] The treasurer was required to make the books available for inspection by the councillors (s. 93), and to prepare and deliver an account of money 'received' and 'disbursed' to the council when required (s. 60). Each year, in March, the burgesses were empowered to elect, as auditors, two individuals qualified to be councillors, provided they were not actually members of the council (s. 37). The borough treasurer was required to submit accounts to these auditors and 'to such member of the council as the mayor shall name on the 1st March of every year' (s. 93),[5] and further provided that 'if the said accounts shall be found correct, the Auditors shall sign the same'. Following the audit, the treasurer was required 'to make out in writing, and ... cause to be printed a full abstract of his accounts' to be made available for inspection by ratepayers, and delivered to them, on application, and 'on payment of a reasonable price for each copy' (s. 93).[6]

The above accounting requirements introduced to achieve a greater measure of openness in the administration of borough affairs, and we will examine, in later chapters, the extent to which the above requirements helped achieve an adequate level of accountability. A few initial comments may help to 'set the scene'. The requirement to prepare and publish an accounting statement, based on fund accounting, could be satisfied by the production of simply a cash statement. Chapter 5 shows that this was how the Act's provisions were initially interpreted, but that the concept of fund accounting was subsequently elaborated to incorporate outstanding assets and liabilities. The problem of accounting for capital expenditure, which naturally flowed from the decision to prepare accruals-based accounts, is examined in chapter 6.

Turning to the audit requirement, the main problem was that MCA 1835 adopted the type of audit introduced for parishes by Hobhouse's Act 1831, ss. 33-6, namely an 'elective' audit. It seems reasonable to ask why the centrally administered audit (called the district audit from 1844) introduced for the poor law, in the previous year (see Coombs and Edwards, 1990), was not extended to these corporations? The simple explanation may be that the boroughs had sufficient influence in Parliament to prevent the introduction of intrusive regulations which they did not favour. There was also, of course, a certain logic behind the concept of elective auditors, which was that they were appointed by and responsible to individuals - the ratepayers - who had a direct interest in ensuring that the municipal affairs were properly conducted. The elective audit may therefore be seen as equivalent to the amateur/shareholder audit already in use among railway companies and soon to be adopted by companies registering under the Joint Stock Companies Act 1844. The changes in the system of audit, deemed desirable as time went by, are examined in chapters 7 and 8.

The need for municipal corporations to inform Parliament, as well as ratepayers, about the application of public monies was recognised with the introduction of a requirement for boroughs to make an annual return of receipts and expenditure 'made up to the last period of audit of the said receipts and expenditure', MCA 1836, s. 10 and MCA 1837, s. 43. The return (a precursor of the local taxation return) was made to the Secretary of State who, in turn, submitted an abstract to Parliament.

The district fund

Accountability was taken a stage further commencing with the establishment of local boards of health in 1848. The borough treasurer was made responsible for maintaining a district fund account and therein recording receipts and expenditures under the Act (s. 87). When located in a borough, the board of health came under the jurisdiction of the borough auditor; all other boards came under the scrutiny of the district auditor. Parliament initially imposed more exacting audit requirement on all local boards (PHA 1848, s. 122), but from 1858 it was accepted that, where the board was the town council, it should be audited in the same manner as other municipal accounts (LGA 1858, s. 60). All local boards were required, however, to make an annual report, in prescribed form, to the Secretary of State, and to publish the same in a local newspaper (s. 76). The Public Health Acts of 1872 and 1875 consolidated all existing public health and nuisance legislation.

The concept of fund accounting was extended by local acts to trading activities with the borough treasurer required to open a separate account for each of these. For example, the Bradford Waterworks Act 1854 stated that: 'the Council shall cause a separate and distinct account to be kept by the Treasurer of the borough, to be called "the Water Account", of all monies received and paid' (s. 7).

Subsequent statutory developments

The audit and accounting provisions of MCA 1835 were repeated, with minor modification, in MCA 1882, ss. 21, 25-8, 62, 139-43, 233. The Municipal Corporations (Audit) Act 1933 permitted municipal corporations to adopt, instead of the elective audit, either the district audit or a professional audit undertaken by members of the accounting bodies listed in a schedule to the Act. The new Act was almost immediately replaced by LGA 1933.[7] This consolidated the existing law, with the accounts and audit provisions relating to boroughs set out in ss. 120, 185, 237-40 and 244-8. The statutory regulations therefore continue to make no reference to the need for the abstract to include a balance sheet, or even for the accounts to be framed on the accruals basis,[8] but the income and expenditure basis was specified for the purpose of the local financial (taxation) return to Parliament (s. 244).

The statutory requirements applying to municipal corporations therefore changed little over the period 1835-1935, but the form and content of their published accounts altered dramatically. We will see that these improvements took place under the close supervision of local authority-based professional accounting body, the CTAI/IMTA (see table 3.3 for numbers). The strong leadership provided, in this respect, may be contrasted with the unwillingness of the private sector-based professional accounting bodies to take the initiative in guiding the reporting practices of limited companies in Great Britain until the early 1940's. Important initiatives during this period covered by this study was the advice issued in 1889 concerning the form and content of the published accounts, and the revised standard form for eleven of the main local authority non-trading accounts issued in 1913.

Table 3.3: The growth in membership of the CTAI\IMTA between 1886 and 1935[1]

	Fellow	Associates	Students
1886	60	8	-
1890	77	20	-
1895	102	41	-
1900	154	59	-
1905	200	84	40
1910	252	187	130
1915	256	218	97
1920	293	179	86
1925	285	288	210
1930	282	387	497
1935	294	588	854

Note 1 In 1901 the CTAI was renamed the Institute of Municipal Treasurers and Accountants.

Source: Poynton, 1960: 143.

Review

It was MCA 1835 that became, with some modification, the basis for the general form of local self government which was developed over the next 100 years, and which remains in operation today. The 1835 Act had provided for the election of a council to act for, and be responsible to, the inhabitants of the borough. The minutes of council meetings were to be made available for inspection by ratepayers, and their accounts were to be audited twice a year. Similar principles were extended to urban and rural sanitary authorities in 1875 (re-constituted as urban and rural district councils in 1894) and to county councils in 1888. The fact that the regulations laid down for municipal corporations established a broad framework for other authorities to follow has been cited as the reason why it became possible for LGA 1933 'to generalise the rules of organisation and function applicable to all local authorities' (Jennings, 1935b: 62). LGA 1933 was, more immediately, based on the findings of the Local Government and Public Health Consolidation Committee (Chelmsford Committee) which drafted a Bill consistent with the existing law. The result of its enactment was that all regulations relating to local authorities were consolidated in a single statute.

NOTES

1 The philosophy of responsibility accounting, which underpins charge/discharge accounting, is a fundamental feature of public sector auditing practices and regulations throughout the period covered by this chapter.

2 *R. v. Fouch* (1841) 2 Q. B., 308, made it clear that the justices had a discretionary power under this branch of the clause entitling them to disallow the cost incurred by the overseers in contesting, unsuccessfully, an appeal against the rate. The amounts had, incidentally, been passed by the auditors of the union.

3 John Hobhouse (later Lord Brougham) was mainly responsible for securing the passage of this Act.

4 Prior to 1835 boroughs had no general power to levy a rate, although there were a few isolated cases where the borough's charter (Kings Lynn and Bristol) contained this enabling provision.

5 The appointment of a 'mayor's auditor' was already accepted practice based on either the borough's original charter or established custom.

6 These publication requirements were carried through to LGA 1933, s. 240(c) and remained in force until municipal corporations were abolished.

7 One important modification was the deletion of 'full' from the previous requirement to 'print a full abstract of accounts'. This change was designed, without success, to discourage the publication of lengthy abstracts,

8 The obligation to use the income and expenditure basis, for the purpose of accounts keeping, was specified in the Accounts (Boroughs and Metropolitan Boroughs) Regulations 1930, SR&O., 1930, no. 30, but the order applied only to borough activities subject to the district audit.

4

RECORD KEEPING IN MUNICIPAL CORPORATIONS

The use of charge/discharge accounting in Britain, in early times, is well documented. It was substantially, though not only, a cash-based system which was widely used, as early as the thirteenth century, to enable the steward to inform the lord of the manor how resources entrusted to him (charged) had been applied (discharged) (Noke, 1981). The system had its origin in the need to report to a higher authority and Jones has demonstrated that it was eminently suitable for application to local government. The first recorded use of charge/discharge by a borough occurred in 1321 (Jones, 1985a: 202).

It equally well known that the system of double entry bookkeeping (DEB) emerged as a an alternative method for recording transactions in the Italian City States, in the thirteenth century (Lee, 1977), and found its way to Britain by about the sixteenth century.[1] We are also certain that DEB eventually emerged triumphant in most if not all advanced economies, though the process of change has received little attention.[2]

We start with some introductory comments concerning the difficulty of distinguishing between different methods of record keeping. We then examine the accounting practices of boroughs before 1835 and note the first signs of the move over from charge/discharge to DEB. Next we examine the action taken by the government in 1835 to improve accountability and suggest its possible impact on bookkeeping within the borough. We then consider pressures building up for the wider adoption of more sophisticated record keeping procedures in the second and third quarters of the nineteenth century, and move on to examine the process of change from charge/discharge accounting to DEB both generally and in relation to the five municipal corporations whose archival records have been investigated for the purpose of this study. Finally, we present our conclusions.

Methods of record keeping

Today, systems of record keeping may be categorised as either single entry or double entry. Single entry is not a particular system of bookkeeping, but is the term used to cover any written accounting record other than double entry. It is in the nature of a homespun system which is nevertheless capable of meeting the needs of (usually) a small-scale organisational entity such as sole trader, club or society. In these cases, the records may, in due course, be used to process transactions in accordance with double entry principles and enable the preparation of a profit and loss account and balance sheet, perhaps for taxation purposes. Where this is not required, the records may simply be used to draw up a statement of receipts and payments, perhaps for presentation to club members. In still other cases - household accounts might be a good example - a memorandum record of selected transactions may never need to be converted into any form of financial statement whatsoever.

Charge/discharge accounting may be seen as a subset of single entry bookkeeping, the distinctive feature being the form of the financial statement prepared from the initial record. There may of course be debates about whether a particular system is charge/discharge[3] in the same way that questions arise concerning whether a particular recording mechanism possesses the precise attributes required to justify the accolade double entry bookkeeping. At the margin, it sometimes boils down to no more than a question of semantics and terminology.

As far as possible, we steer clear of such detailed matters. In relation to charge/discharge, we are not concerned with which set of entries comes first, whether the words charge/discharge are used, or whether the account deals only with cash transactions or also with debtors or stock. The only tests we apply are whether the statement is presented by an agent to some higher authority (in the case of a borough, typically by the treasurer or chamberlain to the town council) which to all intents and purposes sets out in a single financial statement the resources entrusted to the agent during an accounting period and how these financial responsibilities have been discharged.

But even if we take this broad view, the actual classification of a particular accounting system as double entry or single entry (including its subset, charge/discharge) can prove problematic. There is no shortage of examples to prove that the presence of individual features of DEB (e. g., a (cash) account presented in bilateral format, the insertion of the terms debit and credit to head up columns of entries, the use of the terms 'to' and 'by', or even the preparation of a balance sheet) do not necessarily reflect its full scale application. Jones tells us that the churchwardens' accounts for the Parish of Bodicote in 1816 'dabbled' with DEB, exhibiting the first three of these typical characteristics (1992: 53). The county treasurer of Lancashire prepared a charge/discharge account (mistakenly described as a 'balance sheet' by the county archivist) headed up 'debit' and 'credit' for 1774/5 (France, 1952: 155-6). Corresponding information may be found in the Cardiff archives, commencing 1790, where use of the prefixes 'to' and 'by' is also prominent (Cardiff archive: box 2564).

Therefore, even where we have access to the primary records, it may not be easy to make a correct classification, and the difficulties increase if the records are incomplete. The following question was therefore asked in the endeavour to take this study forward: Where the records have not survived, or are incomplete, is there any other evidence that can be used to help decide the method of bookkeeping in use?

One might be tempted to assume that knowledge of the introduction of a new and improved system of bookkeeping would imply the adoption of DEB. But this is not a safe assumption, even in the nineteenth century, by which time it was a growing practice for organisational entities to engage public accountants, as consultants, to advise on improvements in the existing accounting system. Local authorities were no exception. At Liverpool borough, for example, the 'experienced accountant' Bartholomew Prescot reported on the 'mode of keeping accounts', in 1820, and we are told that this led to significant improvements (BBP 1835, xxxvi: 655) in the system of single entry bookkeeping. While Mr Groom, a London accountant engaged by Ludlow, 'made a report, in pursuance of which the accounts have been since consolidated and an entirely new system of keeping adopted' (BBP 1835, xxxvi: 725). This enabled the preparation of an annual statement which disclosed, not only receipts and payments, but also rents due but unpaid.

A second avenue which we have explored is the possibility that the type of bookkeeping record might be inferred from the form of the published accounts. More specifically, we examined the possibility that the publication of only a cash (charge/discharge-type) statement implied the use of single entry bookkeeping, while the preparation of a profit and loss account and balance sheet might be considered suggestive of the operation of DEB. Our findings are that such assumptions could not safely be made, certainly as regards the former relationship.

The unaccountable boroughs

We have seen that, prior to 1835, central government intervention in local financial affairs was motivated by the desire to impose some degree of control over expenditure on poor relief which was mainly responsible for the rapidly increasing rate in some areas. The boroughs, not being responsible for the provision of poor relief,[4] remained almost free from regulation, despite a history dating from the twelfth century. By the 1830's, however, boroughs in some areas were responsible for supplying a significant range of other services. Their early (pre-1835) accounting practices are first examined.[5]

A typical example of a charge/discharge statement is the Court Leet Record of the Borough of Manchester covering the year 1579-80 (figure 4.1). The opening balance confirms cash in the hands of the previous constables and is followed by income from a rate. The expenditure is mainly on military matters and the closing balance identifies the deficit owed to the constables at the end of the year. There are also listed two amounts which the constables failed to collect (Guthrie, 1886: 613).

This type of record is what one would expect in the light of conclusions reached by Jones in chapter 2 ('From the middle ages to c1835') of his study of the history of the financial control function of local government accounting in the UK:

> Our conclusions would be then that charge/discharge accounting was determined by its original feudal context but that it persisted down the years and pervaded the economy as a written manifestation of the 'obligation to serve' imposed by governments of the locality on inhabitants (1992: 67).

More specifically, in the present context, the contemporary method of organising finances within *the borough*, with administration of financial affairs effectively delegated to the chamberlain or treasurer, ensured that this scheme of accountability remained entirely applicable.

Bristol - the oldest of the boroughs covered by this study (it received its charter in 1373) - experienced recurrent problems of financial control and it may be these that led to the appointment of a committee, on 8 December 1784, 'to inspect, correct and improve the manner in which the City accounts are now kept, and to form some more perfect mode of keeping the same in future' (Common council proceedings, 1783-90: fo. 71). But other factors possibly contributed to the need for change. According to Jones 'the [previous] charge/discharge account increasingly demanded subsidiary books of account [which included rent books, day books, books of loan transactions as well as cash books] to the point where these needed to be linked in a structured way (Jones, 1992: 59, 67). We also know that the committee believed that an improved system of accounting would prevent unnecessary expenditure unearthed during the course of their investigations. The outcome of their deliberations was the introduction of DEB in 1785.[6]

It was the City's archivist, Elizabeth Ralph (1953), who initially publicized this change, and we have reexamined these records for the purpose of this study. We are impressed by a number of features.

The system was based on a sequence of journals, rent books, cash books, ledgers, and what are called balances of the ledger books, each set of which runs through to 1929. On account of the 'extraordinary trouble in the

---

Rd. by vs Thomas browensword & Raffe Sorocowld Connstables ffor the Last yere as ensuithe

It.Rd at the hands of Ricd. mortone and Raffe proudloue constables the year beffor [1578-9][1]	viij^{s} vj^{d} [8s.6d]
It.Rd in the Towen and hamells [hamlets] thervnto belonging the same of	xv^{ll} iij^{s} vj^{d} [£15.3s.6d]
	Some is xv^{ll} xij^{s} [£15.12s.0d]

Itm. paid by vs the Connstables afforsaid ffor the vse of the Towen as ensuithe.

Itm. paid To the hands of Sr Edmud Trafford & Mr Edmud assheton ffor the making of soldiars into Ireland	xvj^{s} [£16. 0s.0d]
It paid ffor the cariage of Ricd. bordma to Lancast^{r}	vij^{s} vj^{d} [7s.6d]
Itm mor for the bringinge of Mr. Leaver to Lancast^{r}	iiij^{s} iiij^{d} [4s.4d]
It paid James Dunsture ffor the caridge of a woman being acutt purse to Lancast^{r}	iij^{s} vj^{d} [4s.6d]
	Some is xvj^{ll} xvj^{s} iiij^{d} [£16.16s.4d]
So that the Towen is in o^{r} Dett as apperethe by the accounts	xxiij^{s} iiij^{d} [24s.4d]

Itm Rest vngathered wch wee could not R^{v} of the Laie, Laid by Mr. Robart Langley & george Birch as ensuithe

It in the Towen	xj^{s} viij^{d} [11s.8d]
It ffor the hammell of mostone	xxiiij^{s} [24s]

Raffe Sorocowld
Thomas bronsword

Figure 4.1: Extract from the Constables' accounts, 1579-80 for Manchester

Source: Guthrie, 1886: 619

new mode of keeping the City accounts' the salary of the chamberlain was increased by ninety two pounds and ten shillings (Common council proceedings, 1783-90: fo. 209).[7] The format and content of each set of books remained broadly unchanged over the 144 year period (1785-1929) and, *inter alia,* provided the basis for the calculation of the surplus of income over expenditure which was then added to the stock balance. The 'balances of the ledger books' contain statements which are, in essence, balance sheets, but the entries remain unclassified, although their number falls as time goes by, indicating an element of summarisation.

The comments of the Royal Commissioners appointed to investigate the ancient boroughs, who reported in 1835, make it clear that Bristol's system was not typical of the many which they examined:

> We cannot conclude this notice of the corporation revenue without bearing testimony to the admirable manner in which the books are kept. The accounts are kept by double entry, and a separate rent ledger is used, in which an account is opened with each tenant, the balance only being transferred to the general ledger (BPP 1835, xxiv: 537).

However, the Commissioners also reported that the Bath Improvement Commissioners maintained their accounts on the double entry basis, though 'They were not fully posted up, so as to enable us [the Commissioners] to obtain immediately an actual balance sheet' (BPP 1835, xxiv: 465).

Other instances cited by the Commissioners, in their report, are suggestive but not conclusive evidence of the use of double entry techniques. These include comments: that the books of the Liverpool Dock Estate 'are closely posted' from 1822 (BPP 1835, xxvi: 701); that a balance sheet was printed by the Borough of Haverfordwest for the years 1830/1 and 1831/2 (BPP 1835, xxiii: 377), and that its market account was labelled debit and credit (BPP 1835, xxiii: 379); and that at Chichester 'the balance is entered in the journals ... the receipt and expenditure of which passes to the general debit and credit of the treasurer' (BPP 1835, xxiv: 67). From other sources we are able to discover that, to tighten up control over finances, the Middlesex county treasurer 'was instructed [in 1782] to keep his accounts by double entry; ... and to produce Abstracts of the balances for inspection and audit by a Committee of eleven' (Staff of the County Record Office, 1952: 278).

At Leicester, despite the existence of accounting and audit requirements from the late fourteenth century, there was a history of recurrent financial malpractice; 'indeed, the whole state of affairs in Leicester was an outstanding example of the financial mismanagement of many such corporations, and contributed largely, by the angry opposition which had excited, to the passing of the Municipal Corporations Act in 1835' (Woodcock,

1954: 214). The specific conclusion of the Commissioners was that 'as administrators of the public funds, it is impossible to speak of the corporate authorities except in terms of unqualified censure' (BPP 1835, xxv: 511). The outcome was the transformation of 'the old *Camera* into the new treasurer's department' (Woodcock, 1954: 210); a significant feature of the changes made was the introduction of DEB (Jones, 1992: 56).

The investigation of Cardiff's archives revealed accounting records to have survived for the period 1790-1821 (Cardiff archive: box 2564), comprising the records of the treasurer to the 'Corporation of Cardiff'. The accounts are kept on a cash basis, in the form of a debtor and creditor (charge/discharge) relationship between the council and the treasurer. The record of transactions for 'John Evans in Acco^{t} Current with the Corporation of Cardiff' for 1790 ends with a 'Balance due to Corporation' of £9. 16. 7½ (Cardiff archive: box 2564, book 1). A later statement of transactions between 'The Corporation of Cardiff in Account with Thomas Morgan, Common Attorney', made up to September 1803, shows a 'Balance due to Accountant' of £10. 10. 0. At the foot of the account is the statement that 'This account was this day settled having first examined the same with the vouchers and sworn Thomas Morgan to the truth thereof and a balance of £10. 10. 0 appears to be due to him from the Corporation as witness our hands this 29th day of September 1817'. It is signed by John Wood who is described as one of the bailiffs of the town of Cardiff with the other Bailiff, Edward Thomas, being described as having declined to act (Cardiff archive: box 2564, book 2½). The time lapse between the date of the account being closed, 1803, and the statement, 1817, is explained by the Commissioners on Municipal Corporations, 1835:

> Prior to the year 1817, no accounts of the receipts and expenditure of the corporation appear to have been kept.[8] In that year there was a division among the council, and many questions were about that time agitated respecting the rights of burgesses, and of the governing body. From that period the accounts of the corporation, though never published, have been audited and entered in the books (BPP 1835, xxiii: 329).

The annual accounts continue to be cash-based (Cardiff archive: box 2564, books 5 and 6), but in 1819/20 we find, for the first time, written evidence of an interest in debts outstanding, with the records expanded to incorporate full details of rentals due to the Corporation, i. e. arrears brought forward, rent due, rent received and amount the outstanding from each tenant.

Government (in)action

We have seen that the upshot of the Commissioners' investigations, particularly the suspicion of corrupt practices, was the creation of the modern municipal corporation subject to regulatory controls which included requirements for accounts to be prepared, published and audited. MCA 1835 laid down no rules concerning how the books should be kept, but statements contained in this and subsequent Acts concerning the form the financial statements should take certainly provided no incentive for the adoption of sophisticated recording procedures. In line with central and local government tradition, the requirement or at least implication was that they should be cash-based (see chapter 5).

It does not necessarily follow, of course, that a corporation which prepares cash-based financial statements does not use DEB, and we will show that this happened. But one of the main virtues of DEB is that it facilitates the preparation of accruals-based financial statements and, where this is not a priority, the case for the introduction of a more sophisticated method of record keeping is less strong.

It is unlikely that the government needed to be discouraged from introducing a DEB requirement[9] but, if they it did, there was an influential opponent in the persons of Jeremy Bentham and his disciple Edwin Chadwick. Bentham was a strong supporter of bookkeeping procedures; indeed his interest in social problems led him to devise an ambitious plan for dealing with the poor which consisted of a network of 250 workhouses each containing 2,000 paupers; all under the control of a single giant joint stock company (Hume, 1970: 23). 'In a system of poor-houses of the proposed extent and magnitude good bookkeeping is the hinge on which good management will turn' (quoted in Goldberg, 1957: 218).

Bentham did not consider DEB as appropriate for these purposes, however, nor for the purpose of central government accounting which was the subject of severe criticism in the 1820's and 1830's. Bentham attacked proposals for a change to DEB, in 1830, directing particular criticism at the fictional nature of accounting entries. Further, in his view, a cardinal requirement was that a system of bookkeeping should be clear and unambiguous whereas 'with the exception of the single class designated by the appellation of merchant's, this [DEB] phraseology is utterly unintelligible' (quoted in Goldberg, 1957: 222).

The adoption of DEB

The case for change

The reasons for the adoption of DEB have been identified by Yamey (1956: 7) and reconsidered in the context of the local authority by Jones (1992: 67-8). The records are, as a result, more comprehensive and orderly; the duality of entries provides a convenient check on the accuracy or completeness of the ledger; while the underlying records contain the material needed to prepare the profit and loss account and balance sheet.[10]

[1] Jones (1992) sees the first two factors as of supreme importance, arguing that double entry is 'a better stewardship model than charge/discharge when organisations carried out a substantial number of transactions involving debtors and creditors' (p. 68) which ensures the recognition of liabilities and safeguards against the manipulation of cash flows (p. 137).

Regulations

The importance of the first factor, identified by Yamey, is underlined in General Orders issued by the Poor Law Board to parishes in 1867, and by the LGB to county councils in 1889. In a letter accompanying the 1867 circular, which provided for the adoption of DEB, the Poor Law Board criticised the existing receipts and expenditure statements on the grounds that 'they [the ratepayers] had no information as to the amount of outstanding liabilities' (BPP 1867, xxxiv: 125). This is clear evidence of the assumption (implicit elsewhere, e. g. the Report of the Departmental Committee on the Accounts of Local Authorities, BPP 1907, xxxvii) that DEB, accruals accounting and, presumably, income and expenditure statements, are seen as natural corolaries of one another. This is an assumption of which we make some use but, as mentioned earlier, it must be treated with care. Turning to the 1889 circular, this recommended the use of DEB in view of 'the nature and variety of the transactions to which the accounts of the council will relate' (BPP 1889, xxxv: 441).[11 12]

Despite these findings, much of the debate concerning the adoption of income and expenditure accounting (which is facilitated by the use of DEB), by municipal corporations in particular, was associated with the affairs of their trading organisations (Coombs and Edwards, 1991) and we feel that the ranking of Yamey's three influences in terms of their importance to municipal corporations would benefit from further investigation. This is particularly the case in view of the fact that DEB was increasingly adopted by municipal corporations despite the fact that *neither* the 1867 *nor* 1889 regulations applied to them.

Local initiatives

It was noted above that the transition from charge/discharge accounting to DEB is not always easy to discern even from the examination of accounting records. For a start, the terms charge/discharge are not usually found in the nineteenth-century financial statements of boroughs, although the caption for the Bristol accounts of 1836/7 - 'Thomas Garrard, Treasurer of the City and Borough of Bristol and County of the said City, in account with the Mayor, Aldermen, and Burgesses of the said City and Borough for Year ending 31 August, 1837' - and the typical closing entry - 'BALANCE due to the TREASURER, 31 August 1837 [£]3,350. 19. 1' - are indicative of the charge/discharge philosophy. Also, as mentioned earlier, a system of single entry bookkeeping can of course be elaborated to provide all the material required for an accruals-based profit calculation and balance sheet, and one finds amongst the records of municipal corporations elements of accruals accounting creeping into the various financial statements prepared in the 1840's 1850's and 1860's in circumstance where single entry bookkeeping remained in use (see chapter 5). By way of contrast, it is possible to operate a system of DEB purely on the cash basis thereby automatically generating data suitable only for cash-based financial reports.[13]

The available records of municipal corporations are extensive, but they do not provide a complete picture because not everything has survived and, even if it had, it would not contain all the answers, because not everything of interest to us, today, was recorded. It is for this reason that we make some use of the idea that the type of accounting statement published will be linked with the record keeping system in use. But our findings at Bristol and Bradford (where the primary records have survived and are available for public use) show that this hypothesis is fraught with problems.

Following the passage of MCA 1835, the borough of Bristol, although employing DEB, reported (in accordance with minimum statutory obligations) only cash transactions affecting the borough fund for the next 80 years, moving over to accruals-based financial reporting as late as 1915.[14] Quite clearly the purpose of maintaining the system of DEB, after 1835, was to meet aims other than the provision of information to enable the preparation of a profit and loss account and balance sheet. Presumably these included the provision of a degree of control over amounts due from collectors of rents, and the identification of the extent of the borough's obligations.

The first accounts of Bradford Corporation, following its creation in 1847, are for the year to 1 September 1848, and begin with the amount received from the local improvement commissioners who were previously responsible for providing local services. These accounts are on the cash basis and remain entirely in that format until 1856 when an accruals-based balance sheet and a distinction between capital and revenue are exhibited in the published accounts for the water department. Here we encounter what is potentially an important factor affecting the development of accounting practice - namely the adoption, following takeover, of procedures already in use in the private sector - since we know that the Bradford Waterworks Company (purchased in 1856) kept its accounts on a double entry basis (Bradford archive: ledger 2/4/2/1) and that the corporation continued to use this method for its newly acquired activity (Bradford archive: ledger 2/4/42/1).

The accounting records kept and financial statements prepared for the borough and the district fund continue, however, to be on the cash basis.[15] A major review of the accounting system, in 1872, followed the discovery of a deficiency in the cash balance and the removal of James Harris from the position of borough treasurer. The minutes state that an accountant was called in to examine the accounts and 'requested to prepare a fresh set of books for simplifying the accounts in the borough accountant's office' (minute dated 8 April 1872).

Blackburn & Co produced a new scheme for preparing the books (minute dated 10 June 1872), and a report was subsequently prepared, printed and adopted by the general committee (minute dated 1 January 1873) which contains a number of sections designed to ensure better accounting and financial control. The accountant's duties include 'To keep the necessary cash books and ledgers, by double entry, together with the subsidiary books; to post into the ledgers the respective items of receipts and expenditure to the several heads, and in the manner required in the several acts in force from time to time within the Borough'. The books (journal and ledger) opened in 1872 are on a full double entry basis,[16] though the published accounts continue to be prepared on a cash basis (although distinguishing between capital and revenue) until 1891 when accruals accounting was introduced following the appointment of a new treasurer, T. A. Thorpe.[17]

It is the above findings that led us to the conclusion that the forms of records and reports were not causally related. More specifically, that the continued use of cash accounting is not necessarily indicative of the operation of single entry bookkeeping, and that the introduction of certain aspects of accruals accounting in the published accounts does not necessarily signify the operation of DEB. We therefore limit our assumption of a *possible* causal relationship to the following: that the decision to publish an income and expenditure account and balance sheet, *instead* of or in addition to a cash-based charge/discharge type report, in the second half of the nineteenth century, is increasingly *likely* to involve the *switch* from single entry bookkeeping to DEB.

At Manchester the prominent nineteenth-century accountant, David Chadwick, was auditor of the corporation's trading activities in the late 1850's, while the waterworks accounts for 1859, which contained the first clear distinction between capital and revenue expenditure, were audited by Samuel E. Cottam & Sons, public accountants. Progress elsewhere was slow, however, with cash accounts only being rendered up until 1880 when 'proper balance sheets' were introduced following 'the employment of one of the leading firms in that City [Broome, Murray & Co.] as professional auditors' (*The Accountant*, 11 October 1889: 4).

At Cardiff, the charge/discharge system of cash-based financial reporting, in use in the 1790's, continued in force until the early 1860's. Subsequent developments in accounting practice can be associated with the appearance, on the scene, of public accountants. For example, J. Walkinshaw was called in to prepare a cumulative statement of receipts and payments covering the period from the establishment of the corporation to 1859, which is the year when the borough accounts are for the first time divided into the three constituent elements: receipts and payments on market and slaughterhouse; superannuation fund; and other civic responsibilities. The accounts prepared for the local board of health in respect of 1869 bear the signature of David Roberts, public accountant, and for the first time there is published a separate capital account and list of 'general balances' resulting in the accounts conforming to the double account format.[18]

Returning to the borough fund, we find evidence suggesting the introduction of DEB by 1875 (although it must be admitted that an efficient system of analysis based on single entry would achieve the same outcome). For that year, there are published separate receipts and payments accounts for each of the 'borough fund and markets account', the 'superannuation fund account', and the 'baths purchase account'. The balances from each of these accounts, together with the amount due from treasurer, are listed - debit and credit - and articulate to produce a statement of 'general balances'.

The perceived existence of statutory obligations to publish cash accounts, which possibly conflicted with information requirements, is clearly evident from an examination of archival material at Birmingham, where the town council considered it necessary to maintain two complete sets of books from the early 1850's. In 1851, following the passage of LGA 1848, Birmingham Borough took over responsibility for public health from the Improvement Commissioners. The resultant significant expansion of operations was accompanied by the appointment of Nathan Kimberley as accountant and acting treasurer[19] and the establishment of a dual system of bookkeeping -

cash-based and accruals-based. This meant that the Birmingham accounts (non-statutory) were on a full accruals basis and differentiated between capital and revenue from 1852.

It does not seem that the records were at this stage maintained on a full double entry basis. The stimulus for accruals accounting, at Birmingham, seems to have been the desire for information which was strictly comparable with estimates made, at the beginning of the year, as the basis for setting the rate. In 1857, however, a conflict arose between the finance committee and the public works committee concerning the calculations which had been made, and the outcome was the appointment of 'a professional gentleman' to prepare a set of accounts compiled on the basis of income and expenditure (minute 1589). John Percivall was called in and, together with Nathan Kimberley, submitted a report which identified discrepancies in the accounts prepared for the previous year. The council subsequently resolved that the entire method of accounting should be investigated (1857: minute 2436), and this discovered a complete lack of uniformity in account keeping between committees and recommended that two sets of books be kept for the authority: one for the municipal accounts (the Borough fund), and one for the improvement accounts. Both these accounts to be kept 'on the principle of double entry' (1858: minute 2728).

Conclusion

Based on this study, we may summarise the reasons for the adoption of DEB as follows.

Each of the three authorities adopting DEB up to 1835 - the boroughs of Bristol (1784) and Leicester (1835) and the County of Middlesex (1782) - appear to have suffered from financial irregularities, while at Bristol, at least, DEB was required to cope with the burgeoning number of transactions, undertaken by this wealthy borough, in an efficient and orderly manner. At Birmingham (1858) the need to prepare accounts on the income and expenditure basis to achieve comparability with estimates seems to have been the immediate stimulus. There, and at other boroughs which we find making this change after 1835, the engagement of professional accountants to undertake investigatory or audit work appears to have accompanied the introduction of DEB, though we cannot be certain that it was they who recommended change rather than, possibly, the members or officers. Bradford was the next to make the change in its borough accounts, following a defalcation by the former treasurer, though the water department's records were on a double entry basis from the date this activity was taken out of private hands in 1856.

The point has already been made that one cannot confidently infer the form of the accounting records from the nature of the final report. Certainly,

Bristol, which for sometime after 1835 published only a receipts and payments account in compliance with its minimum statutory obligations, nevertheless continued to operate the system of DEB installed in 1784. But although double entry-based records are obviously perfectly capable of enabling the publication of cash accounts, it is less likely that a system of single entry bookkeeping remains in force where the final accounts take on the form of a profit and loss account and balance sheet. We therefore suggest that DEB was introduced at Cardiff, in 1875, when we find an interlocking set of final accounts published for the first time, and possibly from 1864 when the accounts first made a clear distinction between capital and revenue, as this is likely to have been based on the bookkeeping system which distinguishes between real and nominal accounts. Finally, at Manchester, the preparation of income and expenditure accounts in 1880, following the engagement of a leading firm of auditors to perform this function, is again suggestive of the introduction of DEB at that date. Again, the indications are that one of its trading departments (water) is likely to have used this system since 1856.

The three reasons for the adoption of DEB put forward by Yamey are, therefore, all clearly evident in the above study. Our findings are also fully consistent with Jones' claim that it is 'a better stewardship model' and, in view of the fact that it 'was able to provide the necessary final accounts', its eventual success was inevitable (1992: 68). We would add that all three of Yamey's explanations are of *major* importance in relation to municipal corporations, and that the need for a full account of a corporation's rights and obligations and, particularly with the development of trading activities, to measure profit became paramount as time went by. We have also shown that an important attribute of DEB, specific to local authorities, was that it facilitated the preparation of accounts which could be directly compared with estimates made at the beginning of the financial year.

We can therefore see that the system of charge/discharge accounting increasingly proved inadequate to meet the needs of municipal corporations due to the number, nature and rapidly expanding range of transactions undertaken during the late eighteenth and nineteenth centuries. The move to DEB occurred at different points in time at different boroughs and, even within the same borough, was not adopted at a single date for all activities. A range of factors, which would repay further study, are seen to be responsible for the process of change. But the common outcome for municipal corporations, by 1907, despite statutory regulations that provided no incentive for change and in the absence of General Orders requiring the change to be made, was the widespread adoption of DEB.[20] More specifically, of the 45 boroughs investigated in 1907, just five provincial boroughs stated that the accounts were partially on the single entry system and in one borough wholly on that system (BPP 1907, xxxvii: appendix 1, q. 5).[21]

NOTES

1 The first English text on DEB, by Hugh Oldcastle, was published in 1543.

2 Exceptions include: Haydn Jones, 1985: 39-74; Jones, 1992: chapter 2: 53-90.

3 The following sources deal with the nature of charge/discharge (Jones, 1992: 43-7; Baxter, 1983; Noke 1981; Napier, 1991: 164-5). Charge/discharge statements sometimes included debtors and occasionally stock, in addition to cash transactions, though Jones has shown that local authorities did not cope very convincingly with the inclusion of stock in their financial statements. A possible explanation for these (half-hearted) attempts to include figures for inventory in parish accounts is the wording of the Poor Law Relief Act 1601, Section 2, which required the overseers to report 'such stock as shall be in their hands'.

4 It was the responsibility of the parish council.

5 This builds on the work of Rowan Jones, 1985a using further information from a series of articles published in *Local Government Finance* on the theme of 'Mr. Treasurer' and from the archives of Bristol and Cardiff Corporations.

6 The efforts made to ensure a full statement of assets is impressive, including the following methods of valuation: houses on leases for forty years, renewable, were valued at twice the rack (full market) rent and thirteen years' cheap rent; houses on rack rents at fourteen years' rack rent; and estates let at rack rents at twenty-five years' purchase. The result was an initial credit to the stock account of £137,960. 4. 10. Livock has pointed out that this practice lasted until 1817 when the surveyors recommended that these 'merely visionary' valuations be dropped from the books (1965: 99).

7 This change did not prevent a subsequent chamberlain from defrauding the City in 1822, although it is thought to have aided in his detection (Ralph, 1953).

8 This is not true; accounts were kept at Cardiff in the early 1790's (Cardiff archive: box 2564, books 1 and 2).

9 The chaotic state of central government bookkeeping generally, and that of the Ministry of Munitions in particular, up to the early twentieth century is discussed in Marriner, 1980a.

10 Although Baxter has shown that this can be done (1983: 138).

11 An order issued by the LGB concerning the accounts of local boards in 1881 (BPP 1881, xlvi) makes no specific reference to DEB, but the range of

books expected to be kept and the *pro forma* statements attached to the order are in a format which implies the use of this technique.

12 Double entry bookkeeping was made compulsory for all records subject to the district audit in 1930 (SR&O 1930, No. 30: article 4).

13 It is however possible for such records to distinguish between capital and revenue transactions and between different funds and this happened amongst the corporations examined (see chapter 6).

14 In that year the finance committee reported that the district fund accounts had for some years been kept on the accruals basis 'and this method undoubtedly has the advantage of setting out clearly the position of each committee at the end of the financial year'. They therefore recommended that the borough fund account be at last placed on the same basis as the district fund account (Report dated 5 March 1914).

15 The system of record keeping contained significant aspects of DEB. There is a journal in which the left hand page is headed 'debit' and the right hand page 'credit', and the entries are mirror-images of transactions in the ledger. The 'journal entries' are posted quarterly and, individually, cover a number of pages. In the ledger there are separate columns for the borough fund, district fund, lamp rate fund and water account, rather than separate ledgers for each of these. All the data is cash-based.

16 The extent to which municipal corporations (and other local authorities) continued to operate their system of DEB on the full accruals basis also requires study. In 1910 the borough accountant of Holborn refers to 'a pernicious habit, which appears to be growing up in different quarters, of keeping the accounts on a cash basis, and making them up on an income and expenditure basis at the end of the year' (Pocock, 1910: 170). The failure to maintain debtors and creditors ledgers is criticised on the grounds that one of 'the most useful checks against extravagance or unwise expenditure' is lost and the spending committees 'cannot well be blamed if they exceed their estimates' (Contributed, 1910: 673).

17 The accounts for the second trading activity acquired by the borough - gas - were prepared on the accruals basis immediately following the acquisition of the Bradford Gas Light company in 1871.

18 This system of financial reporting is discussed in chapters 5 and 9.

19 The previous treasurer was the borough's bank manager, H. Knight, 1839-52. This was a common arrangement and probably partly explains the popularity of cash accounting.

20 Evidence presented to this effect were from Adams, district auditor for the North Western Counties District, who believed the system to be in general use (BPP 1907, xxxvii: minute 1621) while Carson Roberts, the doyen of district auditors during the first quarter of the twentieth century, described it as in 'universal use' (BPP 1907, xxxvii: minute 1889).

21 Major residual problems, at least in relation to systems subject to the district audit, were that they were poorly maintained and lacking in uniformity and clarity (Adams, BPP 1907, xxxvii: minute 1626: Carson Roberts, minute 1992). It was possibly these weaknesses which led the District Auditors Society to recommend, at a meeting held on 6 April 1906, that the accounts be kept on the income and expenditure basis and that the ledger accounts on the double-entry basis (Davies, 1986: 22).

5

FRAMEWORK OF ACCOUNTS

Municipal corporations were initially authorised to provide a limited range of services, accounted for through the borough fund, which included the following: policing, the incarceration of offenders and lunatics, and the organisation of elections. The level and range of expenditure increased phenomenally, however, over the next hundred years. In particular, municipal corporations assumed full responsibility for the health and safety of local inhabitants by providing a wide range of services administered through the district fund, and for further improving living standards within an increasingly urbanised society by the establishment of 'trading' services (water, gas, electricity, and tramways) each also accounted for through its own separate fund account.

The figures for rate receipts, in table 5.1, give some indication of the massive increase in scale of municipal operations.

We should therefore not be surprised to find a considerable increase in the size and complexity of published financial statements over time. In the early years these statements often consisted of merely a one page cash account whereas, by the 1930's, published reports of over 300 pages, and often significantly more, were the norm.

This chapter is concerned with the provision of accounting information for external users comprising the following main groups: local electors (up to 1918 this class was restricted to ratepayers; afterwards national franchise rules applied); consumers of municipal services; creditors, and investors in local authority securities; and central government.[1]

The specific objectives are: to examine the development of the financial reporting practices of municipal corporations; to explore the relationship between accounting theory, as embraced by the literature, and observed accounting practices; and to examine, in depth, both the environmental factors responsible for accounting change, and the specific influences which proved crucial at particular points in time.

Table 5.1:[a] Municipal corporations' rate receipts

Year	£
1839-40	197,000[b]
1882-83	7,417,414[c]
1913-14	27,038,124[d]
1932-33	102,957,115[d]

Notes

a Over the period covered by this table the overall cost of living did not increase. Computed price indices (1661 = 100) being: 1840, 111; 1883, 88; 1914, 91; 1933, 103 ('Back to an Age of Falling Prices', *The Economist*, 13 July 1974: 62).

b Appendix to Report on Local Taxation, 1870: 72.

c Statistical abstract for the UK, c. 4463: 32.

d Statistical abstract for the UK, 1938, cmd, 5627: 228-9.

The key practices

The accounting practices of municipal corporations first received detailed attention from the literature in a series of leading articles published in *The Accountant* in 1884, ten years after that journal was first published.

> Accounts have been made up, printed, and circulated, but the defective and often erroneous manner in which they were constructed, their incompleteness, and the meagreness and often entire absence of proper explanations, prevented any but an extremely small section of the ratepayers from obtaining even a tolerable notion of the financial position of the body corporate. (20 September 1884: 3)

Given the rivalry between various groups of accountants beginning to emerge at this time, comments contained in a journal which focused principally on affairs within the private sector should not be accepted without question, and this chapter will help to show whether this highly influential journal presented a true and fair view of the prevailing practices.

At the start date (the creation of the municipal corporation) and the end date for this study (by which time their system of financial reporting was well developed) there existed broad uniformity between the accounting practices of all boroughs. In the early years a statement setting out cash received and paid on the borough fund was published; in 1935 it was the common practice to publish for each fund an accruals-based revenue account, capital account, and balance sheet, together with an aggregate balance sheet which summarised the overall financial position of the entity. An overview of the development of financial reporting practices between these dates is given in table 5.2.

Table 5.2 consists of five pairs of columns that focus, effectively, on three developments: the introduction of accruals accounting (columns I and II); the adoption of the double account format (columns III and IV); and the publication of the aggregate balance sheet (column V). It must be emphasised that each of these developments normally occurred gradually, within each municipality, which makes it difficult to ascribe precise dates to the adoption of a particular practice involving an equal degree of complexity and sophistication at each corporation. The columns headed 'First' refers to the first sign of the adoption of each of the five key practices within a single department, while columns headed 'All' indicate that the practice was in use, to an extent, in all departments in existence at the specified date.

We will illustrate these points by reference to Cardiff Corporation's accounts. These were on the cash basis until 1864 when, following assumption of responsibility for health, we find the following information published: an 'Abstract of the Accounts of the Cardiff Local Board of Health' for the year to 31 August which is confined to revenue transactions and contains a small number of items owing and owed; a 'Balance Sheet' which sets out loans raised, capital expenditure, amounts owing and owed, and cash balances. By 1869 capital transactions are separately reported in the 'Sewerage Works and Special Improvements Account'. In addition, the net balance of capital from the 'Improvements Account' is listed, together with balances arising in respect of revenue transactions, in a financial statement entitled 'General Balances'. At this stage the essential features of the double account system, which requires the maintenance of a separate capital account (see later) are therefore in place, though the accounts themselves remain substantially on the cash basis.

In 1876 we find the first signs of accruals accounting in the borough fund, a distinction made between capital and revenue transactions, and the double account system fully operational, but it is not until 1897 that the activities of all departments appear to be on the full accruals basis. The first sign of what might be loosely described as an aggregate balance sheet appeared in the borough accounts for 1861 when the cash balances arising in respect of the three separate activities (the superannuation fund, market and slaughterhouse, and mainstream borough fund activities) are summarised under the heading 'general balances'. The first full scale aggregate balance sheet, together with other major innovations in financial reporting practice discussed below, was published in 1897.

The notes to table 5.2 are indicative of the fact that accounting innovation at the five corporations was spread over the period 1850 to 1922; in other words a 72 year time span from the initial movement away from cash accounting to full accruals accounting conforming to the double account system and summarised in the aggregate balance sheet. The outcome was achieved first at Birmingham (1855), then at Manchester (1887), Bradford (1891), Cardiff (1897) and, finally, Bristol (1922). Although not evident from table 5.2, it was always the adoption of a key practice by the borough fund which was the last stage
(sometimes contemporaneously with its adoption by certain other departments) in the achievement of broad uniformity of accounting practice within a municipality.

Before examining these developments further below, we need to acknowledge certain limitations in the scope and coverage of this analysis. The development of the following financial reporting practices, used from time to time by the five municipal corporations studied, is not examined.

* Sinking fund transactions: Birmingham (reported in 1852); Bradford (1864); Cardiff (1866); Manchester (1860).
* Summary of loans raised and repaid: Birmingham (1863); Bradford (1866); Bristol (1837); Cardiff (1896).
* Inventory of properties: Birmingham (1868); Bradford (1873); Bristol (1895); Cardiff (1897).
* Information concerning estimates: Birmingham (1874); Bradford (1873); Bristol (1906).
* Statistics and/or comparative figures: Bradford (1873); Bristol (1895); Manchester (1890).

Neither do we consider, in detail, changes in the nature of the terminology used (e. g. income and expenditure, revenue and expenditure or profit and loss), its reliability (e. g. the use of the term expenditure to describe what we call today payments, and the term balance sheet to describe a statement of receipts and payments), and variety (e. g. the use of a wide range of captions to describe the balance sheet) except where it is relevant to the main thesis. Finally, we are not concerned with variations in layout (e. g. whether assets appear on the right and liabilities on the left hand side of the balance sheet or

Table 5.2: Development of financial reporting procedures - key practices

	I Accruals		II Accruals based balance sheet		III Capital/Revenue distinction		IV Double account system		V Aggrega balance sh	
	First[1]	**All[2]**	**First**	**All**	**First**	**All**	**First**	**All**	**First**	
Birmingham (1838)	1852	1852	1852	1852	1852	1852	1860	1860	1855	18
Bradford (1847)	1856[3]	1891	1856[3]	1891	1856[3]	1872	1857[3]	-[5]	1852[4]	18
Bristol (1373)	1895[6]	1915	1895[6]	1915	1895[6]	1895	1895[6]	1915	1895[6]	19
Cardiff (1324)	1864[7]	1876	1869[7]	1876	1864[7]	1876	1869[7]	1876	1861[4]	18
Manchester (1838)	1850[7]	1881	1870[3/8]	1881	1859[3/8]	1881	1880[3/8]	-[9]	1887	18

Dates of incorporation are given in brackets.

__Notes__:

1 First evidence of use of practice within municipal accounts
2 Practice in use by all departments/funds.
3. Waterworks.
4. Cash balances of various departments.
5. Borough account balance sheet never separated into capital and revenue sections.
6. Change probably made before this date.
7. District fund accounts.
8. Change probably made on this date but possibly earlier.
9. Separate revenue account and capital (improvement) account balance sheets in respect of the borough (city) fund until superseded by rate fund in 1925.

vice versa) or in the ordering of data (e. g. the sequence of items in each column in the balance sheet or revenue account).

Financial reporting

Cash versus accruals accounting

In this section we consider: the continued support expressed in certain quarters for cash accounting; the case for accruals accounting; the nature of the 'key' accounting practices identified above, and the broad arguments put forward for their adoption.

The case for cash accounting We have seen that MCA 1835 obliged town councils to make available to ratepayers an abstract of the treasurer's accounts. The precise form of these accounts was never specified, but the requirement for the treasurer to keep 'true accounts of the sums of money by him received and paid' (5&6 Will. 4, c. 76, s. 93) implied publication of a cash-based operating statement rather than an income and expenditure account and a balance sheet. It was perfectly natural that the Act's provisions should be interpreted in that manner in view of the fact, demonstrated in chapter 4, that the essential features of the charge\discharge method of accounting (mainly a cash-based system) remained in common use. The tendency of some corporations, at least, to place a narrow interpretation of the provisions of the Act might help to explain the decision of Bristol Corporation to publish cash-based reports of transactions on the borough fund through from 1835 to 1915, despite the fact that DEB was introduced in 1785 (see chapter 4). It might also explain the decision of Birmingham Corporation to maintain two complete sets of books from 1852, the year when the corporation also made the decision to prepare accounts on the accruals basis. This state of affairs persisted until 1870 when a scheme of accounting was designed to enable the statutory cash accounts to be extracted as well as providing the basis for what were considered to be the corporation's main accruals-based accounts.

The continued use of cash-based accounting in certain quarters during the late nineteenth-century, under the banner 'receipts and payments' or 'receipts and expenditure',[2] has been attributed, in part, to the district auditor's insistence on the cash basis to account for those areas where he had jurisdiction (Swainson, 1895: 70; Greatrex, 1897: 41; but see BPP 1907, xxxvii: minute 6320). As usual, however, experience varied from place to place. According to Thomas Abercrombie Welton, head of the accounting firm, Welton, Jones &

Co., an ex-president of the ICAEW and chairman of the finance committee of Wandsworth Borough

> in Wandsworth, when I first became a member of the finance committee, the accounts were kept on that [receipts and payments] system ... which I understood had been in use for many years. I was not satisfied with that system, and when the district auditor, Mr Carson Roberts, suggested a change to income and expenditure, I welcomed the alteration, which I had imagined we were not at liberty to make (BPP 1907, xxxvii: minute 6320).

The opposition of council members and the continued existence of cash-based statutory reporting requirements also served as stumbling blocks to progress (*Financial Circular*, November 1898: 1-3; Greatrex, 1897). The existence of a perceived legal obligation also to report receipts and payments was neatly satisfied by some municipalities using a three column presentation which showed cash flows in the first column, accruals in the second and income and expenditure in the third (Jones, 1992: 96; see, for example, Manchester Borough's accounts for 1900).

There were also some who continued to dispute whether accruals accounting was the superior option. The 1907 Departmental Committee pointed out that the cash approach had the 'merit of simplicity' (BPP 1907, xxxvii: para. 27), while specific objections 'of a general character' to the accruals approach included 'the undesirability of admitting into account, as final records, items that may have to be estimated' thereby introducing 'an element of uncertainty' as well as unavoidable 'delay in closing the accounts' (para. 35). Further, the Permanent Secretary to the LGB expressed the view, in 1903, that the 'advantage that has been felt in having actual cash accounts kept is that it shows what the ratepayers do actually pay during the particular year' (BPP 1903, vii: q. 78).

As late as 1899, correspondence emanating from the County Accountant's office, Trowbridge, expressed doubt about whether the form of accounts prescribed by the Board of Trade for trading undertakings, for the purpose of government returns, permitted the use of accruals accounting. It was pointed out that each of the terms income and expenditure was 'only conspicuous by its absence'; also that the *pro forma* capital account, headed 'receipts and expenditure', can only be taken to imply the need to use the cash basis (Dring, 1899: 46-7).

The Accountant identified, as an additional complication, the fact that 'each member of the Corporate Treasurers' and Accountants' Institute seems to have started with the idea that all that was needed, in order to bring about a uniform system of accounts, was that every other municipality should adopt the form of accounts employed by his own [municipality]' (1897: 330).

The case for accruals accounting Bolton's borough treasurer, George Swainson, in his inaugural address, as President, to the newly created CTAI, in 1886, criticised prevailing reporting practices and drew attention to 'one very large borough in England whose accounts occupy 200 pages, in no place can you find a clear statement of assets and liabilities' (*Proceedings*, 1886: 5). *The Accountant* confirmed that there are 'many corporations ... who simply give a statement of their receipts and payments' (11 November, 1884: 3). Indeed, up to the end of the nineteenth-century, leader writers for professional journals continued to perceive a need to advocate the adoption of accruals accounting (*The Accountant*, 13 February 1897: 172; *Financial Circular*, November 1898: 1).

The relative merits of cash and accruals as the basis for financial reporting were considered by the 1907 Departmental Committee which lists the advantages of the latter as follows: it records every step of a transaction thereby protecting against negligence and irregularity; it enables the statement of an entity's profit and loss and financial position; it records values; and it provides a stable and homogeneous basis for statistics.

The drawbacks of cash accounting were seen to be: that it is an incomplete representation of events for reporting and control purposes; that it provides scope for delaying payments in order to manipulate the accounts and influence the level of rates (BPP 1907, xxxvii: paras 26-39). Further advantages claimed elsewhere for accruals accounting, in the context of the local authority, were that it provided a better basis for the purpose of setting the rate (Cooke, 1887: 167), and for demonstrating the extent to which actual results varied from the estimates (Guthrie, 1886: 615).

Distinguishing capital from revenue

Many of the municipal corporations, newly created in 1835, possessed little or nothing in the way of corporate assets (Bristol was an important exception). Indeed some of them inherited net liabilities, and it was necessary to borrow money to finance the supply of new services. Loans were raised by special Acts of Parliament or under Provisional Orders which also made provision for repayment.

The basic philosophy underlying these regulations, and many others applying to loan sanctioning, was to guard against the creation of permanent loan capital and ensure that local authorities did not overborrow; the test being whether repayment was made within the life of the asset acquired. The obligation to repay loans within prescribed periods, and to rate accordingly, implied a need to separate capital transactions (the historical record of the amount raised and repayable) from revenue items, with the latter including provision for the redemption of the debt.

In a stewardship environment, with officials keen to demonstrate financial probity and compliance with statutory obligations, the natural outcome was to provide ratepayers with a detailed statement of capital raised, and therefore repayable out of the rates, and how the money had been spent. This treatment gained momentum from the 1850's onwards as corporations increased their borrowing in order to meet their statutory obligations to provide health and sanitary services under LGA 1848 and to undertake the supply of gas and water in response to governmental encouragement (Falkus 1977: 139). We have seen above that this information occupied a great deal of space in the annual abstract, but it required no departure from a cash-based financial reporting system.

The double account system

The double account system of financial reporting is able to combine the attributes of charge\discharge accounting (stewardship orientation) with commercial accounting (profit calculation). The distinguishing feature of the double account system is that it divides the conventional balance sheet into two parts, with capital raised and spent reported in one statement (the capital account) and the remaining items in the other (the general balance sheet). This method was used by public utilities operating in the private sector around this time (Edwards, 1985). A leader in *The Accountant*, 1893, summed up one of the main arguments for the double account system as follows:

> ... no one would [then] be deceived into supposing that there was any necessary connection between the amount of expenditure appearing to the debit of the capital account and the actual value of the works existing as the result of that expenditure (1893: 718).

Support for this method on the basis that it provided a sound stewardship record of capital transactions[3] came from a number of quarters (Swainson, 1895: 72; Harris, 1903: 221; Miller, 1905: 20).

The double account system was used by transportation and public utility companies from roughly the mid-nineteenth century onwards, but it would be wrong to assume that municipal corporations adopted procedures developed within the private sector simply as a convenient 'off the peg' solution to their reporting requirements. As noted earlier, the statutory financing obligations imposed on local authorities *naturally* led to the development of procedures which contained the main features of the double account system - a separation between capital and revenue transactions, although it is possible that they imported from the private sector the final element required - the general balance sheet - to complete the reporting package.

There is one noticeable difference between the statutory form of general balance sheet prescribed for private sector companies compared with that used by local authorities. The private sector general balance sheet was to contain only the balance transferred from the capital account (railways, 1868) or total figures for both capital raised and capital spent (gas, 1871; electricity 1882; and railways from 1911). Both of these presentations may be found, at various times, in the accounts of the municipalities examined, but in three of the five cases the consensus format (neither Bradford nor Manchester published a general balance sheet in the conventional format for the borough fund,[4] see table 5.2) involved re-stating all the major balances from the capital account. For this purpose, the municipality's balance sheet was divided horizontally into two sections, with the upper section containing capital items and headed 'capital accounts' and the lower section captioned 'revenue balances' or 'income and other accounts' (figure 5.1).

The aggregate balance sheet

The aggregate balance sheet (figure 5.2) brought together the year-end balances for each of the funds and departments, and its purpose was to provide a 'bird's eye view' (McCall, 1930: 96) and 'disclose in one statement the financial position of the authority as a whole' (Whitehead, 1931: 118). Bradford's accounts for 1900 refer to the fact that 'the financial position ... may be seen at a glance by reference to the aggregate balance sheet'. Guthrie is similarly enthusiastic seeing its virtue as 'condensing' the individual results of each department 'so as to exhibit in the briefest form the grand total of the true balance sheet of the city' (1886: 615).

The precise content of the aggregate balance sheet varied depending upon the range of services supplied, the bookkeeping system in force, and presentation of data in the individual fund accounts. Some boroughs (e. g. Bradford from 1891) maintained a distinction between expenditure on capital account and revenue account in respect of each fund; others (e. g. Manchester, 1887) made no such distinction. The horizontal format for the aggregate

BOROUGH FUND ACCOUNT.

BALANCE SHEET, 31st March, 1900.

LIABILITIES.	£ s. d.	£ s. d.	Folio	£	s.	d.
Capital Accounts.						
Cardiff Corporation Redeemable Stock		60,458 11 7				
Cardiff Corporation 3% Redeemable Stock ..		46,309 4 9				
		106,762 16 4				
Less, Funds for Redemption, viz.:						
Loans Fund Account	11,095 11 11					
Redemption Fund Account ..	6,604 2 7					
		17,699 14 6				
		89,063 1 10				
Loans	26,447 7 4					
Less, Paid off by Instalments 19,430 6 2						
Sinking Fund provided 321 18 5						
	19,752 4 7					
		6,695 2 9				
			24	95,758	4	7
Capital Account (Balance)—						
Due to Treasurer on Capital Accounts ..		204,358 3 7				
Due to Urban Authority Account ..	416 5 4					
Due to Water Works Account ..	70 4 6					
		486 9 10				
Sundry Creditors		788 3 3				
			24	205,632	16	8
Excess of Capital Expenditure and other Assets over Liabilities derived from the following sources, viz.:—						
Loans Fund Account	11,095 11 11					
Redemption Fund Account	6,604 2 7					
		17,699 14 6	24			
Loans repaid	19,430 6 2					
Sinking Fund in hand	321 18 5					
		19,752 4 7	24			
Sale of Sites—Post Office Site ..		800 0 0	..			
			..	38,251	19	1
Carried Forward				339,643	0	4

ASSETS.	£ s. d.	Folio	£	s.	d.
Capital Accounts.					
By Expenditure on Works and Undertakings ..	343,296 3 3				
By Expenses raising Corporation Stock, including Discount on Issues	651 15 5				
	343,947 18 8	24			
Less, Premium received with Stock Issues	5,104 18 4	24			
		..	338,843	0	4
By Investment *re* Sale of Sites—					
Consols £847 13s. 7d., Post Office Site		..	800	0	0
Carried Forward			339,643	0	4

Figure 5.1: Borough fund account balance sheet, Cardiff Corporation, 1900

BOROUGH FUND ACCOUNT.

BALANCE SHEET, 31st March, 1900 (continued).

LIABILITIES.	£ s. d.	£	s.	d.
Brought Forward		339,643	0	4
Income and other Accounts.				
To Police Pension Fund		18,158	4	9
To Fire Brigade Pension Fund		821	7	7
To Surplus *re* Exhibition, 1870 (per contra)		510	4	7
To Sundry Creditors—				
County Council of Glamorgan	4,142 1 7			
Technical Instruction Committee	252 0 0			
Welsh Intermediate, &c., Committee	252 0 0			
Various	4,247 18 1			
	8,893 19 8			
Less, on Capital Accounts (p. 30)..	788 3 3			
		8,105	16	5
To Suspense Account—				
Severn Navigation Commissioners for Interest to 31st December, 1899 (per contra)		1,936	19	8
To Cardiff Corporation Act, 1894, Cost of Obtaining (Borough Fund Share)				
Amount provided out of Revenue (per Contra) ..		2,670	0	4
To Revenue Account—				
Excess of Income over Expenditure to 31st March, 1899 (p. 29)	30,253 9 0			
Add, Excess of Income over Expenditure, year ended 31st March, 1900 (p. 1)	961 6 11			
		31,214	15	11
£		403,060	9	7

F. R. GREENHILL,
Borough Treasurer.

31st August, 1900.

ASSETS.		£ s. d.	£	s.	d.
Brought Forward			339,643	0	4
Income and other Accounts.					
By Investments of Police Pension Fund—					
Loan *re* Cardiff Free Library Building		4,017 1 2			
Purchase of £11,941 14s. 0d., 2¾% Consols		12,755 11 11			
			16,772	13	1
By Amounts due from other Departments—					
Cardiff Burial Board Account		29,572 2 2			
Less, Amounts due to other Departments—					
Urban Authority Account.. 1,317 10 11					
Less, on Capital Accounts (p. 30) 416 5 4	901 5 7				
Waterworks Account .. 94 4 10					
Less, on Capital Accounts (p. 30) 70 4 6	24 0 4				
Electric Lighting Account	125 4 5				
		1,050 10 4			
			28,521	11	10
By Amount due by Treasurer—					
On Income and other Accounts			5,728	19	6
By Sundry Debtors—					
Overseers *re* Borough Rate		1,054 2 5			
Free Libraries Committee		742 10 9			
Sundry Tenants		36 6 8			
Magistrates' Clerk		210 16 8			
Severn Navigation Commissioners		1,936 19 8			
National Provincial Bank of England, Surplus *re* Exhibition, 1870 (on deposit)		510 4 7			
Various		628 6 1			
			5,119	6	10
By Cardiff Corporation Act, 1894, Cost of obtaining (Borough Fund Share)			2,670	0	4
By Cardiff Corporation Bill, 1900					
Promotion Expenses to date (p. 27.)			4,079	17	8
By Cash in hands of Officials—					
Borough Treasurer		500 0 0			
Head Constable		10 0 0			
Medical Officer of Health		5 0 0			
Cashier, Finance Office		10 0 0			
			525	0	0
£			403,060	9	7

DAVID JONES,
Mayor's Auditor.

A. MAURICE BAILEY, A.S.A.A.,
DAVID SHEPHERD, F.C.A,
Elective Auditors.

C. E. DOVEY, F.C.A.,
Auditor.

AGGREGATE BALANCE SHEET, 31st MARCH, 1900.

Assets.

Account.	Page in this Abstract.	Expenditure on Works, &c. — Capital. £ s. d.	Expenditure on Works, &c. — Revenue. £ s. d.	Sundry Debtors. £ s. d.	Investments &c. £ s. d.	In Banker's hands. £ s. d.	Cash in hands of Officials. £ s. d.	TOTAL. £	s.	d.
CITY FUND	188—191	1800167 3 2	40215 19 1 Stock on hand 219 0 5	253889 1 11	61255 19 11	123949 15 3	1511 1 0	2281208	0	9
GENERAL DISTRICT RATE FUND	292—293	1162914 17 6	...	25209 16 4	...	12623 1 7	8736 13 10	1209484	9	3
WATER FUND	356—357	3120589 9 7	...	42899 1 2	...	14859 14 0	130 0 0	3178478	4	9
TRAMWAYS FUND	394—395	192663 19 8	Stock on hand. 663 5 9	827 19 5	...	...	40 0 0	194195	4	10
GAS FUND	422—425	621565 15 3½	Stock on hand. 25739 15 11	78720 4 5½	...	32833 15 0	100 0 0	758939	10	8
ELECTRICITY FUND	450—451	202568 3 8	Stock on hand. 19886 11 5	13675 17 1	...	...	50 0 0	236180	12	2
FREE LIBRARY FUND	462—463	...	40417 10 7	...	...	36 14 4	22 8 7	40476	13	6
CARTWRIGHT MEMORIAL HALL FUND	468—469	...	432 5 3	...	...	40343 5 3		40775	10	6
CITY COURT FUND	476—477	...	...	378 1 5	...	1327 10 7	100 0 0	1805	12	0
POLICE PENSION FUND	484—485	...	...	338 5 4	21920 0 0	367 4 1	...	22625	9	5
SEMON CONVALESCENTS' HOME FUND	492—493	...	1655 6 4	58 12 1	*15500 0 0	1301 13 6	10 6 5	18525	18	4
FIRE INSURANCE FUND	498—499	...	...	...	...	15689 6 0	...	15689	6	0
TECHNICAL COLLEGE FUND	508—509	...	Buildings, Furniture, &c. 45645 9 6	46 0 4	...	...	26 16 0	45718	5	10
ADDED DISTRICTS	614—615	262746 13 0	4710 1 8	10217 2 7	2200 0 0	...	4 2 0	279877	19	3
SUNDRY PROPERTIES (as per Inventory)	665	...	70151 11 5	...	...	...	...	70151	11	5
Do. do. Added Districts	667	...	1655 8 8	...	...	...	...	1655	8	8
	£	7363216 1 10½	251392 6 0	426260 2 1½	100875 19 11	243331 19 7	10731 7 10	8395807	17	4

Liabilities.

Account.	Mortgage Debt. £ s. d.	Sundry Creditors. £ s. d.	Owing to Banker. £ s. d.	TOTAL LIABILITIES. £	s.	d.	BALANCE—Excess of Assets. £ s. d.	TOTAL. £	s.	d.
CITY FUND	1666389 10 5	48323 19 4	...	1714713	9	9	566494 11 0	2281208	0	9
GENERAL DISTRICT RATE FUND	536495 18 0	14313 16 0	...	570809	14	0	638674 15 3	1209484	9	3
WATER FUND	2702991 9 8	46963 19 10	...	2749955	9	6	428522 15 3	3178478	4	9
TRAMWAYS FUND	143375 0 0	4311 1 1	9958 15 8	157644	16	9	36550 8 1	194195	4	10
GAS FUND	474494 5 4	34344 1 11	...	508818	7	3	250121 3 5	758939	10	8
ELECTRICITY FUND	183574 3 6	8128 13 2	1537 17 9	193240	14	5	42939 17 9	236180	12	2
FREE LIBRARY FUND	...	375 13 4	...	375	13	4	40101 0 2	40476	13	6
CARTWRIGHT MEMORIAL HALL FUND	...	...	...	...	...	...	40775 10 6	40775	10	6
CITY COURT FUND	...	29 16 9	...	29	16	9	1775 15 3	1805	12	0
POLICE PENSION FUND	...	...	...	...	...	...	22625 9 5	22625	9	5
SEMON CONVALESCENTS' HOME FUND	...	107 6 10	...	107	6	10	18418 11 6	18525	18	4
FIRE INSURANCE FUND	...	...	...	...	...	...	15689 6 0	15689	6	0
TECHNICAL COLLEGE FUND	...	871 2 10	13813 15 9	14684	18	7	31033 7 3	45718	5	10
ADDED DISTRICTS	148906 15 7	6940 2 0	7748 11 2	163595	8	9	116282 10 6	279877	19	3
SUNDRY PROPERTIES (as per Inventory)	...	...	...	...	...	...	70151 11 5	70151	11	5
Do. do. Added Districts	...	...	...	...	...	...	1655 8 8	1655	8	8
	5856227 2 6	164709 13 1	33059 0 4	6053995	15	11	2341812 1 5	8395807	17	4

* Presented by the late CHAS. SEMON, Esq.

MEM.—The question as to what extent Capital expenditure, under the head of Street Improvements, Sewerage, and other works of an unrealisable character may be fairly subject to annual reduction as assets in view of the operation of their Sinking Funds, finds no common solution: the periods allowed for the extinction of debt bear no agreed relation or measure of value to the period of utility in respect of which the undertakings were projected, the amounts therefore are retained in the respective Balance Sheets at their actual cost on the one hand, and the position of the Sinking Fund from its inception with regard to the Mortgage Debt on the other. The increment or decrement in the value of lands for improvements has no generally accepted data and does not enter into these calculations.

In addition to the Assets above-mentioned (£8,395,807 17 4) the Corporation own sundry properties which have been presented at various times (but which are not recorded in the Account Books of the Corporation) amounting to about £110,000, including Peel Park, estimated, as per Surveyor's valuation, at £80,000, and Bradford Moor Park Area with Surplus Lands (see page 136) at £12,400, together with Park Lands in the recently Added Districts.

Mem. as to Bank Balance—

	£ s. d.
In Banker's hands	243331 19 7
Owing to Banker	33059 0 4
Net Amount in Banker's hands (see pages 623 and 631)	£210272 19 3

GEO. A. THORPE, F.S.A.A.,
CITY TREASURER.

Figure 5.2: Aggregate balances sheet, Bradford Corporation, 1900

balance sheet was used at Cardiff and Birmingham, but at each of the other three boroughs a tabular format was used from the outset.

Each of the innovations considered in this section of the chapter obtained a strong foothold and complete adoption in most cases; the exception was the failure of Bradford and Manchester to implement fully the double account system for the purpose of the borough fund, although a clear distinction was always maintained between capital and revenue transactions.

The process of accounting change

We now examine the main factors responsible for the adoption of accruals-based financial reporting.

The regulatory framework

We have seen that MCA 1835 provided for the publication of an audited abstract of accounts, while LGA 1858 obliged local boards of health[5] to make an annual report of 'receipts and expenditure' on the district fund to the Secretary of State, and to publish the same in a local newspaper (21&22 Vict., c. 98, s. 76). These broad requirements remained unaltered until the third decade of the twentieth century when we begin to find evidence of *statutory* recognition of the need to move towards accruals accounting (see below). We must therefore look instead to the local government sector's professional accounting body for evidence of regulatory pressure to bring about accounting change.

The CTAI's determination to standardise financial reporting practices appears to have been influenced by stinging criticisms contained in the authoritative *Burdett's Official Intelligence*[6] and in the columns of *The Accountant*. Swainson tells us that these publications had complained that 'it was impossible for several corporations to prepare an accurate balance sheet of their assets and liabilities' (1889: 29).

The CTAI therefore requested the LGB to exercise its power, under PHA 1875 (38&39 Vict., c. 55, s. 245), to issue an Order prescribing a form of accounts for municipal authorities acting as boards of health. Failure to respond to this request caused the CTAI to take the initiative in a letter (dated 24 October 1889) circulated to its members, which comprised mainly borough accountants and treasurers:

> the proper plan of keeping the whole of the accounts of every corporation is that of including the income and expenditure of each

> year, the income being shown on the right hand page of the published abstract, and the expenditure on the left hand page. Each set of accounts should include a balance sheet, embodying the whole of the ledger balances, the stock of stores, the outstanding liabilities and assets, which should include outstanding (and collectable) rates, and the balance shown on the revenue account. It is desirable that there should be shown for every fund, a revenue account, a capital account, and a balance sheet. It is also desirable that a general or aggregate balance sheet should be inserted in every abstract. The borrowing powers, capital expenditure, and sinking funds, should be clearly shown (*Proceedings*, 1890: 5-6).

The letter urged each member to, 'as far as the circumstances of your case will allow, adopt the above suggestions, if you have not already done so'.

Progress was slow according to the President of the CTAI:

> The published accounts of some corporations are still merely summaries of receipts and payments, while others are complete statements of income and expenditure for the year ... [and] ... I doubt whether it will be possible to attain anything like uniformity in the mode of publishing abstracts of corporation accounts until some prescribed form of accounts is issued with authority by the Local Government Board (*Proceedings*, 1894: 13).

We may infer from table 5.2, however, that the CTAI was encouraging the adoption of procedures *already* used by the more enlightened municipal corporations. The favoured procedures were being used by four of the corporations covered in this study by 1889; only Bristol (for reasons considered below) was slow to change.

The broad question of uniformity was considered by Joint Select Committee on Municipal Trading 1903 which favoured the principle of uniform accounts, but was doubtful whether it would be possible to prescribe a standard form suitable for all municipal and other local authorities, having regard to the varying conditions existing in different districts (MacMillan et al, 1934: 26). The 1907 Departmental Committee re-examined the matter and reported that progress was being made, but that there remained ample scope for further improvement. It seems that the receipts and payments basis was used by very many smaller authorities[7] and, '[although] most of the larger authorities follow more or less comprehensive systems of income and expenditure ... there is little uniformity as regards the form in which the abstracts of the accounts are presented to the ratepayers' (BPP 1907, xxxvii: 589).[8] The case for standardisation was also spelled out.

> [Otherwise] direct comparisons [between authorities] may often be fallacious and misleading. But such uniformity as can be obtained is no doubt desirable in itself: the possibility of comparison, even if incomplete, tends to foster interest in the accounts, and to stimulate criticism and investigation which may lead to substantial improvements in administration. (BPP 1907, xxxvii: 601)

Standardisation was considered, by the 1907 Departmental Committee, to be both desirable and achievable, and its report contained proposals consistent with the general instructions issued by the CTAI to its members in 1889. Attached to the report are recommended standard forms of accounts for electricity, gas, water, and tramways, and for non-trading activities. The accounts are based broadly on the double account system of financial reporting (BPP 1907, xxxvii: 615, Schedule A-E), of which the initial draft was prepared by the IMTA whose contribution is gratefully acknowledged (BPP 1907, xxxvii: 611). No immediate steps were taken to give effect to the above recommendations.

In the years that followed, annual meetings of the IMTA record unsuccessful attempts to persuade the Board of Trade to issue prescribed standard forms of accounts.[9] The IMTA therefore decided to take the initiative, in 1913, of issuing to its members standard forms for eleven of the main local authority non-trading accounts.[10]

A statutory development of significance was contained in SR&O, 1930, no. 30, issued by the Ministry of Health under the District Auditors Act 1879. The Order covered the accounting practices of municipalities only to the extent they were subject to the district audit (e. g. education) but, according to a contemporary authority, 'the regulations are of great interest and importance, representing as they do, an official pronouncement regarding the application of the principles of accountancy to the transactions of local authorities, and it is probable that many authorities, to whom the regulations do not apply compulsorily, will follow the principles enunciated therein' (MacMillan et al, 1934: 27). According to Carson Roberts the regulations 'were considered and agreed by the IMTA and the Association of Municipal Corporations before being promulgated by the Minister and were also submitted to the Association of Urban District Councils and accepted by that body as appropriate for its members' (1930: 386).

The new regulations, however, although covering the main principles of record keeping and financial reporting - specifying use of the double account system and the income and expenditure basis - did not tackle the precise form of published accounts. Nor did LGA 1933 which merely re-enacted existing legislation with few modifications. We will see, however, that other factors had already conspired to achieve fundamental change in the form and content of published accounts.

Public accountants

From 1835 to 1933 there was a statutory requirement for municipal accounts to be audited by two officials elected by the local inhabitants. In 1884, the absence of a requirement for these individuals to possess an accounting qualification and the perceived lack of professionalism on the part of the corporations' financial officers (the CTAI was not formed until 1885) were the subject of attack from an editorial in *The Accountant*.

> There are probably few kinds of accounts which would require more skilful treatment in the form of setting them forth than those of municipal authorities, but it is very unlikely indeed that any improvements which time or circumstances might render necessary would be effected from within. There are many corporations now who simply give a statement of their receipts and payments ... it is questionable if there could be found in most of these corporations officials capable of doing this [preparing a balance sheet] in a correct manner. (8 October 1884: 3)

These criticisms must again be interpreted mindful that this journal was keen to advance the interests of its principal readership (chartered accountants) and, in the next section, we show that local initiatives provided an important impetus for accounting change before 1884. Nevertheless, there is ample evidence of the initial involvement of public accountants in the affairs of municipal corporations being associated with significant developments in accounting practice.

The public accountant, W. R. Kettle, was called in to audit Birmingham corporation's recently established accruals-based accounts for 1855, in which year an aggregate balance sheet was first prepared. At Bradford, a major review of the corporation's accounting system was mounted on 13 February 1872 (Birmingham archive: minute 526), following the discovery of a cash deficiency in the treasurer's office. The minutes state that

> the Chairman and Messrs Alderman, Brayshaw Scott, and I. Dawson be and they are hereby appointed a sub-committee to investigate the books of the Borough Accountant with power to call in the assistance

> of a Public Accountant and that in the meantime Mr [James] Harris be suspended from further execution of the duties of his office. (13 February 1872: 526)

The public accountant, a Mr Blackburn,[11] called in to examine the accounts, found that money had been advanced to Harris, as treasurer, for the payment of wages and other disbursements and that 'he was unable to account for the whole thereof and that the extent of the deficiency amounted to £507. 4. 0½' (4 March 1872: 549). As noted in chapter 4, Blackburn was then 'requested to prepare a fresh set of books for simplifying the accounts in the borough accountant's office' (minute dated 8 April 1872: 561).

A second example occurred at Manchester where David Chadwick was auditor of the corporation's trading activities in the late 1850's, at a time when they were transferred from the cash basis to the accruals basis.[12] Progress elsewhere in the borough's accounts was slow, with cash-based accounts being rendered up until 1880 when 'proper balance sheets' were introduced following 'the employment of one of the leading firms in that City as professional auditors' (*The Accountant*, 11 October 1889: 4). The firm appointed was Broome, Murray & Co., chartered accountants, one of whose partners, Adam Murray, wrote on municipal finance. A few years later this firm was replaced by Thomas, Wade, Guthrie and Co., chartered accountants, where Edwin Guthrie, was an even more prominent contributor to the literature. Guthrie confirms the influence of professional accountants on the financial reporting practices of Manchester, drawing attention to the fact that they 'have been steadily elaborated in the direction of simplicity, comprehensiveness, and precision' (Guthrie, 1886: 615).

The contribution of professional accountants to the development of municipalities' financial reporting practice receives confirmation from prominent municipal treasurers of the day. Lister Woodhouse (President of the CTAI 1900-1) tells us that Burnley's auditors 'year after year suggested fresh improvements in the accounts' and 'I do not remember a single suggestion being rejected' (1894: 433). While George Swainson, the borough treasurer of Bolton, quotes with evident approval *The Accountant*'s observation that 'whatever improvements have been made from time to time in the manner in which the accounts of corporations are stated are in almost every instance a result of the representations of a chartered accountant, acting either as a borough accountant or as a professional auditor' (1895: 72).

Local initiatives

In the preceding section, it has been suggested that accountants brought in from outside played an important part in the development of municipal financial reporting practice during the nineteenth century, although in a number of cases it has been impossible to state more than the fact that the new appointment and an accounting innovation occurred in the same year. In this section we consider cases where improvements appear to have been the result of initiatives from the corporation's officials, usually the treasurer, and the extent to which the need for improvement arose from an increase in the size and complexity of the corporations' activities.

In 1851, following the passage of LGA 1848, Birmingham Borough released responsibility for public health from under 'the rule of a self elected body of [Improvement] Commissioners [which] had long been resented as out of harmony with modern ideas and as being unsuited to the fast growing requirements of the town' (*Birmingham Daily Post*, 26 December 1888). We have seen that Birmingham Corporation then adopted a dual system of bookkeeping (cash-based and accruals-based) and financial reporting, which meant that its (non-statutory) accounts were on the full accruals basis and differentiated between capital and revenue from 1852. As was normal practice, piecemeal changes in the direction of distinguishing clearly between different activities and achieving a more organised format continued during the next decade or two. An important step towards the full accruals accounting occurred in 1859 when it was decided that 'a detailed account of the stock and plant of the corporation be kept, and an account of stock in each department be taken annually' (1865 minutes: 5094).

In 1870 W. R. Hughes, appointed treasurer in 1867, 'thoroughly revised the system of accounts, and substituted one blue book'[13] for the previous system (Briggs, 1952: 125-6). The inefficiency of operating two separate systems had become evident to Hughes, and seems to have arisen from the need to prepare the statutory abstract up to 1 September, whereas the calendar basis was favoured for the purpose of preparing accounts to be used by the members and published annually in the month of January (Borough treasurer's report, minute 5848). The revised form of accounts put forward by Hughes, and adopted for the purpose of 1870's accounts, aimed at a one third reduction in the combined length of the white and yellow books. Writing a couple of decades later, Hughes tells us that further 'improvements have been made in this book year by year and it is considered by the competent authorities to be a model of municipal finance' (1889: 181).

The result was that the blue books 'increased from being pamphlets to large volumes' (Briggs, 1952: 126). Indeed, it seems that the accounts had become too long and a finance sub-committee was set up, at the turn of the century, working in conjunction with the treasurer and the professional auditor, Howard S. Smith,[14] reflecting concern that 'the blue book has grown to such a size that it really prevents persons interested in the city accounts from studying it'. The committee's findings were put into effect for the purpose of the 1901 accounts which are preceded by a memorandum specifying the changes designed to improve the overall format and reduce its length by some 200 pages. This was achieved by merging and condensing material and deleting unnecessary repetition. For example, instead of separate statements for receipts and payments and income and expenditure, a single statement employed a four column presentation which adjusted cash flows for opening and closing debtors and creditors.

The first accounts prepared for Bradford Corporation are in respect of the year to 1 September 1848. They are on the cash basis and remain in that format until 1856 when three of the key practices identified in table 5.2 - accruals accounting, an accruals-based balance sheet and a distinction between capital and revenue - are exhibited in the accounts for the waterworks acquired from the Bradford Water Works Company in that year.

We have seen that revelations surrounding the discovery of Harris's defalcation, in 1872, resulted in the engagement of the accountants, Blackburn & Co, who produced a new scheme for preparing the books. It also saw the appointment of John Hamer, previously the borough accountant of Salford, as treasurer. These changes were together probably responsible for an expansion and general improvement in the form, order and content of the corporation's accounts for 1872 and 1873.

The next significant development occurred soon after the promotion to treasurer, in 1889, of the corporation's accountant, T. A. Thorpe. In 1891 the borough accounts are at last placed on the accruals basis; the presentation adopted was first to list all receipts and payments and then, at the end of the statement, make the adjustments required (debtor and creditor) for conversion to the accruals basis - a procedure criticised, in some quarters, on the ground that the accounts fail to show the income and expenditure of individual departments comprising a particular fund. There is also published for the first time an aggregate balance sheet.

Bristol's district fund accounts exhibit all five key characteristics from 1895, which is the first year that financial information for this aspect of the municipality's operations survive, but the archives show that they were on the full accruals basis before that date. A committee, appointed in 1894 to consider transferring the borough fund accounts from the cash basis to the accruals basis, expressed broad satisfaction with existing practices. It noted that published data already exceeded statutory requirements and observed 'that they may with advantage to the public be still further amplified'. With that objective in mind it was decided to adopt 'so much of the forms used at Birmingham,

Bradford and Liverpool, as may be considered applicable'. A number of useful additions were made to the accounts in the form of supplementary data, but the only significant change in the form of the borough accounts was to distinguish for the first time between capital and revenue transactions (Report dated 7 February 1894).

Twenty years later the finance committee was asked once again to examine auditing and accounting matters. It reported that the accruals basis 'undoubtedly has the advantage of setting out clearly the position of each committee at the end of the financial year' and recommended that the borough fund account be at last placed on the same basis as the district fund account (Report dated 5 March 1914).

A possible explanation for the slow rate of change, at Bristol, is the persistent use of 'home grown' talent for appointments to the position of borough treasurer. John Harford, treasurer from 1855 to 1881, was 'in harness' for 65 years, having served his apprenticeship in the office of the previous borough treasurer, Thomas Garrard, who himself spent 54 years working for the corporation. Harford's successor, John Tremayne Lane, also worked his way up from the position of clerk and remained as treasurer till 1921. The appointment of W. Legh Smith, previously the City accountant at Hull, in 1921 may have been a breath of fresh air. In the following year an aggregate balance sheet was introduced for the first time, together with an 'epitome' summarising the major financial developments at Bristol. Both changes are highlighted by Legh Smith in his brief report on the contents of the published abstract.

We have seen that, at Cardiff Borough, cash-based financial statements setting out transactions between the treasurer and the corporation were prepared at least as early as 1790. These were therefore already in a format consistent with the requirements of MCA 1835, and statements continued to be prepared in that manner until the early 1860's.

A distinction between capital and revenue expenditure was made in the district fund account for 1864; the first year for which accounts for that fund have survived. The substantial increase in borrowing required by the municipality to discharge its responsibilities as a health board is likely to have motivated the need for an improved system of accounting and financial reporting.[15] Piecemeal improvements in the financial reporting system include the adoption of the double account system for the district fund in 1869 and the application of four of the five key practices (aggregate balance sheet excepted) to the borough fund in 1876. All these developments took place before the City began to undertake trading activities, starting with the acquisition of the waterworks in 1879.

The system of financial reporting changed little between 1876 and the mid-1890's when the position of the elective auditors came under review. In

1895, the elective auditors, Oswald Coleman (a chartered accountant) and Alfred Maurice Bailey (an incorporated accountant) refused to continue to act as mere figureheads (the real audit having been undertaken by a professional accountant - David Roberts - since 1869) and insisted on doing a more thorough job, each claiming £22. 1s for his services and making recommendations including the suggestion that the accounts be made up half yearly in accordance with MCA 1882 (45&46 Vict., c. 50, s. 27).[16] The town council resisted efforts to introduce a more effective elective audit, but there is evidence which suggests that the auditors' actions caused the corporation to review its financial reporting practices.

A resolution dated 22 April 1895, established a committee to consider 'unsatisfactory estimates' and see what could be done with the 'object of reducing the rate'. The committee carried out a wide ranging review and recommended: that the borough treasurer's claim that he was understaffed be investigated; that work correctly charged to capital be identified and authorized by the council, and afterwards sanction for borrowing be obtained from the LGB; that there be added to the annual financial statement a district stock account showing the properties of the corporation in kind and value; that separate ledger accounts be kept showing the income and expenditure on a fortnightly or monthly basis, so that each committee 'would be able to keep a close watch over its own affairs' (1895 minutes: 436-44). A meeting of the special finance committee on 27 April 1896 'discussed the principles upon which the liabilities and assets of the corporation might be published in the treasurer's annual accounts distinguishing between remunerative and unremunerative works, and directing the borough treasurer with regard to certain forms submitted as applicable thereto' (1896 minutes: 2215).

The published accounts for 1897 distinguish, for the first time, between remunerative and unremunerative expenditure and also include: a much fuller balance sheet for each fund; an aggregate balance sheet for the borough as a whole; and an inventory 'statement of liabilities and assets'.[17]

At Manchester, the first evidence of accruals accounting is again found in the early accounts for the district fund, this time in 1850. Progress was slow, however, and it is only in the waterworks accounts for 1859 and 1870 that we respectively find evidence of a distinction being made between capital and revenue expenditure and the preparation of an accruals-based balance sheet. It has been previously pointed out that the borough accounts remained on the cash basis until very late, and it was only the engagement of professional accountants, as auditors, around 1880 which resulted in their major revision. In the mid-1880's the corporation decided that 'having regard to the rapid growth of the business of the corporation; it appears necessary that the entire system of corporate finance should come under review' (minutes: 7 January 1885). A sub-committee consisting of the mayor and six others collected information from other boroughs, including Liverpool, Birmingham and Glasgow, and concluded that the 'published financial accounts of this corporation are now conspicuous for their fullness, clearness and simplicity' (minutes: 22 October 1885).

Assessment and Conclusion

The purpose of this chapter has been to identify and explain the development of the financial reporting practices of municipal corporations over a one hundred year period, at the end of which the essential structure which remained in force until municipal corporations were abolished in 1974 had been created.

We have addressed these objectives by identifying five key accounting practices, tracking their development and considering factors responsible for observed changes. A reference point for this analysis was *The Accountant*'s (1884) criticism of the backward state of municipal accounting. We have seen that the move towards the adoption of the key practices was well underway prior to 1884. Thirty two of the 50 dates listed in table 5.2 are pre-1884, as are 13 of the 25 dates applying to the adoption of these practices *throughout* the corporation. This does not mean that the key practice was *fully* implemented on the dates specified, and the municipal corporations covered by this survey were of course large, but it does suggest that progress was rather more significant than claimed in *The Accountant*. Moreover, the criticism of the local authority practices, by implication, compared with those of limited companies seems totally unjustified; until the passage of the Companies Act 1929, limited companies typically published a two or three page document comprising a brief directors' report and a summarised balance sheet.

We have seen that a common pattern of evolution occurred at all five corporations and the various steps in the process have in most cases been identified. It has naturally proved more difficult to identify the precise causes of change. The incentives for local authorities generally to publish information has been studied by Rowan Jones, who has applied the central government-based economic model of Anthony Downs to the local level (1992: ch. 5). Put very succinctly, Downs believes that there is no incentive for the electorate to seek accounting information: if they favour a political party, the information will not affect their decision; if they do not have a preference, the accounting information will be of no interest to them. At local level, Jones makes the additional point that there is no incentive to seek out accounting information for the purpose of lobbying because the cost would outweigh any possible benefit. Jones' further analysis of the groups interested in the provision of accounting information - 'the statutory nexus', comprising councillors, officers, ratepayers, clients, electors and the government, (1992: 122) - leads him to the conclude that none have any incentive to influence the accounting function except the government. And their involvement is designed to impose controls over the elected councillors (1992: 138).

As postulated by Jones, we have found virtually no empirical evidence to suggest that innovation was a response to the demand from ratepayers for more or better information. With ratepayers the intended recipients of accounting reports, it might have been expected that their interest would rise in line with the growing financial demands imposed upon them through rising local taxation. Memorials were found at Cardiff (Cardiff archive, box 503) and Birmingham (1855 minutes: 786) objecting to various items of expenditure, but no criticism was discovered of the accounting practices themselves. There is also some evidence of national associations of ratepayers criticising local authority accounting methods, but not a great deal. For example, evidence presented by James Walker on behalf of the National Chambers of Trade and the Association of Trade Protection Societies to the 1907 Departmental Committee expressed concern over the continued rise in rates and recommended 'in the interest of the community' the introduction of statutory regulations similar to those put forward by the CTAI in 1889 (paras 3674-886). The general impression gained is that ratepayers and their associates were sometimes vociferous in their condemnation of the level of local taxation but that they did not see the content of published accounts as relevant in reinforcing their objections.[18]

In another respect, the lack of ratepayer interest in the accounts is not entirely surprising. From about the 1880's onwards, the length of the 'blue book' increased phenomenally in response to the level of accounting sophistication employed in their preparation and range of services offered. Abstracts of more than 200 pages became the norm and 400/500 or even 600 pages were by no means unknown. Early on there was considerable variation in terminology and the many financial statements published were often poorly presented but, even when a more stereotyped format was developed, the accounts were unlikely to have been comprehensible to anyone without specialist financial expertise. According to Allen:

> The criticism is frequently heard that the published accounts of local authorities are so complicated as not to be readily understood, and so full of detail as to be confusing. Not one rate payer in a thousand ever makes a serious attempt to peruse and understand these accounts, and of the few who do, ninety-nine out of a hundred give up in hopeless despair and, perhaps, express disgust. (1912, preface)

Indeed, we have seen comments from municipal officials to the effect that the reason for change was to improve the readability and comparability of the accounts. An important development, in this respect, was the publication of the epitome, described as 'a short report setting out in a concise and non-technical form the salient features of the year's financial transactions' (*Financial Circular*, February 1927: 43; see also Sutcliffe, 1927). A further initiative was the inclusion of graphical presentation which was pioneered, at Sheffield, during the first decade of the twentieth-century (Allen, 1912) and was adopted for the purpose of Manchester's accounts by 1920 and Cardiff by 1926. However, the indications are that these innovations were made more in the endeavour to interest the ratepayer in a municipality's financial affairs than as a response to any demand for better information.

We also agree with Jones' contention that statutory regulations exerted an important impact on the financial reporting practices of local authorities in general and municipal corporations in particular, but we believe that they have done so in only certain limited respects. Their influence has been principally in the direction of encouraging the publication of detailed *cash-based* financial statements which distinguish between amounts spent on capital account and on revenue account. In other words, the statutory requirements explains the adoption of key practice 3, but not the others.

This study provides empirical support for Jones' contention that accounting innovation was supply driven rather than demand led, and also demonstrates the determination of *two other groups inside* Jones' statutory nexus (the officers and the council) and *one outside* (the accounting profession) to develop the reporting package far beyond statutory obligations. The statutory support provided for the publication of cash-based accounts proved an obstacle to the move towards accruals accounting, but it was one that was overcome. The factors bringing about accounting change were many and varied. In the endeavour to identify individual factors, there has been inevitable over-simplification since, in many cases, change was no doubt the result of a combination of events, not all of which are reflected in surviving archival material.

Having said that, the main influences were the need to account more effectively for growing municipal expenditure, with the distinction between capital and revenue dictated by statutory obligations. Changes usually became apparent, first in respect of expenditure designed to ensure that the borough was a healthier place in which to live (the district fund), secondly in the provision of trading services, finally spreading through the entire borough accounts. The sequence was similar in the case of accruals accounting; a technique which was presumably adopted because it was judged to possess the range of virtues identified earlier in this chapter.

Town councillors took the voluntary step of engaging professional auditors in addition to the elective auditor, and there is evidence, particularly at Manchester but also elsewhere, to suggest that the former both encouraged and advised on the subject of accounting change. The dominant force bringing about improvement, however, seems to have been the members and officers (particularly the treasurer) of the corporation, with the latter more likely to prove innovative when engaged from outside rather than promoted internally.

In this context, it is worth noting that the findings from this study are consistent with recent research into users of local authority accounts. Collins *et al*'s 'layered schema of potential users' sees councillors and officers as most prominent followed by central government; the general public together with pressure groups trail a poor third (1992: chapter 2). One might therefore imagine that councillors appointed to committees would have been keen to obtain full financial information concerning the results of departments for which they were responsible and, once this information was available, it was simply convenient to combine together the reports of each committee to produce the accounts for the borough as a whole. In circumstances where there was concern to demonstrate financial probity in respect of public money, little or no competition, and minimal evidence of accounting data being exploited by ratepayers to embarrass the town council, what could be more logical?

NOTES

1 It is of course acknowledged that the security provided by the rating system effectively eliminated the need for financial information to assess risk.

2 These terms appear to have been regarded as synonymous by the legislature and, to a large extent, by corporations throughout the nineteenth century.

3 Capital transactions were reported in a separate capital account and also appeared in summarised form in the balance sheets published by municipal corporations.

4 Bradford mixed capital and revenue items together in the balance sheet while Manchester prepared separate balance sheets for the capital transactions and revenue transactions.

5 Within the borough, the town council acted as the board of health (LGA 1848, 11&12 Vict., c. 63, s. 12).

6 This annual publication was compiled by Henry C. Burdett, Secretary, Share and Loan Department, London Stock Exchange, from 1882 to 1908.

7 This reference is to parishes and district councils.

8 A further criticism was that 'in many cases the general results of the authority's operations are obscured by the mass of detail shown' (BPP 1907, xxxvii: 587).

9 It seems, however, that the forms attached to the 1907 Departmental Committee's report, except for the electricity accounts which continued to be prepared in the 'old [1883] form' for the purpose of returns to the Board of Trade, 'have been so generally used that they are by common consent received as standard forms' (*Proceedings*, 1913: 56).

10 It is noted that the IMTA had previously (1905) issued, in conjunction with the Municipal Tramways Association, a 'Suggested Standard Form of Tramway Accounts'. The general move towards standardisation was completed as a result of action taken by the IMTA in 1938 and 1955. For a discussion of these provisions see *FIS*, 1972, and for subsequent developments see Jones and Pendlebury (1982).

11 Probably either J. or J. H. Blackburn of the firm Blackburn & Co., Bradford, founder members of the ICAEW.

12 Chadwick has also been described as 'instrumental in commencing the accounts of the borough' of Salford (Guthrie, 1886: 627).

13 The term blue book was used to distinguish it from the white book and the yellow book previously in existence; the new term gradually achieved widespread acceptance throughout local government as the appropriate description for a corporation's published abstract.

14 Smith had been clerk to the corporation, some time earlier, but resigned in 1867 when his application for promotion to the position of treasurer was unsuccessful; Hughes being appointed instead.

15 The accounts for the year show £48,000 borrowed from the Atlas Assurance Company to finance the construction of the city's sewerage system.

16 It had become quite common for municipal corporations to make up just one set of accounts for the year, usually to 31 March, but the legality of this practice was uncertain.

17 This last-named statement seems to have been regarded as a financial virility symbol by certain late-Victorian municipal corporations, and represents a 'rough and ready' attempt to calculate the extent to which a corporation's infrastructure had been financed by past generations. It is discussed further in chapter 6.

18 Much later, in 1933, the Ratepayers' Association of Tredegar and District successfully arranged for Bedwelty Urban District Council's accounts be examined by a professional accountant (*Rex v. Bedwelty, ex parte Price*, 1934 1KB 333).

6

CAPITAL ACCOUNTING: THEORY AND PRACTICE

It is tempting to assume that accountants have adopted a critical attitude towards the evaluation of alternative accounting methods only in recent years.[1] This is not so. It is no doubt the case that there are cycles of intense activity and periods of relative calm and, because we know relatively little about our accounting past, a resurgence of critical comment naturally produces a tendency to conclude that matters are the subject of radical comment for the first time. Such a conclusion is usually wrong.

The late nineteenth century was a time when many of our modern accounting practices took shape, but it was the accounting treatment of capital expenditure within local authorities which possibly gave rise to the most intense public debate. The consensus view, such as it was, was achieved neither quietly nor easily, with one contemporary observer likening the dispute to the 'story of the two knights who fell to fighting over the question of whether a shield was gold or silver, each of them having seen one side only' (Miller, 1905: 15). The real issues sometimes became obscured as a result of local rivalries, differences in professional backgrounds and the failure to draw a clear line between matters of law and matters of policy. The existence of intense feelings shows itself in the use of colourful and even insulting language in the professional press, with attempts made by *Financial Circular* (the official organ of the CTAI) to obtain monopoly control of the debate and carefully censor the information it chose to publish; an alleged policy which, the rival publication, *The Accountant*, was naturally happy to make public (Swainson, 1898: 204-5).

The year 1884 saw the accounting treatment of capital expenditure and the accounting practices of municipal corporations begin to receive close attention from the literature. Matheson's celebrated *The Depreciation of Factories* was first published while, in the autumn of that year, eight leading articles in *The Accountant* dealt with various aspects of municipal accounts. We will seek to show that, by the time the 1907 Departmental Committee met, most of the issues had been substantially resolved, in the sense that there was general agreement concerning the minimum standards of financial policy and accounting practice (closely inter-related matters in the case of local authorities) deemed to be consistent with long term financial viability. Beyond this minimum, a wide variety of accounting practices continued to be comfortably accommodated, reflecting the different policies adopted by individual authorities in the light of local conditions.

The remainder of this chapter is structured as follows. The first part examines three environmental factors essential to a proper understanding of the debate; the economic significance of trading undertakings; the use of loan regulations to help control the actions of local officials; and the fundamental difference that eventually emerged between capital accounting of private sector companies, on the one hand, and municipal corporations on the other. We then move on to examine the theory and practice relating to the four main aspects of the capital accounting problem: identification; presentation; valuation; and amortisation. Finally, we present our review and conclusions.[2]

The environment

Trading undertakings

Today we are concerned with the vast amount of economic power wielded by multinational companies. At the beginning of the century, in Britain, it was the activities of municipal corporations which were the subject of close public scrutiny. We have seen that MCA 1835 laid down a basic framework for their organisation and accountability which remained in operation, with periodic modification, until 1974. The initial Act provided for the financial effects of a strictly limited range of activities to be recorded through the borough fund but, as time went by, central government encouraged the boroughs to extend the range of services offered, and this led to the development of 'trading undertakings'. The first two were water and gas, to which were added electricity and tramways by the turn of the century.

The activities of local authorities developed at a rapid rate over the period 1884-1935 (table 6.1), but it was the upsurge in the provision of municipal trading services in the 1890's - almost all corporations had established electrical undertakings by 1903 (Harris, 1903: 218) - that generated an enormous interest in their level of indebtedness. Burdett (1890) reports the total amount owing by local authorities as £195 million in 1889 (p. 38), of which £141 million related to municipal corporations (p. 44). Between that date and 1905, municipal debt increased by £250 million compared with a growth in the national debt of just £100 million (*The Accountant*, 17 June, 1905: 737). Against this background, the accounting treatment of capital expenditure was considered, by many, to reflect financial policies which had

Table 6.1: Local authority expenditure on principal services, 1884/85 - 1934/5 (£m)

SERVICE	1884/85	1894/95	1904/05	1914/15	1924/25	1934/35
Education	3.9	7.8	22.1	32.8	73.9	86.9
Police	3.5	4.7	6.1	8.2	19.2	22.3
Highways	6.7	9.3	13.5	17.7	45.8	47.5
Public Health	*	*	10.1	14.1	32.8	49.7
Poor Relief	7.4	8.5	11.5	12.9	31.4	36.2
Lunacy	1.7	2.0	3.4	4.6	8.1	11.8
Housing (Excluding small Dwelling Acquisition)	0.3	0.3	0.5	0.9	17.5	44.4
Principal Trading Services (Gas, Water, Electricity, Harbours, Tramways)	8.6	11.6	22.4	42.3	88.6	119.1
Miscellaneous Services	12.0	15.5	18.1	19.8	37.6	36.9
Total Expenditure other than Out of Loans	44.1	59.7	107.7	153.3	354.9	454.8
Expenditure out of Loans	10.4	13.4	31.4	21.8	70.3	80.7
TOTAL	54.5	73.1	139.1	175.1	425.2	535.5

* Details not available, included in miscellaneous services.

Sources: Annual Report of the Ministry of Health, 1932-33, Cmd 4372
Statistical Abstract for the UK, BPP 1937/8, xxvii,1.

Table 6.2: Key statistics for selected municipal corporations, 1890-1930

	Popul-ation	Rateable Value	Receipts from Rates	Loans Raised	Loans outstand-ing	Debt per head	Remune-rative Loan	Unnumera-tive Loan
	000	£000	£000	£000	£000	£	£000	£000
1890								
Birmingham	461.8	1786.4	363.1	8790.4	7443.9	16.7.4	4899.7	3900.9
Bristol	232.2	1019.6	203.7	9051.8	5507.5	2.7.5	1400.0	8911.8
Cardiff	135.0	7730.9	728.6	1309.8	3199.1	8.17.7	8109.5	4988.5
Bradford	240.5	1025.1	206.5	5425.8	4469.8	18.17.5	3228.9	2196.8
Manchester	484.9	2781.0	385.1	1031.4	7332.7	15.2.0	7005.0	3306.4
1900								
Birmingham	514.9	2348.8	560.1	1344.6	1080.2	21.0/0	8338.5	5103.4
Bradford	233.7	1149.7	270.8	6925.8	5108.1	21.4/5	4263.3	2662.5
Bristol	320.9	1482.0	378.0	2098.2	1169.5	3.3/5	2587.0	1837.5
Cardiff	185.8	1029.0	206.1	2221.7	1847.2	10.0/0	2161.3	9521.7
Manchester	543.9	3109.6	847.1	7070.7	1621.0	29.4/5	1416.5	5842.4
1910								
Birmingham	364.8	2927.4	820.8	2213.8	1705.3	30.5	1463.3	7505.2
Bradford	291.3	1557.7	513.4	1199.6	8069.4	27.7/10	7112.2	4784.0
Bristol	377.6	1854.4	622.5	1044.0	8138.4	21.11/20	7070.1	3370.5
Cardiff	195.3	1140.7	334.9	5223.4	3972.4	20.7/10	3147.4	2737.2
Manchester	710.6	4293.2	133.5	3166.1	2198.5	32.7/10	2147.4	1618.7
1920								
Birmingham	840.2	5069.6	215.2	2882.7	1810.4	21.11/20	1785.6	1097.1
Bradford	288.5	1700.3	808.5	1445.7	8491.2	29.9/20	8664.7	5793.0
Bristol	357.0	1896.6	615.1	1130.9	7472.6	20.19/20	7620.9	3688.3
Cardiff	182.2	1222.2	421.2	5926.0	3527.0	19.7/20	2916.9	3009.0
Manchester	714.3	4541.9	221.5	3751.1	2202.7	30.17/20	2563.6	1187.4
1930								
Birmingham	981.0	6735.3	333.4	-	4585.9	46.3/4	3531.6	1052.2
Bradford	289.2	2667.2	140.4	-	1941.4	67.3/20	1332.9	6085.7
Bristol	391.3	2855.2	138.1	-	1789.1	45.3/4	1489.5	3003.3
Cardiff	224.2	2081.6	772.4	-	8914.8	39.3/4	6681.5	2233.2
Manchester	746.5	7047.0	335.7	-	4238.6	56.4/5	3379.7	8589.3

Source: 1890 and 1990 figures. Burdett, Henry C. *Burdett's Official Intelligence*, London: Spottiswoode. 1910, 1920 and 1930 figures. Secretary of the Share and Loan Department (ed.) *The Stock Exchange Official Intelligence*, London: Spottiswoode.

considerable significance for the financial stability of these massive entities and, beyond that, the general state of the economy. According to the borough treasurer of West Ham

> one charge, and perhaps the most important of all, is that municipalities are not making adequate provision for depreciation of their trading undertakings, thereby causing the community to run a grave risk of finding themselves one day in practically an insolvent position. (Harris, 1903: 218)

At the same time there was a strong suspicion, in certain quarters, that the depreciation question was simply being exploited by those steadfastly opposed to municipal trading[3] based on the conviction that such services were best provided by the private sector. Not surprisingly, much of this opposition came from the directors of companies offering services identical to those supplied by municipal trading undertakings, and from their representative bodies (for example, the London Chamber of Commerce, *Proceedings*, 1899: 11).

Each of the five municipal corporations dealt with in detail in this study operated trading undertakings, and an indication of their overall level of operations is given in table 6.2. Writing in 1878, Bunce probably described the broad experience of most large municipal corporations when he observed that the 'development of a vigorous corporate life in the town' of Birmingham had been achieved in three stages: the establishment of the town council's right to govern, which was achieved in 1851 'after a contest of 13 years duration'; 'the construction of public works conducive to the health, the comfort, and the dignity of the municipality'; and the provision of trading services - water and gas - under 'the mayoralty of Mr Chamberlain ... thus extinguishing monopoly for the common benefit' (1878: 252-3). Water and gas undertakings were acquired from local companies in 1874, and the electricity undertaking in 1899. Birmingham Corporation also took over responsibility for the provision of tramways in 1904, having previously leased the lines to various local companies.

Bradford acquired water and gas operations from local companies respectively in 1854 and 1871. The logic underlying the latter purchase is evident from discussions contained in the corporation's minute books. Concern with the quality and availability of gas, supplied to local inhabitants by the Bradford Gas Light Company (formed 1821), gave rise to the appointment of a smoke prevention committee to consider whether it would be better for the corporation to undertake this activity. As was often the case, when a municipality was contemplating reform, other boroughs were circulated with a request for relevant information. It was discovered that 'in one or two instances' (only Manchester was mentioned by name) the works were initially established by the borough, enabling it 'to effect all their public improvements without there being any rate for the purpose' (minute book no. 1). The committee further discovered that boroughs who instead acquired the works from an existing company obtained one or more of the following benefits: reduced charges; improved quality; and 'a considerable profit to apply for the benefit of the town'. An investigation of the Bradford Gaslight Company's accounts resulted in the discovery that it had abused its position by retaining and re-investing monopoly profits instead of reducing the price charged. Presumably this discovery increased the municipality's determination to complete the purchase and, in due course, the price was agreed at £210,000 (*ibid*).

Bristol ranked second only to London as a port and trading centre at the beginning of the nineteenth century (Harvey and Press, 1988: 1), and the provision of adequate docking facilities naturally concerned the borough council. It appears that these were increasingly mismanaged, by the Bristol Dock Company, 'to the detriment of local trade and industry' (Harvey and Press, 1988: 2). This led to the docks being taken over, in 1848, to become that city's first trading undertaking. The high level of expenditure involved, in this operation, is borne out by the accounts for 1860 which show unredeemed debt of £478,280.

In other respects Bristol's town council proved not to be a successful disciple of socialist principles. This does not seem to have been entirely due to lack of effort. Soon after acquiring the docks, the council, acting as the local Board of Health, resolved to consider the desirability of acquiring the two local gas companies, formed in 1817 and 1823 (minutes, 26 November 1852: 106). Consideration was given in the 1870's and the late 1890's to the possibility of acquiring the Bristol Water Works Company, established in 1846. A report dated 28 February 1877 cites both concern with the present level of charges and the conviction that the acquisition would prove remunerative, to the borough, as reasons for the planned take-over. The archives refer to the difficulty of agreeing terms, but the failure to proceed seems also to have been due to opposition from local citizens: 'Many improvements suggested by the council were passionately opposed. The newspapers give reports of lively town meetings where the ratepayers negatived schemes put forward by the council, being unwilling to pay the necessary rates ... ' (Ralph, 1973: 45). It may well be that local inhabitants had in mind the cost of the docks, and did not want to add to this already substantial commitment.

The Bristol town council's experience with tramways contains further evidence to suggest that the successful promotion of trading activities was not one of its achievements. The construction of a tramways by local authorities was authorised by an Act of 1870, in recognition of the growing size of certain towns and the level of population in their suburbs. The initial question, at Bristol, was whether the tramway should be built (at this time local authorities were not authorised to operate a tramway) by the borough or by private contractors. Advocates of municipal ownership 'reasoned that tramways, like water or gas, were "natural monopolies"; and should not be entrusted to private concerns because of the danger of high fares and low safety standards' (Harvey and Press, 1988: 138-9). Opponents expressed concern 'that transport undertakings involved high risks and that under council ownership, without the discipline of market forces, tramways might well lapse into unprofitability and become a charge on the rates' (Harvey and Press, 1988: 139). The town council decided to go ahead, but iron prices then rose sharply 'causing a minor financial crisis and a major loss of nerve' (*ibid*). A much truncated line was leased, amidst much embarrassment, to the Bristol Tramways Company, created by the efforts of local solicitors Stanley & Wasbrough.

The single public utility service, successfully established by the City, was the electric lighting works begun in 1891, eight years after the decision was initially taken to proceed (Report of the Electricity Committee, 19 October 1885).

Cardiff acquired its water undertaking from the Cardiff Water Works Company (established 1851) in 1879 at a cost of £320,000. The move to expand the provision of trading services again did not proceed smoothly. The possibility of acquiring the Cardiff Gas-Light & Coke Company was also the subject of a thorough investigation, commencing in 1889, with the views of other corporations and urban sanitary authorities canvassed to help assess the desirability of the proposed course of action. Purchase was recommended but, in the face of strong opposition, channelled through the Cardiff Ratepayers' Association, which attracted considerable press coverage, the plan was dropped. A similar scheme for acquiring the local tramway company, in 1890, was shelved, but new lines were eventually constructed in 1898 following its eventual takeover by the corporation. The building of an electricity had works commenced in 1895.

The principles of public ownership were applied earliest, and in the most comprehensive manner, at Manchester where its Police Commissioners established a publicly owned gas works in 1817. The extent of the commissioners foresight is reflected in the fact that 'up to 1860 only a few towns sought to copy Manchester's pioneering role' (Wilson, 1991: 197), including only Bradford from this study which, as we stated, acquired a waterworks in 1854. Manchester retained its leading role, establishing its waterworks in 1848, electricity works in 1894 and tramways in 1902. It also spent over £5 million on the construction of its ship canal in the late 1890's.

The profitability of trading activities The 'cardinal principles' of Birmingham's financial policy, laid down at an early stage, are worth noting as these had clear implications for the Corporation's system of accounts:

> that capital expenditure should be defrayed out of moneys borrowed by the issue of stock or by mortgages ... ; that the revenue-producing undertakings, with the exception of Water, should always be self supporting; that the accounts of the separate departments should be kept quite distinct; and that each specific new investment should be provided with a sinking fund that would extinguish the debt within a prescribed period (Briggs, 1952: 123-4).

The special position of water is also referred to by Joseph Chamberlain, mayor of Birmingham 1871-4: 'When the purchase of the waterworks comes before you it will be a question concerning the health of the town; the acquisition of the gas works concerns the profits of the town' (quoted in Waller, 1983: 304). This comment was probably based on his knowledge of the 'Manchester model' which 'remained a source of inspiration for many local authorities seeking a viable financial solution to their problems' (Wilson, 1991: 184). The gas works established by Manchester's Police Commissioners generated profits of £230,000, by 1842, which was used to subsidise other municipal activities (Wilson, 1991: 192). Wilson argues that it was the initiative, at Manchester, which 'succeeded in establishing municipal trading as a legitimate feature of local government' (Wilson, 1991: 194).

A corporation's financial policies were usually given formal recognition by a privately promoted local act or a provisional order. For example, the Bradford Improvement Act of 1854, 'for better supplying with water the Borough of Bradford and the County of York', provided that any surplus, after meeting operating costs, should be applied 'in aid of the sinking fund until the money raised under the powers of the Act shall be paid off, after which any remaining surplus may be applied under the direction of the council for the benefit of the inhabitants and the improvement of the borough' (s. 40). The Bradford Corporation Gas and Improvement Act of 1871 (s. 64) set out the application of revenue raised in the more formal manner which became the common practice, namely that the corporation should apply revenue to meet outlays in the following order:

1. In paying the costs and other expenses incidental to raising and levying rates and rents and borrowing money.
2. In the payment of interest on borrowed monies.
3. In providing a sinking fund.
4. Payment of expenses of managing and maintaining the Gasworks.

5. In improving and extending the Gasworks.
6. In any manner the corporation may think best for the improvement of the borough and for the public benefit of the inhabitants.

In view of the fact that the corporation was usually the sole local supplier of the services it chose to provide, the extent to which revenue was available for each of the specified purposes depended principally on pricing policy. If the objective was to break-even, the aim would be to generate revenue sufficient to cover expenditures 1-4; any surplus would result in the possible subsidisation of either future generations of gas consumers (item 5) or of the services supplied to non-gas consumers (item 6); any deficit, in the absence of a reserve fund, would either be a charge to rates or recorded as a liability to the rate fund in the trading undertaking's balance sheet.

An indication of variations in departmental 'profitability', resulting from differential policy decisions regarding prices, is given in tables 6.3 (Birmingham) and 6.4 (Bradford). The first of these shows considerable variation in the results of Birmingham's four trading undertakings. Electricity produced an overall surplus transferred to the rate fund of nearly £0.5 million, gas £2 million and tramways £0.7 million. By way of contrast the water department received an overall subsidy in excess of £1.9 million, justified on the grounds that 'the supply of water is largely in the nature of a health service, and it is a duty of local authorities to maintain a good and efficient supply' (Jones, 1940: 83). We can also see that there were considerable variations in profitability over time; even the water committee produced small profits each year between 1888 and 1899.

The purchase of the Bradford Gas Light Company was described by Cudworth as 'of vital importance to the interests of the borough' (1881: 179) and by 1881 had 'already been of great pecuniary advantage to the ratepayers of Bradford' generating 'profits ranging from £25,000 to £30,000 per annum, to be appropriated in reduction of the rates of the borough' (Cudworth, 1881: 180). For the years 1901-21 (table 6.4) we find certain similarities with the pattern of results at Birmingham; water showing an overall loss and the other departments profits. Again there is considerable variation between maximum profits and losses, with water generating a surplus in 13 of the 21 years covered by these calculations. Not shown in the table is the fact that gas produced surpluses in relief of the rates amounting to £413,227 prior to 1901 whereas, over the next 20 years, it produced a overall surplus of just £35,185

Loan regulations

As previously stated, the municipal corporations, newly created in 1835, had little or nothing in the way of corporate assets - indeed some of them inherited net liabilities - and it was therefore necessary for them to borrow money to finance the supply of new services. MCA 1835 conferred no explicit power to borrow, but such action was tacitly approved since the Act made it clear that the treasurer was responsible for monies borrowed 'which have been already instituted or which may hereafter be instituted by way of mortgage or otherwise' (Page, 1985: 115).

Loans were raised by special Acts of Parliament, or under provisional orders, and to facilitate the passage of this specialist legislation a number of 'clauses' Acts were passed in the 1850's. Of particular interest is the Commissioners Clauses Act 1847 which contained specimen rules covering the raising and repayment of loans, including the creation of a sinking fund for the latter purpose (Page, 1985: 116-19). Drawing on these provisions the Bradford Corporation Act 1858, for example, authorised the corporation to borrow £200,000 for the construction of a new and altered water supply, and obliged it to set aside each year, out of the Water Account, a sum equal to one fiftieth of the amount borrowed to a Sinking Fund to be applied to repayment of the loan (s. 50).

It seems, however, that some of the early local regulations placed no limit on the period of the loan, while provisions contained in other private Acts were ignored (*The Accountant*, 29 November, 1884: 4). The government's response was to lay down explicit conditions for the approval of a new loan, and the Municipal Corporations (Mortgages) Act 1860 was the first *general* statute to place a limitation on the loan period (in this case 30 years, s. 1)[4] and lay down specific obligations for repayment (s. 2).

The basic philosophy underlying these regulations, and others applying to loan sanctioning, was to ensure that local authorities did not over borrow, with the test being whether repayment was made within the life of the asset acquired. The desirability of acquiring particular assets was generally regarded as a matter of local policy, though subject to scrutiny by the LGB. There is general agreement that, in the early days, the loan repayment periods were excessive and highly variable - between five and one hundred years - even for assets within the same category (Woodhouse, 1893b: 969). According to Swainson, presenting his presidential address to the inaugural meeting of the CTAI, Parliament was

> Apparently floundering about according to the whim or crotchet of individual members of each committee, veering first in the direction of stringency and then of latitude ... until, like a ship without a rudder or compass, promoters of Improvement Bills and their Parliamentary agents are driven to their wits' ends what to ask for. (1886)

Table 6.3: Analysis of contributions of trading undertakings to the rate fund of Birmingham City Council 1875 to 1934/35

Year	Gas	Water	Elect.	Tramways
	£	£	£	£
1875	25,000	-	-	-
1876	30,000	-	-	-
1877	25,000	-	-	-
1878	25,000	-	-	-
1879	25,000	-	-	-
1880	25,000	-	-	-
1881	27,500	-	-	-
1882	25,000	-	-	-
1883	25,000	-	-	-
1884	28,465	(4,997)	-	-
1885	25,000	(7,643)	-	-
1886	19,227	(5,468)	-	-
1887	25,773	(2,020)	-	-
1888	25,000	106	-	-
1889	41,649	2,878	-	-
1890/1	30,000	2,845	-	-
1891/2	22,144	3,612	-	-
1892/3	27,966	4,092	-	-
1893/4	24,552	26,923	-	-
1894/5	30,448	12,226	-	-
1895/6	25,000	17,718	-	-
1896/7	35,520	25,812	-	-
1897/8	50,336	28,614	-	-
1898/9	30,320	15,409	-	-
1899/1900	29,821	(6,479)	-	-
1900/01	33,821		-	-
1901/2	34,000		-	-
1902/3	34,000		-	-
1903/4	32,031		-	-
1904/5	50,677		-	-
1905/6	54,526		-	-
1906/7	58,546	(753,166)	-	
1907/8	61,564		-	12,000
1908/9	65,313		-	35,000
1909/10	75,459		10,008	29,499
1910/11	75,498		10,256	32,914
1911/12	78,904		16,793	44,253
1912/13	83,974		20,237	47,272
1913/14	81,017		21,635	56,352
1914/15	68,810		25,134	44,972
1915/16	37,351		35,385	30,000
1916/17	26,274		25,498	50,000
1917/18	26,649		27,795	-
1918/19	30,758		25,263	25,000
1919/20	-		20,008	15,000
1920/21	-		15,324	-
1921/22	-		-	-
1922/23	-		-	-
1923/24	-		12,500	-

Table 6.3 (cont.): Analysis of contributions of trading undertakings to the rate fund of Birmingham City Council 1875 to 1934/35

Year	Gas	Water	Elect.	Tramways
	£	£	£	£
1924/25	42,256	(1,276,034)	31,000	27,000
1925/26	42,000		31,000	40,000
1926/27	41,200		31,000	40,000
1927/28	41,200		31,000	40,000
1928/29	51,200		41,000	55,000
1929/30	41,200		31,000	40,000
1930/31	41,200		-	40,000
1931/32	41,200		-	10,000
1932/33	25,000		-	10,000
1933/34	35,000		-	20,000
1934/35	-		-	6,500
	2,029,837	(1,915,572)	461,836	700,762

Table 6.4: Depreciation etc., Bradford, 1901-21

Profit appropriation

	Water	Gas	Electricity	Tramways
	£	£	£	£
Unappropriated, 31.3.1901	5,173	13,679	10,190	3,813
Profit[1]	(55,206)	35,185	162,189	522,737
Applied as follows:				
Relief of rates	(47,500)	(25,556)	(27,742)	(176,035)
Reserve & renewals	-	-	-	(312,142)
Depreciation & renewals	-	-	(63,698)	-
Other purposes	(11,360)	(31,489)	(80,939)	(38,373)
Unappropriated, 31.3.1921	(108,893)	(8,181)	-	-
Maximum annual: profit	20,499	55,082	18,956	60,826
loss	(73,880)	(14,499)	(3,419)	(16,634)

Reserves, depreciation and renewals account

	Electricity	Tramways
	£	£
Balance 31.3.1901	18,554	12,382
Transfer from profit	63,698	312,142
Reserve and renewals	-	(239,047)
Depreciation and renewals	(75,699)	-
Balance	6,553	85,477

Note 1 Profit after transfer to sinking fund

As time went by, there was an increasing tendency for the LGB to insist on 'rapid repayment of debt' (Miller, 1905: 16). The practice of fixing the loan period at less than the expected life of the asset, sometimes significantly so, produced strong criticism from local officials (Stevens, 1899: 55).

We will see (below) that the above inconsistencies had significant implications for accounting practice.

Contrasting corporation and company developments

The capital accounting debate resulted in comparisons being made, often unfavourable, between the practices of municipal corporations, on the one hand, and those of private sector companies on the other, and it is probably true to say that the failure to appreciate clearly the differences between these entities, in terms of their objectives and financial structure, were factors which made the resolution of certain issues a slow process. The assumed superiority of capital accounting methods deemed appropriate for companies is a little curious, however, since actual practice remained in considerable turmoil. Many manufacturing and trading companies omitted depreciation altogether, while others treated it as an appropriation of profits, with the amount deducted depending on the level of profit. Within private sector-based public utility companies, whose activities were directly comparable with the trading activities of municipal corporations, the use of quite different accounting treatments merely added to the confusion. Moreover, although the literature does seem to have accepted that manufacturing and trading companies *ought* to depreciate fixed assets, there was a strong feeling that public utility companies were doing enough by charging only maintenance, repair and renewal costs to revenue. It seems fairly clear that Hopper's observation that we today have 'private sector problems posing as public sector solutions' (1986: 13) is closely parallelled by events occurring one hundred years ago.

It is probably fair to say that the system of local authority accounting for capital expenditure has been shaped by the controls relating to borrowing, since these institutions are required to make provision for the repayment of principal through the revenue account, unlike private companies which may issue permanent capital. A comparison of the accounting treatments eventually considered generally desirable for capital raised, spent and repaid by companies and corporations, set out in table 6.5, will serve as a useful reference point for the discussion which follows.

Table 6.5: Financing capital expenditure in limited companies and municipal corporations (£)

	Limited Company				Municipal Corporation			
	1	2	3	4	1	2	3	4
Share capital	100	100	100	100				
Loan capital[5]					100	100	100	100
Accumulated depreciation			100					
Sinking fund account							100	
	100	100	200	100	100	100	200	100
Fixed assets at cost		100	100			100	100	
Cash	100		100	100	100		100	100
	100	100	200	100	100	100	200	100
Profit before capital charges			100				100	
Less: Depreciation			100					
Sinking fund			—				100	
Profit			-				-	

Interest charges ignored throughout.

A limited company and a municipal corporation are each established to undertake an activity which requires an investment of £100. The limited company issues shares and the municipal corporation loan capital producing the respective financial positions set out under (1). Each entity uses the cash to purchase the required fixed asset giving the position set out in (2). Trading results are identical over the life of the asset and in each case produce a profit before capital charges of 100; in the case of the limited company depreciation is charged of this amount, while, in the case of the municipal corporation, similar total transfers are made to a sinking fund account producing the financial positions shown under (3). In both cases the fixed asset is now valueless and may be deleted from the balance sheet giving (4). The limited company may now be liquidated resulting in capital being returned to the shareholders while the amount borrowed by the municipal corporation must be repaid.

The following further contrasts made between the two types of entities are worth noting before attempting to evaluate the conviction, strongly held in some quarters, that municipal corporations should do *more* than merely provide for the repayment of loan finance. According to William Wing (a chartered accountant)

> the sinking fund is in effect what a depreciation fund *would be* [emphasis added] if a private enterprise were to set aside a portion of its profits to meet the replacement of capital at the end of any given number of years. The depreciation fund so provided would, however, remain in the business. It may be in cash at the bank, stock, book debts, or other assets, or applied in reducing liabilities, including repayment of capital, but it is quite optional as to how that depreciation fund shall be invested. (1903: 133)

The implication that municipal corporations did more to ensure financial stability is echoed by Miller (a practising accountant and founder member of the ICAEW) who pointed out that he has 'never heard that a limited company is bound to earmark this money and so to speak hold it in trust for future renewals of its plant'; the money may be used to finance further capital investment or to pay off any loan capital, and he then inquires 'why, then, is a local authority to be regarded as delinquent for acting on the same lines?' (1905: 16). A leading article in *Financial Circular*, at about the same time, exclaims: 'imagine all our railways and trading companies compelled to do that [repay capital] out of current revenue. How the dividends would be affected: and yet that would be a reasonable comparison' (1903: 278).

The accounting treatment of capital expenditure

The development of accounting for capital expenditure in local authorities and the private sector of the economy gave rise to four main problems which we now consider, namely: identification; presentation; valuation (original cost, replacement cost, market price, etc); and amortisation.

The identification of capital expenditure

The treatment of capital expenditure in the published accounts of municipal corporations received careful attention as a direct result of the furore surrounding the entire omission of fixed assets from the Glasgow Police

Commissioners' Accounts (*The Accountant*, 5 August 1893: 685-7; 12 August 1893: 701-2; 19 August 1893: 717-8). This treatment, linked with the inclusion of related loan finance in the balance sheet, resulted in the disclosure of a deficit erroneously implying an unsound financial position. A little later, the borough treasurer of West Ham surveyed 11 large English towns and identified the following four treatments: to omit the expenditure from the balance sheet altogether; to omit all capital expenditure except land and buildings; to include the whole of the expenditure as an asset; to include the whole of the expenditure, in the first instance, and to reduce it as the loans were repaid (Harris, 1893: 952). The result is what Harris describes as an 'extraordinary anomaly', that in the first two cases a deficiency would be reported, and in the third case a surplus, despite the fact that in all three cases the underlying facts are identical (1903: 216).

However, it does seem that, by 1907 (BPP 1907, xxxvii: Appendix I: para. 14), the usual practice of English and Welsh boroughs was to capitalise expenditure on fixed assets and, as early as 1893, *The Accountant* observed that the Glasgow treatment was 'directly at variance with the most invariable practice in England' (30 September 1893: 811).[6] This is perhaps not surprising in view of the fact that the immediate write-off would produce an enormous burden on the rates and run counter to the stewardship objective of disclosing the manner in which money raised had been spent.

Presentation of fixed assets in the balance sheet

The two questions to be considered here were: whether it was necessary to distinguish between different categories of fixed asset; and the appropriate location for the balances credited to the sinking fund and loans repaid, that is, whether they should be shown amongst the liabilities as sources of finance or whether they should be deducted from the capital expenditure so as to give a net figure in the balance sheet.

It was recognised, at a fairly early stage, that there were important differences in the value of the fixed assets belonging to a corporation depending upon their use. This led to the development of the following four, sometimes overlapping, terms:

* Realisable assets, that is assets which could possibly be sold, such as gas works and town halls.
* Unrealisable assets, such as street improvements and sewers.
* Remunerative assets, that is assets which produced revenue such as trading undertakings and markets.

* Unremunerative assets, such town halls and street improvements.

Based on this terminology, the following three categories were developed by Swainson and used for the purpose of Bolton Borough's 1894 accounts: realisable and remunerative outlay (covering, for example, waterworks, gasworks, markets, etc.); realisable but unremunerative outlay (parks, town halls, surplus lands etc.); unrealisable and unremunerative outlay (street improvements, bridges, main sewers, etc.) (1894: 603-4; 1895: 72).

The question of whether fixed assets should be shown in the balance sheet gross or net drew the following forceful comments from Birmingham's borough treasurer, clearly mindful of the stewardship role the corporation's accounts were intended to serve:

> the balance sheets then represent facts showing how much out of monies raised by loans has been expended, how much of the loan has been repaid, and how much still remains outstanding. They do not show the actual realisable value of the assets: this can only be done by a re-valuation of property every year, and when it was ascertained no good purpose would be served. (Clare, 1902: 110)

This was also a matter on which Swainson held strong views, giving rise to a fierce debate between himself and the treasurer of the adjoining Borough of Burnley. Woodhouse favoured the statement of capital expenditure at gross cost on the grounds that the repayment periods for similar assets varied a great deal, thereby in no way reflecting actual depreciation and undermining comparability (1893a: 881). The statement of capital expenditure, net, was based on the contrary view that the repayment period was closely in line with the asset's expected useful life. Scarborough's auditor, a professional accountant, changed the accounts of trading and non-trading departments to comply with this format, based also on the conviction that it was a simpler and neater presentation more easily comprehended by the ratepayers (Bradley, 1893: 783-5).

Swainson's preference fell somewhere between the two extreme views. Although broadly of the view that capital expenditure should be shown gross, he believed that unremunerative assets (sewerage and sewer outfall works, and public improvements) which 'rapidly deteriorate, and have no real selling value' should be written down by the amount of the loan repaid (1893: 927). The argument with Woodhouse, which ensued, saw Swainson make an unsuccessful attempt to enlist the 'authoritative' support of Adam Murray (*The Accountant*, 16 June 1894: 540). As usual, Swainson continued his crusade unabashed, and re-framed the Bolton Borough accounts in accordance with his ideas (1894: 603-4).

The Departmental Committee found that boroughs frequently distinguished between different types of fixed assets, with the most common classification being that developed by Swainson. In the vast majority of cases assets were valued at gross cost; in those cases where assets were shown net, the deduction was stated so that the user could see how the balance had been arrived at. The following unusual treatments are singled out for special mention.

> In Bolton and a few other boroughs the value of street improvements, etc., shown under the third of these divisions [unremunerative and unrealisable], is written down by the amount of loans repaid.
>
> In Bristol 'the corporate estate consists of lands, farms, houses, etc., and other property belonging to the borough fund are not valued or included in any balance sheet; 'and in Manchester and some other boroughs only realisable properties are introduced into the balance sheet' (BPP 1907, xxxvii: appendix I: para. 14).

Clearly a high degree of uniformity had been achieved in this area by 1907.

Cost or value

An attempt to revolutionise the content of municipal accounts, which deserves consideration in view of the major impact it might have had on the apparent financial position of municipalities, was whether to report assets at cost or value.

One argument put forward by the advocates of change was 'that certain people connected with the Stock Exchange occasionally attach what I consider an undue importance to the nominal amount of assets shown in the abstract of accounts' (Woodhouse, 1894: 436). Another reason seems to have been the desire to show a strong balance sheet, as epitomised by use of the following terms - balance of assets; property, assets, capital expenditure etc. in excess of liabilities; and surplus of assets - in the published balance sheets, to describe the difference between reported capital expenditure and loans outstanding (BPP 1907, xxxvii: Appendix I: para. 14(b)). One perceived advantage to be gained from disclosing a healthy surplus was to emphasise the financial strength of an entity (*The Accountant*, 26 August 1893: 739) and make borrowing easier:

> the splendid results achieved by Manchester in the high price obtained for their last issue of ship canal stock, only a few days ago, proves

> how important it is for all towns who can do it to show that their realisable assets exceed their total debt. (Swainson, 1894: 603)

The innovative Manchester Corporation adopted a system of quinquennial valuations, and the conviction that values might be of interest to ratepayers was given affect in the financial accounts of other corporations. At Cardiff, for example, the finance committee instructed:

> Heads of Departments to prepare and submit to the various Committees concerned an inventory of all moveable Plant and effects, including furniture, &c., belonging to the Corporation on the 31st March 1896, in respect of each Establishment and Undertaking, in order that such inventory, when the money value therein is approved by the respective Committees, shall be forwarded to the Finance Committee for inclusion among the Assets to be published in the Treasurer's Annual Accounts with particulars of method by which the result is arrived at. (1896 minutes: 3041)

An appendix to the 1897 accounts contains a 'Statement of Assets and Liabilities' in which the first entry is the balance transferred from the capital account captioned 'Excess of assets over liabilities'. To this is added a range of other assets belonging to the borough to arrive at 'total assets over liabilities' £688,452. Items added are: materials and stocks purchased out of revenue; fixed assets purchased out of revenue; miscellaneous properties at the borough engineer's valuation, less amounts included at cost in capital account; rentals on properties not in capital account capitalised at rental x 27 years (echoing the treatment at Bristol, in 1785, referred to in chapter 4); the balance on revenue account. This may be seen as a rough attempt to calculate the extent to which the infrastructure of Cardiff Borough had been financed, in 1899, by past generations.

These kinds of innovation received both support and criticism from the contemporary literature. A letter published in *The Accountant* made the important point that the appropriate valuation depended upon whether a corporation was to be looked upon as a going concern or one about to be liquidated and, if the former, then cost was the appropriate choice as in the case of private sector organisations (26 August 1893: 738-9). Criticisms of periodic valuations were that: valuations varied greatly depending on location, thereby causing considerable confusion (Woodhouse, 1894: 435-6); the aggregate balance sheet would lack a common denominator unless all the assets were revalued, which no one seems to have suggested; that no two valuers would agree on the same figure (Woodhouse, 1893b: 968); and that values were irrelevant because the real security for creditors was the borough's rateable value (Miller, 1905: 16). Positive arguments in favour of the use of cost were that local authority accounts should be considered stewardship documents (Woodhouse, 1894: 436) setting out 'an historical summary of the receipts and payments on capital account' (Miller, 1905: 14).

The outcome of the debate, so far, may be summarised as follows: there was general agreement that capital expenditure should be reported in the balance sheet and that the appropriate figure was original cost.

Amortisation of capital expenditure: theory

We now turn to the question of whether assets should be written off over time and, if so, at what rate. We first examine the case for creating a sinking fund only, and then identify the significance for this approach of (i) the relationship between loan periods and asset lives and (ii) the use of 'repairs and renewals' accounting. We next examine the arguments for the inclusion of a depreciation charge, and conclude with an analysis of the possible alternative uses of a reserve fund.

Sinking Funds and Loan Repayments. George Swainson quoted, with evident approval, the following extract from *The Accountant* dated 23 March 1895:

> there can we think be nothing more illogical than the method adopted by some corporations, of depreciating their assets at such a rate that, when the loans out of which the assets were created are redeemed, these assets will have been written down to zero in the accounts. (1895: 73)

We will see that the editors of *The Accountant*, and Swainson, later changed their minds.

The accounting treatment of capital expenditure was given careful consideration in evidence taken before the 1903 Select Committee. The President of the Society of Accountants and Auditors believed that the sinking fund 'operates sufficiently well to render the question of depreciation a secondary matter' (Wilson, minute 1049), and this view received strong support from a number of witnesses, including Liverpool's internal auditor who believed that the sinking fund corresponded to the depreciation fund in the private sector (Barrow, minute 1566).

Lawrence Dicksee is perhaps the best known, and most highly respected, writer on accounting matters around the turn of the century. His position as the first British professor of accounting (at the University of

Birmingham) and his broad experience of accounting matters probably enabled him to take a fairly impartial view of the various claims and counter-claims. In a lecture presented to the Chartered Accountants Students Society of London, in 1907, he observed that 'the charge against revenue in respect of the sinking fund may, under these peculiar circumstances [where the life of the asset approximated to the period of the loan, which he considered to be government policy], be regarded as being the statutory equivalent for, and as taking the place of, the ordinary businessman's charge for depreciation of assets' (1907: 484). The inconsistency pointed out by Forster (1907: 128-31) between this assertion and Dicksee's earlier expressed commitment to the need for a depreciation charge at least shows that the was familiar with all the arguments when reaching his later assessment.

In a similar vein Harmood-Banner, sometime president of the Association of Municipal Corporations, argued, when president of the ICAEW (1904-5), that 'the strength of municipal credit generally, including municipal trading, lies in the compulsory sinking fund, a model method of depreciation' (quoted in Forster, 1907: 149).

The Loan Period A number of contributors to the debate argued that the adequacy of the sinking fund as a surrogate for depreciation depended, from the practical viewpoint, on the relationship between the loan repayment period and the fixed asset's useful life. It was mentioned, earlier, that there was a tendency for the LGB to specify shorter repayment periods, as time went by, but this reflected, to some extent, the changing nature of municipal expenditure, with more being spent on trading undertakings. These fell within the first of the three categories popularised by Swainson, namely realisable and remunerative outlay. The Scottish chartered accountant Alexander Murray, ex-treasurer of City of Glasgow, was one of the few who drew attention to the need to make a careful distinction between these different types of expenditure when discussing loan repayment periods and the depreciation question (1903: 785), but his advice was often ignored.

When the Select Committee on Repayment of Loans met (1902) one of the LGB's assistant secretaries made a clear statement that the period of repayment was determined by the assumed life of the works or undertaking (cited in Murray, 1903: 784). There is fairly widespread agreement, however, that the Board's practice differed significantly from its stated policy, with instances cited of the reduction from the normal 25 years allowed in the case of electricity works to 21 years, and a massive further proposed reduction to 12 years successfully resisted (Stevens, 1899: 55). The perceived reasons for these reductions were to err on the safe side in situations of uncertainty (e. g., where there were concerns with the possibility of technological change), and to hand on property uncluttered by debt to 'future generations [who] will in all probability have heavy enough burdens of their own to bear' (Murray, 1903: 784). This was seen as an excursion into the domain of municipal policy making, however, and likely to affect the willingness of corporations to undertake further investments (Forster, 1907: 145).

The 1907 Departmental Committee recognised that an equality between loan repayments periods and asset lives was by no means a foregone conclusion, but took the view that it was a reasonable working assumption which had the following virtues: it was based on independent authority and therefore prevented arbitrary or capricious fluctuations in the amount set aside; and was probably as good an estimate as could be obtained by any central authority attempting to fix the rate of depreciation (BPP 1907, xxxvii: para. 59).

Repairs and Renewals Advocates of the sinking fund as an adequate answer to the 'depreciation question' quite reasonably pointed out that, in addition, the costs of maintaining and repairing the asset were charged to revenue, so that (in the case of an electricity undertaking) 'the ratepayers will, in 20-5 years inherit a fully equipped undertaking free of debt' (Stevens, 1899: 53). The council of the CTAI agreed (1904) that as the result of 'constant repairs ... the life [of an asset] is usually extended far beyond the original period sanctioned' (quoted in Forster, 1907, at 165).

In response to the criticism that depreciation occurs which is not covered by repairs and renewals, Woodhouse drew attention to the fact that appreciations in the value of land provided adequate compensation (1893a: 881). A novel suggestion, drawing on the statutory requirements then applying to railway companies, was for the introduction of a requirement for management to certify whether the assets 'have during the past year been maintained in good order and repair' (Miller, 1905: 17).

The Depreciation Question The question of whether local authority assets should be depreciated became a matter of fierce public debate, in 1888, following revelations by Mr. Alderman King that the Manchester Corporation Gas Committee had included such charges for some years past:

> would any sane man, if the works were his own, value annually the street mains, for instance, (which have, of course, a date of death inherent in them, and at which date they must be renewed), at the amount they cost ... the only mode is to estimate, with the best intelligence you can apply, what the probable lifetime of the same is,

> and then to spread the cost of such items over the period of that life by an annual percentage. (1888: 496)

Support for this view, interestingly initially expounded by a non-accountant closely connected with local government, came from many quarters. Alexander Murray believed that the need for depreciation *and* sinking funds followed from the fact that 'the two are quite distinct and different in character, the former being a provision for the maintenance or replacement of assets, the latter having to do exclusively with the repayment of borrowed money' (Murray, 1903: 783). He went on to confirm that this was the approach adopted, in general, by the Glasgow Corporation.

Strong support for the inclusion of a depreciation charge was also expressed in evidence presented to the 1903 Select Committee, but close questioning indicated that advocates of this scheme were either not in full possession of the facts or pleading a special case. Sherley Price (a mechanical engineer) referred to 'the absolute necessity of writing off depreciation' (BPP 1903, vii: minute 1282), but was shown to have experience only of private sector organisations. Fells (joint author of the celebrated *Factory Accounts*, first published 1887) insisted that depreciation and the sinking fund were quite different matters, that depreciation should be accounted for as 'a charge upon the ordinary course of working or receipts' (minute 3329), and that it was presently very inadequately provided for by English boroughs (minute 3543). It was established, however, that Fells considered himself to be speaking on behalf of the Industrial Freedom League, in this matter, which was an organisation formed to attack municipal trading (minutes 3546-52). Glasgow's accountant, Dalrymple, was also convinced that depreciation should be charged, while Alexander Murray (from the same city) believed it should be made a legal requirement (minute 2423).

Proponents of the 'double charge' sometimes argued, alternatively, that this approach was required to deal with the possibility of premature obsolescence, particularly in the case of electricity and tramways, and to deal with the inclusion of short lived items among the total range of assets financed by a single loan equal to the average life of the concern's assets - the 'equated' loan period. Dicksee illustrates this point by reference to capital expenditure on an electric lighting undertaking whose constituent assets varied from 12 years in the case of meters to 80 years in the case of the buildings (1907: 485).

Opposition to the inclusion of a depreciation charge dates from King's initial outburst. Editorial comment in *The Accountant* drew attention to the fact that King was advocating a double charge which forced the present generation to make a gift of municipal assets to the next and asked: 'why should the present generation do anything of the kind?' (4 August 1888: 492). The leading chartered accountant Adam Murray believed, probably correctly, that the Manchester treatment was exceptional and sarcastically asked whether 'the trading accounts of municipal corporations are incorrect and misleading, except those of the Manchester Gas Committee' (1888: 522). He accepted King's conclusion that depreciation and liquidation of debt were two different things but pointed out that, in the case of local authorities, the fact is that 'they are both effected from the same source - out of profits' (1888: 523).

The claim made by Towers (1901) that the depreciation question, at least for electricity undertakings, should be resolved in favour of making a charge caused borough treasurers, attending the lecture, to stand up one after another and voice their strong disagreement. Bateson drew on personal experience to point out that he was associated with the first municipality to supply electricity (Blackpool in 1880) and that, if you redeem your capital within 25 years, there is no need to make any provision whatsoever for depreciation (discussion of Towers, 1901: 115). Stevens (of Brighton) blamed the press for the failure to distinguish between companies and corporations, leading to 'of late a great movement ... to induce corporations to make large advances towards this depreciation reserve' (discussion of Towers, 1901: 107). Miller similarly takes the editors of *The Accountant* to task as having caught 'the epidemic [of expressing doctrinaire views] and is not yet convalescent' (1905: 15).

In accounting disputes, as in other controversies, the parties to the debate often do little more than repeat their earlier entrenched position, pay no attention to the substantial arguments of their opponents, and instead focus on trivial matters where they believe a debating point can be won. There is thus a tendency to ignore any possible compromise which might obtain 'the best of both worlds'. The appropriate compromise solution in this case, worked out by Bolton for their tramways, was first to carry the amount of the depreciation charge to the depreciation fund and to pay out of it the debt instalment falling due (Murray, 1903: 785). This 'topping-up' approach was put forward for general application in a report prepared by the council of CTAI in 1904 (quoted in Forster, 1907: 165).

A further reason why it proved difficult to resolve the problem arose from the failure to distinguish between statutory requirements and matters of policy. As we have noted earlier, *The Accountant* (4 August 1888: 492) recognised that the effect of the double charge was to provide a gift for the next generation. It was not until the beginning of the twentieth century, however, that the 'danger of confusing statutory obligations with the suggestions of prudence' received careful attention in the literature (Miller, 1905: 15). According to Miller, 'the magnitude of the depreciation fund [is] the test of sound finance irrespective of the efficiency of the undertakings themselves' (*ibid*). Another reason for making the charge, put somewhat piously by Miller was:

> I think we may well wish to leave the world or our little corner of it better than we found it, we may well wish to lighten the burdens of our successors, and to take a broader view of the matter than the strictly legal official one. (Miller, 1905: 16)

These sentiments are echoed by Dalrymple who believed that 'every municipality should look forward to a time when its undertaking will be entirely free of debt' (1905: 264) and Forster who believed that 'they should endeavour by means of these trading or revenue-producing undertakings to do something for the benefit of their successors (1907: 157).

Depreciation and Income Tax At the beginning of the twentieth century Swainson implored his colleagues to turn their attention to the matter of depreciation, not simply to help secure financial stability or provide an improved performance measure, but because of tax implications. Income tax rates, which had remained between 6d and 8d in the £ between 1885-1900, nearly doubled to 1s in 1901 and 1s. 2d in 1902, and stayed at around that figure until the First World War when it increased to 5s in the £. Bolton Borough council used only a sinking fund for many years, but replaced this by the 'the commercial system of depreciation', based on the 'topping-up' system, in the endeavour to convince the Inland Revenue of the need to provide some relief in this area.

Swainson tells us that the Inland Revenue had never allowed the repayment of loans or sinking fund items to be deducted for tax purposes (Swainson, 1901: 735; see also Towers, 1901: 104), but that relief was given for actual expenditure on repairs and renewals. In the case of water and gas, where the capital outlay had usually been made some years earlier, where the rate of technological development slow, and where current expenditure on repairs and renewals substantial, the Inland Revenue's ruling gave little cause for concern. It was in relation to the new trading undertakings - tramways and electricity - where heavy investments were being made and technological progress was rapid that Swainson saw a particular need to negotiate tax relief for depreciation. It seems that, in the 1880's, when Bolton's accounts included no charge for depreciation, attempts to obtain some allowance for the old track of the tramways fell on deaf ears, and 'I thought it wise to revise our methods of account keeping, and recommended the tramways committee to adopt the commercial system of depreciation for their municipal trading' (Swainson, 1901: 737). Clearly Bolton was in the forefront of negotiating new concessions, with Swainson pointing out that Bedford was the only other town where depreciation had been allowed by the income tax authorities, in that case an allowance of 5% on expenditure on mains and machinery. Interestingly, they do not appear to have included this charge in their published accounts.

The decisions reached by the Income-tax Commissioners would not, of course, necessarily remain consistent over the whole country, but one might imagine that the inclusion of a carefully calculated depreciation charge would have attracted tax relief in view of the successful use of an even more blatant ploy described by Towers. Apparently deductions equal in amount to repayments of loans of sinking fund payments were sometimes permitted by the Income-tax Commissioners provided the deduction was covered by the word "depreciation"' (1901: 104).

The CTAI turned its attention to the tax treatment of capital expenditure in the years that followed, and a series of meetings were held with representatives from the Board of Inland Revenue, the Municipal Tramways Association, the Incorporated Municipal Electrical Association, the Institution of Gas Engineers, the Association of Water Engineers, and the Incorporated Association of Municipal and County Engineers (*Proceedings*, 1908: 39). The objective was to reduce the number of appeals made by municipal trading undertakings against income tax assessments, and the widely divergent treatment in different parts of the country. The result of these negotiations (IMTA, 1908: 165-76) was the introduction of rates of write-off for most of the assets comprising tramways and electric lighting undertakings. No depreciation whatsoever was allowed for gas and water undertakings, although repairs and renewals (and it seems replacements, with the old cost written-off rather than the new where there was an element of improvement) allowed as before. The arrangements outlined above were made towards the end of the period covered by this chapter, but it will be suggested below that there is no strong evidence they had a major impact on subsequent accounting practice.

Reserves It was common practice for provisional orders or special Acts of Parliament, authorising the establishment of particular trading undertakings, to include a clause providing for the establishment of a reserve fund, out of profits, normally not to exceed one tenth of the aggregate capital expenditure. The reserve fund might be used to meet trading losses, extraordinary claims and, sometimes, the cost of extending or renewing the works. These regulations sometimes also, or alternatively, made provision for the establishment of a separate repairs and renewals fund to help equalise the cost of these expenditures over a number of years. In either case the practice was to invest, separately, an amount equal to the balance to the credit of the reserve fund, in order to guarantee its availability when required. We are told that such funds had been established by virtually all boroughs by the time that the 1907

Departmental Committee met (BPP 1907, xxxvii: Appendix I: para. 16(a)), though the adequacy of sums set aside was, of course, a separate matter.

These reserves were often looked upon as a means of dealing with the problem of premature obsolescent and the cost of replacing short life assets where the expiration of the equated loan period and the opportunity to re-borrow remained in the distant future (Dicksee, 1907: 485). Further, the fund was seen by some as a means of providing for depreciation, causing Forster to comment sarcastically that its advocates were 'thereby putting a threefold burden on its [the municipalities] shoulders, and providing not only for the discharge of its liability, but for its [the assets] replacement twice over' (1907: 127). In general, however, the reserve fund was looked upon as an alternative to the depreciation fund. Indeed, some believed that the statutory reserve fund was intended to take the place of depreciation, and that municipalities were therefore precluded from also making a charge. For example, this view was expressed by the LGB in response to an inquiry from the Pontypridd Urban District Council concerning the district auditor's advice that they should establish a depreciation fund (Williams, 1904: 292). The LGB was also of the opinion that the revenue of the gasworks had to be applied in the manner indicated by the Act and that this did not appear to permit the establishment of a depreciation fund. Continued uncertainty concerning the precise legal position was indicated in the Report of the 1907 Departmental Committee (BPP 1907, xxxvii: para. 60).

The view of the Municipal Electrical Association (1902) later supported by the Borough Treasurers Association was that, in relation to electrical undertakings, no depreciation need be charged provided that the operations were maintained in a thorough state of efficiency, but that a reserve fund 'should be formed, up to the limit allowed by the provisional order, before any contribution is made in relief of the rates' (Harris, 1903: 220). As noted earlier, the proposed standard forms of accounts reproduced in the 1907 Departmental Committee's Report, accepted this approach; they contained entries for sinking funds, renewals funds, and reserve funds, but made no mention of depreciation which the report, elsewhere, described as a matter to be decided upon in the light of local conditions and unsuitable for central direction (para. 60).

Amortisation of capital expenditure: practice

There was a statutory requirement for boroughs to repay capital out of revenue, and even if they did nothing by way of upkeep there still remained the land and buildings and odd items of machinery representing 'a clear gift to posterity at the expense of the present generation of ratepayers' (*Financial Circular*, December 1903: 278). But all corporations seem to have done more than this. At the minimum they maintained the asset in working condition, while the vast majority also established a reserve fund. We will first consider the policy decisions of individual corporations and then look at the broader picture.

Individual corporations The amounts transferred to variously named funds established to take account of the decline in fixed asset values, over time, is set out at ten yearly intervals between 1890-1930 in table 6.6. Birmingham's published accounts refer to depreciation on only one occasion; a depreciation fund for water of £4,000 was established in 1876, but the entry was reversed the following year. By 1882, however, transfers to reserve funds for gas and water amounted respectively to £64,441 and £50,000. These do not show up in table 6.6 for the period 1881-90, due to the fact that *Burdett's* records, for that period, only transfers to a 'depreciation fund', but amounts do of course appear under the broader captions employed from 1910. The table also shows that Bradford charged modest amounts for depreciation of both its electricity works and tramways in the 1890's but, afterwards, instead operated a reserve and renewals account (for tramways) and a depreciation and renewals account (for electricity), with an overall summary of the transactions, between 1901-21, given in table 6.4.

Despite the considerable variety in accounting practice, both between individual entities and over time, it is quite clear that certain boroughs gave serious attention to the depreciation question and attempted to tackle it in a systematic manner. The experimentation of the Manchester Gas Committee with depreciation accounting - substantial transfers were made each year from 1862, when the works was established, until 1891 (the accumulated charge is £688,744 in the 1890 annual accounts) - was discontinued in 1892. It subsequently made only modest transfers to the variously described depreciation, renewals and reserve fund accounts as indicated in table 6.6. Other municipalities took up the depreciation gauntlet; for example Burnley had charged £130,000 against revenue, by 1893, in addition to the £144,000 repaid through the sinking fund (Woodhouse, 1893a: 881), while Bolton charged depreciation and met loan repayments out of the amounts set aside (Murray, 1903: 785; Swainson, 1901).

At Bristol, following the establishment of the electricity department in 1893, small amounts were written off in respect of depreciation, and modest transfers made from profit to build up a reserve fund and depreciation fund of £10,000 and £6,000 respectively by 1905. In the following year

Table 6.6: Depreciation etc charged by selected municipal corporations, 1890-1930

		Gas	Water	Elect.	Tramw.
		£000	£000	£000	£000
1881/90	Depreciation Fund				
	Birmingham	-	-		
	Bradford	5.5[1]	7.8		
	Bristol	N/A	N/A		
	Cardiff	N/A	-		
	Manchester	32.8	-		
	Total: Transfers	38.3	7.8		
	Expenditure	4,176.6	9,503.9		
	%	0.9	0.1		
	All corporations				
	Total: Transfers	124.6	10.6		
	Expenditure	13,819.7	31,979.4		
	%	0.9	0.03		
1891/1900	Depreciation Fund				
	Birmingham	-	-		
	Bradford	-	-	2.6	3.8
	Bristol	N/A	N/A	-	N/A
	Cardiff	N/A	-	-	N/A
	Manchester	-	-	-	N/A
	Total: Transfers	-	-	2.6	3.8
	Expenditure	6,477	15,022	5,943	4,949
	%	-	-	0.1	0.1
	All corporations				
	Total: Transfers	91.6	9.4		
	Expenditure	28,420[2]	49,969	[3]	[3]
	%	0.3	0.01		
1909/10	Depreciation, renewals and reserve fund				
	Birmingham	-	0.2[4]	9.0[5]	23.5
	Bradford	-	-	5.0[7]	12.4
	Bristol	N/A	N/A	3.1[6]	N/A
	Cardiff	N/A	-	9.6	11.0
	Manchester	-	-	-	70.0
	Total: Transfers	-	0.2	26.7	116.9
	Expenditure	6,477	20,769	5,943	4,720
	%	-	-	0.4	2.6
	All corporations				
	Total: Transfers	159.2	33.4	160.2	733.7
	Expenditure	26,772	67,229	25,253	40,77[illegible]
	%	0.6	0.01	0.6	1.8

le 6.6 (cont.): Depreciation etc charged by selected municipal corporations, 1890-1930

		Gas	Water	Elect.	Tramways
		£000	£000	£000	£000
'20	Depreciation, renewals and reserve fund				
	Birmingham	19.0	-	60.0	151.5[10]
	Bradford	-	-	-	14.8[8]
	Bristol	N/A	N/A	5.0	N/A
	Cardiff	N/A	-	-	21.9[9]
	Manchester	16.3	-	5.8	80.2
	Total: Transfers	35.3	-	70.8	268.4
	Expenditure	7,578	23,023	8,212	6,796
	%	0.5	-	0.6	1.8
	All corporations				
	Total: Transfers	261.2	20.8	398.6	946.5
	Expenditure	34,235	78,567	43,026	50,283
	%	0.8	0.02	0.9	1.9
'30	Depreciation, renewals and reserve fund				
	Birmingham	152.2	-	144.5	230.9
	Bradford	-	0.2	-	137.1
	Bristol	N/A	N/A	4.0	N/A
	Cardiff	N/A	-	-	45.6[1]
	Manchester	20.1	53.6	-	75.0
	Total: Transfers	172.3	53.6	148.5	488.6
	Expenditure	11,995	31,990	31,910	11,479
	%	1.4	0.2	0.5	4.2
	All corporations				
	Total: Transfers	522.1	161.2	1,149.7	1,489.3
	Expenditure	57,539	118,404	144,817	83,329
	%	0.9	0.1	0.8	1.8

Not applicable
Taken from accounts
Includes electricity
Figures unavailable
Contingency fund
Renewals fund
Reserve fund
Depreciation and renewals fund
Depreciation and contingencies fund
Depreciation fund
Reserve fund and suspense account

the method of accounting for fixed assets was altered on the recommendation of Professor Dicksee. The depreciation charge was written back to profits, while the other two amounts were credited to the newly created 'reserve (for renewals) fund account'. Also credited to this account, from revenue, was £2,500 described as the 'difference between the provision for renewal of assets recommended by Professor Dicksee and the amount of the statutory repayment of loans' (1906 accounts: 140). We can therefore see that the 'topping-up' system is in operation, with the rates used possibly those set out in Dicksee's paper published in *The Accountant* in the following year (1907: 485). A separately calculated depreciation charge, for the electricity plant, appears as a contra entry in the balance sheet, being deducted both from the balance on fixed asset account and from the combined amounts transferred from revenue for loan repayments and renewals. The accumulated write-off at the end date for this survey, 1935, was £1,280,469.

Depreciation also became a major issue at Cardiff, during the first decade of the twentieth century, with the first cause for concern being whether it was legal for a municipal corporation to create a depreciation fund. In a report to the finance committee (29 May 1903: 74), Cardiff's town clerk expressed the opinion that it was illegal, but revised his opinion on the basis of advice subsequently received from the Municipal Corporation Association. The Association's view seems to have been that a depreciation fund may be regarded as part of the 'working and establishment expenses and cost of maintenance of the undertaking', which was the first call on electricity revenue under Section 52 of the Cardiff Electric Lighting Order, 1891.

Moving on to the calculation of the charge, it was the view of the technical staff and the treasurer that the tramway lines required to be replaced at the end of 15 years, while the equated loan period was fixed at 30 years. Allcock, the City Treasurer and a leading member of the IMTA, clearly felt the Tramways Committee had prevaricated long enough:

> The fear that the rates of the City might be called upon to assist in the building up of depreciation funds has, on several occasions, been discussed by the council, but perhaps I may be allowed to submit that the source from which the money is derived does not operate on the abstract question of depreciation, it is either a fact that the wear and tear of the machinery, &c., is greater than that represented by the amounts set aside for sinking funds - (in which case extra provisions should of necessity be made) or it is not a fact, and until this question is definitely agreed upon and settled, it will I think be quite clear to the committee that I cannot complete by report (Treasurer's report, 1909: 4).

> the committee that I cannot complete by report (Treasurer's report, 1909: 4).

The treasurer calculated that the cost of reconstructing the 30 miles of track, in 15 years time, would be £120,000, at which date the balance on the sinking fund would amount to only £46,912, leaving a shortfall of £73,088. The treasurer's recommendation was for an additional charge to meet the forecast deficit.

The strength of the treasurer's argument was conceded and the committee increased the charges accordingly. Transfers to the electric tramways depreciation account, subsequently made, were used partly to meet the cost of renewing and replacing fixed assets, leaving an accumulated surplus of £293,118, in 1935, then described as 'capital expenditure defrayed out of revenue'. Not surprisingly, the amounts transferred were the target of political comment (Councillor Saunders, minutes 1913-14: 152), resulting in the borough treasurer being instructed to report on the possible use of these balances in relief of the rates. The eventual decision was to leave the fund untouched, in contrast with the action taken by certain other boroughs and by private sector-based companies wishing to report higher profits and/or pay larger dividends both before and after this date.

A further example of the care taken to achieve a sensible resolution to the depreciation question is contained in the evidence presented to the 1903 Select Committee by Richard Barrow, Controller and Auditor of the City of Liverpool. 'I consider it is the duty of financial advisers of corporations to obtain all the information from the corporation engineers and from all other sources, which are open to them as to the life and character of the undertaking' (BPP 1903, vii: minute 1564). Futher:

> I not only obtain from them the facts within their own experience, but I obtain from other sources the facts and experience of other municipalities and other trading undertakings as to the prospective liability there would be in respect of the undertaking then under consideration (minute 1566).

This information was used, by Barrow, 'with regard to the proposal to transfer a proportion of our tramway profits' to a depreciation fund.

The broader picture The accounting practices of municipal corporations, around the turn of the century, are detailed in the Report of the 1903 Select Committee (BPP 1903, vii: Appendix A). This shows that depreciation charges represented, on average, just 0.2% of total capital outlay. The Appendix also represented, on average, just 0.2% of total capital outlay. The Appendix also reveals that only 55 (out of 319) corporations made transfers to depreciation, reserve, renewal or contingency funds, though it seems likely that these were the larger boroughs.

The broad development of capital accounting practice over the period 1890-1930 is indicated by table 6.7, though it must be realised that this table does not distinguish between transfers to depreciation, reserve and renewals funds. The table shows a significant increase in the proportion of corporations making transfers, and an examination of the data from which this table is derived reveals some large amounts being set aside by individual corporations. The amounts remain a fairly modest percentage of total capital expenditure, even in these latter cases, but it must be remembered that they are *additional* to the loan repayment provisions. Many corporations set aside no amount whatsoever which seems a little strange in view of the availability of tax concessions, discussed earlier, since the early years of the century. Possible explanations are either that the corporations were not making a profit (so there was not tax benefit to be obtained by including a charge in the accounts) or that the inclusion of a charge in the published accounts was not a condition for the granting of relief for tax purposes.

Accounting practice and profitability The returns made by municipal corporations in respect of their reproductive undertakings for the period 1902-6 (BPP 1909, xc) show that transfers to various named depreciation funds depended upon whether profits were sufficient for the purpose. For example, Portsmouth created a reserve and renewal fund under its Electric Light Order 1890, s. 52(5), which amounted to £20,289 at 31 March 1906. At Swansea, by way of contrast, profits were low and no use could be made of similar powers (p. 171). The importance of the availability of profits is again stressed by the actions of the South Shields Electricity Committee, where depreciation charges depended upon the level of profits and no fixed contributions were made (p. 156).

The fact that corporations sometimes varied the amount of the depreciation charge depending on the level of profits was confirmed by Carson Roberts in evidence presented to the 1907 Departmental Committee: 'Naturally the tendency is towards full recognition of this special depreciation in the accounts of those local authorities who have a profit to dispose of, and in a contrary direction in other cases' (BPP 1907, xxxvii: minute 1933). Why did boroughs do this? Possible reasons become apparent when we consider the implications, for the borough, of making a deduction which caused trading undertakings to report a deficit. In these circumstances it would be necessary

Table 6.7: Transfers to depreciation, reserve and renewals funds by municipal corporations 1890-1930

Year	Number of Corporat-ions	Gas		Water		Electricity		Tramways	
		*%	+%	*%	+%	*%	+%	*%	+%
1890	48	56	41	77	14	Not Applicable		Unavailable	
1900	70	49	29	70	16	64	24	Unavailable	
1910	85	47	55	68	28	86	58	75	61
1920	90	51	45	70	24	87	55	77	62
1930	121	47	63	71	42	84	68	69	67

Notes

*% Proportion of municipal corporations supplying service

+% Proportion of 'supplying' corporations making transfers to depreciation, reserve and renewals fund.

Source: 1890 and 1990 figures. Burdett, Henry C. *Burdett's Official Intelligence*, London: Spottiswoode. 1910, 1920 and 1930 figures. Secretary of the Share and Loan Department (ed.) *The Stock Exchange Official Intelligence*, London: Spottiswoode.

to: carry the deficit forward and attempt to recover it out of revenues generated in future years, perhaps requiring an increase in prices charged to consumers, or; make a transfer from the rates in aid of the undertaking by way of subsidy, or; make a transfer from the rates and create a debtor/creditor relationship with the rate fund. The position was exacerbated where municipal undertakings were recently established (most particularly electricity), with the result that they incurred large fixed costs, including heavy loan charges, at a time when they were operating well below full capacity. In these circumstances, authorities were naturally reluctant to create additional burdens on the rates which might fuel the debate against municipal trading.

In the opposite situation, where profits were buoyant, increased transfers to a depreciation or reserve fund might be made to 'mop up' monopoly profits and thus avoid pressure for price cuts and instead use the resources to maintain physical capacity, undertake expenditure for which it might possibly be difficult to obtain LGB approval, or simply to set aside something for a 'rainy day'.

Review and conclusion

The debate surrounding the appropriate accounting treatment of capital expenditure by municipal corporations was intense, wide ranging and, in the main, constructive. It involved borough treasurers, borough accountants, auditors, town councillors, engineers, ratepayers and academics. In presenting their arguments, these individuals were naturally influenced by their background and experience, and some were extremely stubborn.

There is relatively little evidence of local authority officials with public sector-based views lining up in direct conflict with chartered accountants. Perhaps the reason for this is that most of the parties had some knowledge of, experience of and sympathy for the somewhat diverse practices employed by companies compared with corporations. Indeed, the most intense arguments appear to have been *between* municipal officials. The following characterisation of local authority officials in these earlier times is provided in the Chartered Institute of Public Finance and Accountancy's official history:

> They were for the most part men of tough fibre and strong personality, though others were remembered for their old fashioned courtesy ... They were hard workers and hard masters, making great demands both on themselves and their staffs. Generally they were given to strongly held opinions, with not too great a respect for those of others, and they were forthright in expressing them; they were never mealy mouthed. (Sowerby, 1985: 4)

This comment certainly applies to Swainson who placed the responsibility for failure to solve the depreciation question squarely upon the shoulders of the CTAI. We have seen that this body took the initiative, in 1889, of issuing guidance concerning the range of financial reports to be published by municipal corporations, and there were early signs (1894) that it would also provide advice concerning the content of those accounts. The executive committee expressed 'their opinion that in matters of municipal accountancy the Institute is the proper body to decide what in their opinion is the right course to adopt where they find variation in the treatment of any portion of municipal finance' (quoted in Swainson, 1901: 735). Swainson presented a major paper on depreciation to the 1895 Annual Meeting of the CTAI, and this was referred to the executive committee to see what further steps might be taken in the direction of uniformity. The executive committee concluded that

> Mr Swainson's paper, having been printed *in extenso*, and circulated for the better information of the members, they are individually better able as to decide as to the adoption of any of the recommendations contained therein which might be applicable to the accounts under their control. (*ibid*)

Swainson concludes that, as a result, 'the influence of the Institute in making its power felt through the accountancy profession and Parliament was reduced to a minimum' (*ibid*).

But although the CTAI\IMTA provided no explicit leadership on the depreciation question, its advocacy of standardised formats, taken a stage further during the early years of the twentieth century, provided indicators concerning the appropriate treatment of fixed assets. We have seen (chapter 5) that the recommended forms of accounts for each trading activity, attached to the Departmental Committee's Report 1907, were based on a draft prepared by the IMTA. These forms make no mention of depreciation, and an indication of divergent views held concerning the respective methods appropriate for corporations and companies is obtained by comparing the 1907 proposed forms for electricity accounts with those issued (in 1893) under the Electric Lighting Act 1882, s. 9 for use by electricity undertakings, whether operated by companies or corporations. The following observed differences are given particular significance by the fact that the remaining entries are substantially the same. Whereas the 1893 forms contain entries in the revenue account for depreciation of buildings, plant and machinery and in the net revenue (appropriation) account for transfers to reserves, the 1907 forms contain only entries for transfers to a renewals fund and to a reserve fund in the net revenue account.

The CTAI/IMTA therefore provided no explicit support for borough officers keen to include a charge in circumstances where the borough council, for one reason or another (e. g. the desire to avoid a politically sensitive rate increase), were opposed to financial reporting procedures favoured by the experts. Some treasurers were no doubt more capable of standing their ground than the individual - castigated by Swainson as not having 'the backbone of an invertebrate jellyfish' (quoted in Sowerby, 1985: 4) - who questioned the wisdom of forming a Treasurers' Association on the grounds that it might impair his relationship with his employers.

We have also seen that the issues were also considered sufficiently important to be the subject of investigations by government committees in 1903 and 1907. The former made no mention of depreciation in its report, while a *laissez faire* view is evident in the following extract from the latter's report:

> With regard to the depreciation of assets, the amount to be provided in any case depends necessarily on the nature of the asset itself and the special conditions attaching to it, and cannot be regulated by a general standard or scale. The repayment of debt, so far as it goes, may properly be regarded as provision for depreciation; but it is possible that the period allowed for repayment may be excessive, and therefore in some cases further provision may be necessary. (BPP 1907, xxxvii: para. 79(l))

The outcome of the capital accounting debate was that municipalities obeyed the legal requirement to establish a sinking fund to repay money borrowed, and adopted the sensible course of maintaining assets in an efficient condition out of revenue as and when the expenditure was incurred. These actions alone were likely to have been more than adequate to maintain capital intact. In contrast to the conclusion reached by Jones (1986: 139-40), some local authorities did much more, although the range of accounting practices employed, and the level of financial allocations made, varied a great deal. The decision to establish a repairs and renewals fund, a reserve fund, or a depreciation fund depended on a whole host of local conditions and circumstances including the obligations imposed in a special Act of Parliament, the profitability of the undertaking, pricing policy, the existence of local competition, financial prudence, and the desire to use trading profits in relief of the rates.

The lack of direction provided by the CTAI/IMTA or the government may be cited as responsible for the continued variety in capital accounting practices, but it is important to recognise the fact that almost all municipal corporations maintained a sinking fund and charged repairs against revenue by the beginning of the twentieth century. To go beyond this was a policy decision which the central authority quite rightly left to local officials. In addition, it must be remembered that for municipal corporations, unlike limited companies, the variety in accounting practice was linked with full disclosure so that the ratepayers and creditors were able to assess, if interested, the financial significance of the procedures adopted.

Municipal undertakings of course enjoyed considerable privileges. They were local monopolies and relatively free from competition, and they could always look to the rates to subsidise over-spending and trading losses. This may well explain their much greater willingness to borrow compared with limited companies (who were run by many of the same people) in the latter decades of the nineteenth century. It is also important to point out that the loan repayment rules were not just the municipal equivalent of private sector depreciation; they actually required an equivalent amount of cash to be set aside which helped guarantee financial stability. Moreover, where a decision was made to set up a reserve fund or a sinking fund, the same 'liquidity rules' applied, so that there was no problem finding the cash when, for example, the tramway track fell due for replacement. The other side of the coin was that the decision to depreciate did not involve a 'mere bookkeeping entry'; the action required an equivalent amount of cash to put the accounting policy into effect.

Municipal undertakings involved huge investments and reported modest amounts, overall, by way of profits - the usual policy was broadly to break even, and the ratepayers 'dividend' was the local availability, at a reasonable price, of services needed to improve living standards. The municipal corporations seemed to have achieved this objective. In the long run, the actions of prudent corporations did not benefit local ratepayers as much as might have been expected. Compensation on nationalisation of gas (1946) and electricity (1947) was based on loans outstanding with no allowance for revenue financed assets owned at that date.

NOTES

1 For example, the present debate on capital accounting in local authorities which has centred on the work of the Capital Accounting Steering Group, 1990.

2 Capital accounting in local authorities has previously received attention from Rowan Jones, 1985b, and 1986: 138-49.

3 Attacks on municipal trading were based on the view, often dominated by self interest, that such services were best provided by the private sector. A series of seventeen articles published in *The Times* between August and November 1902 were instrumental in adding fuel to a debate which had started

towards the end of the nineteenth century. See also Dicksee's views quoted in Williams, 1904: 293.

4 PHA 1875, MCA 1882, the Electric Lighting Act 1882, and LGA 1888 each laid down a period of 60 years, while the Tramways Act 1870 specified 30 years. All these periods were subject to variation by special Act or provisional order.

5 In practice borough treasurers often delayed raising the loan until construction was complete, with an overdraft initially used to finance the investment. The advantage of this ploy was that it delayed the need to make annual transfers to the sinking fund.

6 The Glasgow Police Commissioners' treatment was possibly exceptional, even in Scotland. However, some drew a clear distinction between the approach in Scotland, where substantial charges for depreciation of municipal assets were common, and 'the anti-Glasgow school' which regarded the sinking fund as sufficient on its own (Williams: 1904: 295). This difference in practice may be due, partly, to the fact that provisional orders and special Acts obtained by Scottish towns sometimes required a charge to be made in the case of tramways, and sometimes other municipal assets (Murray 1903: 786) while, on the other hand, the loan redemption period was often much longer than for their English and Welsh counterparts.

7

MUNICIPAL AUDIT - A PROFESSIONAL POWER STRUGGLE

The decision, made in 1835, to subject municipal corporations to the elective audit was perfectly natural, and chapter 3 draws attention to the fact that it may be seen as the local authority equivalent of the amateur/shareholder audit. The elective audit was also the only feasible option at that time. A professional audit would have been impractical due to the lack of professionally qualified personnel, while any attempt to introduce a government audit would have been stoutly resisted. Moreover, a centrally controlled audit would have been difficult to justify in view of the fact that municipal corporations were at that time almost entirely self-financing. As time went by conditions changed; the rising flow of finance from central government to municipal corporations increased the case for a centrally controlled audit to monitor the use of public money, while the fact that municipal corporations began to undertake trading activities strengthened the case for a commercial audit.

The purpose of this chapter is, therefore, to explore a power struggle between various pressure groups keen to replace the elective audit by either a professional audit or one administered by the LGB through the office of the district auditor.[1]

The elective audit

We have seen that the elective audit, initially introduced to cover transactions on the borough fund, was extended to the district fund in 1848 (PHA 1848, s. 122). The right of the elective auditor to go further and examine the accounts of trading undertakings was a contentious issue in some boroughs; while in others the position was clarified by local Act of Parliament. For example, the Bradford Waterworks Act 1854, s. 7 stated that:

> the Council shall cause a separate and distinct account to be kept by the Treasurer of the Borough, to be called 'the Water Account', of all monies received and paid under the powers and provisions of this Act, and such accounts shall be open to the inspection of all persons

> interested, and shall be audited and published in such and the like manner as accounts are required to be audited and published by 'The Public Health Act, 1848'.

The suitability of the elective audit became the subject of government enquiry in 1874. The Select Committee on Boroughs (Auditors and Assessors) was appointed to consider whether the district audit, which originated from the desire to achieve administrative control over expenditure on poor relief and was in the process of being extended to other local authority activities (Coombs and Edwards, 1990), should be applied to municipal corporations. An important advantage claimed for the district audit was the power to disallow unauthorised expenditure and surcharge officers for amounts wrongly spent.

It was quite natural that the Committee should take a great deal of evidence from town clerks, and most of these expressed strong support for the *status quo*. According to Manchester's town clerk, Sir J. Heron:

> one elective auditor [at Manchester] is agent for an insurance company ... and he is a man exceedingly well versed in accounts. The other auditor is a gentleman in business, who was selected, I may say for his intimate acquaintance with and knowledge of accounts. (minute 631)

Heron further explained that all payments came before the auditors who carefully carried out their duty to examine the authority for payments made. However, Heron's conclusion that the audit was as 'complete and efficient as the Poor Law [audit]' (minute 789) was quite possibly weighted to counter the case for its replacement by the district audit. Similar sentiments were expressed at Hull where 'none but competent and suitable persons acted as elective auditor' (minute 1873).

Not all town clerks were entirely happy with the elective audit. Cambridge's auditors were described as 'not sufficiently alive to their duty' (minute 1114) when failing to discover a major fraud by the treasurer in 1869, although there is some indication that council officials placed restrictions on the auditor's ability to examine documentation which may well have prevented them from doing a proper job. The deputy town clerk of Sunderland drew attention to the failure of the town's elective auditors to discover a deficiency which was subsequently brought to light by a public accountant employed to prepare the municipality's accounts (minute 1355-6).

The Committee's decision not to recommend any change was justified on the grounds that sufficient safeguards existed against extravagant and improper expenditure. For example, a disallowance of expenditure could be achieved by *certiorari* to the High Court,[2] although this was dismissed, by one witness, as a 'very tedious and troublesome process' and 'one must be very much a patriot indeed to carry it out' (BPP 1874, vii: minutes 1631-2). The easier option was to resort to a second protection, i. e. that of 'attending the audit and objecting to the accounts' (minute 1631).

The Committee's Report repeated one of the traditional arguments against the introduction of a government controlled audit, namely that it would 'occasion an unnecessary interference with the independent local self-government in boroughs' (BPP 1874, vii: 5). Even the discovery that payments were often made for items beyond the council's strict statutory authority was turned to the borough's advantage. Nottingham borough council had arranged unauthorised vaccinations of 4,000 people to quell a small-pox epidemic, and much was made of the failure of the board of guardians - subject to the district audit - to take any initiative, although 'the action ought to have begun with them' (minute 185).[3] In this context, the assistant secretary to the LGB, D. B. Fry, proved to be an ineffective advocate for the district audit.

> [minute 1713] I suppose that you would say that it was quite within the province of the auditor to have disallowed such a charge as that which was made at Nottingham with regard to vaccination against small-pox? - [Fry's reply] Certainly, if it was an unlawful expenditure.
>
> 1718 And let the people die in the meanwhile? - [Fry's reply] That might be the result in a particular case, but of course the corporation would be the judges of what they were to do.

The staunch defence of the elective audit proved successful, and the audit and accounting provisions of MCA 1835 were repeated, with minor modification, in MCA 1882 (ss. 21, 25-8, 62, 139-43, 233). However, the overall impression gained from the evidence presented is that, in 1874, the elective audit was usually a fairly ineffective exercise, undertaken mainly by amateurs, with its continuance favoured by council official because it did not entail interference from central government, it cost very little and did no harm.[4] This situation was to change dramatically over the next 25 years.

The attack on the elective audit began, in earnest, in the editorial columns of *The Accountant* in the mid-1880's, and the simple explanation may be that a young and vigorous profession was keen to seize the opportunity to extend its services to a rapidly expanding sector of the economy. The immediate motivation or 'excuse' for the onslaught was the perpetration of frauds, undetected by the elective auditors, and the increasing tendency of municipal officials to voice dissatisfaction with the existing service.

Frauds were committed at the Wigan Corporation over the extended period 1870-84, leading *The Accountant* to

> question whether in view of the history of these Wigan frauds, which may be taken as a fair sample of others, it is likely that town councils will much longer be permitted in such cases to act as the final judges as to the necessity of having an audit ... by qualified accountants? (*The Accountant*, 4 October 1884: 5)

Attention is also drawn to the condition of the accounting system at York where 'the cash book in the surveyor's office was accessible to all the clerks, its contents remaining unbalanced seemingly for years ... and we might quote further in the same strain' (*The Accountant*, 11 October 1884: 6).

At Kidderminster, we are told that 'the Chamberlain expressed his opinion that the present system of auditing in that town was a farce' (*The Accountant*, 23 February 1884: 4), with the ineffectiveness of their work exacerbated by the recent tendency for 'easy-going' auditors to be succeeded by auditors who give 'a most offensive form of publicity to some things which are regrettable, a few unanswerable, many simply too contemptibly small for any mention' (*The Accountant*, 11 October 1884: 5). In this latter context, the journal focuses on the elective auditors' criticism of the accounts of the Borough of Burslam. This caused the corporation to call in a firm of chartered accountants who found that criticisms made by the elective auditor were entirely without foundation and reflected considerable naivety in financial matters. *The Accountant* concludes: 'as shoes are made by shoemakers, so audits to be of the least use should be conducted by professional auditors' (6 August 1887: 451). And: 'it is no reflection on the class on men who have usually filled that office to say that their acquaintance with accounts is, on the average, less than is required of a second-rate bookkeeper' (11 October 1884: 5).

One of the perceived problems associated with the post of elective audit was, therefore, the absence of any requirement for this official to possess a professional qualification. Other criticisms, emanating from municipal officers, were seized upon by the accounting press keen to strengthen its case for reform. One objection was that the post of elective auditor provided local ratepayers' associations and other political pressure groups with the opportunity to support the appointment of people whose principal role was to criticise policy rather than to carry out an audit. The influence of these Associations is reflected in the decision of candidates to sometimes style themselves the ratepayers' association's representative in the belief that this would improve their likelihood of success.

The particular concern of these associations was the burgeoning expenditure of town councils. For example, Manchester Corporation's accounts were 'subject to the most bitter and persistent attacks' from the Manchester Ratepayers' Association, in 1884, but, again, 'grave charges of gross mismanagement and downright fraud broke down utterly when they came to be examined and tested', in this case through an investigation headed by Registrar Lister (*The Accountant*, 25 June 1887: 369-70). It was estimated that costs amounting to £6,000 were unnecessarily incurred (*The Accountant*, 6 August 1887: 451). A further allegation of abuse of the elective auditor's position is given by Butterworth, the borough accountant for Hastings, who describes a thirty-two page pamphlet, written by an elective auditor, 'which is from beginning to end an attack on municipal trading in general, and of the borough in question in particular' (1908: 147). A Mr Waycott of Devonport similarly believed that people were 'elected to the position through political influence and were incompetent to carry out the work' (Butterworth, 1908: 160).[5]

The above accusations may not have been without foundation. However, it would seem not unreasonable for there to be consultation and even collaboration between elective auditors and ratepayers' associations in view of the fact that they shared a common concern to protect the interests of local ratepayers. This philosophy received support from evidence presented to the 1903 Select Committee, by Manchester's elective auditor, who favoured retention of both professional and elective audits on the grounds that the latter 'exercise a sort of oversight which the professional auditors could not profess to do, owing to the exigencies of time' (BPP 1903, vii: minute 2832).

A further perceived strength of the elective audit was that ratepayers might find it easier to approach the incumbent to discuss matters which they thought needed to be investigated, such as the suspected supply of goods to the corporation by a company where, perhaps, a director was also a member of the committee purchasing the goods (Williams, minutes 2843-66). Williams also reminded the Committee of the following fundamental features of the elective audit, namely that it drew strength from the concern of local inhabitants to control local expenditure, while their appointment by the ratepayers rendered them immune from the influence of municipal officials (minutes 2818-9). The latter point was reinforced by rules which made it clear that they were not entitled to remuneration for work on the borough accounts. The weaknesses in the practical application of these ideals stemmed from the general lack of interest in the work of the municipal auditor, despite the best efforts of ratepayers' associations, and the fact that there seems to have been nothing to stop a municipality from paying elective auditors if they chose to adopt this course.

Evidence presented to the 1874 Committee states that Manchester 'had a contest once or twice, but it is extremely rare' (minute 631). At Hull, where a contest was held each year between 1865-72, the elective auditor polled just 87 votes and 73 votes respectively in each of the last two years when the electoral roll amounted to upwards of 20,000 voters. A dispute between council officials and the elective auditor at a time of local concern with the level of municipal expenditure might increase the turnout, such as in Cardiff in the mid-1890's when 3091 ratepayers voted (*The Accountant*, 10 October 1896: 810), but local interest would soon evaporate. Even at Birmingham, where there was considerable anxiety around this time with the level of expenditure undertaken by the water committee, interest was not sustained (BPP 1903, vii: minutes 1795-6).

A further concern of municipal officials, which surfaced in the 1890's, was that the cost of the elective audit might become excessive, since it would depend upon the amount of time that the elected officials choose to devote to the audit of the district fund where they were entitled to a payment of two guineas per day. Indeed, we are told that in some towns contests for the position of elective auditor were extremely frequent owing to the fact that they could charge for their services (*Financial Circular*, February 1897: 63). We also note the following exchange between a member of the 1903 Select Committee and Birmingham's elective auditor W. G. Floyd (an incorporated accountant): 'I am not talking about money; you did not seek this office for the remuneration it gave, did you? - Most people do, I think' (BPP 1903, vii: minute 1832). At Birmingham the elective auditor was paid 56 guineas (minute 1753) which compares well with the fees paid elsewhere (table 7.1). At the other extreme, we sometimes find professional accountants willing to supply their services as elective auditor free or at a figure below the market rate. Floyd also informed the Committee on Municipal Trading 1900, that 'I regard it as being a sort of advertisement. I wanted to come to the front a little in connection with City affairs' (BPP 1900, vii: minute 1767).

Despite a few exceptions, it seems likely that the following summed up the position in 1903 fairly well:

> The elective auditors are poorly paid, or are unpaid altogether, little interest is taken in their election, and although in some cases they are able to lay a finger on a particular irregularity, it is not clear that they could not make the same discovery in the capacity of active ratepayers. (BPP 1903, vii: vi)

There is evidence, however, to suggest that municipal officials were opposed to the elective audit, not because of its ineffectiveness, but because they were wary of the powers that the auditor could potentially wield. This is manifested by the failure of some officers to permit full access to the corporation's records. And where the elective auditor did attempt to criticise existing practices and suggest improvements, there is evidence to suggest that their initiative was unwelcome. In Birmingham, for example, the elective auditors, F. Taylor (accountant) and W. A Parker (auctioneer) produced an extensive report on the treasurer's accounts for 1885 (Birmingham archive: minute 14106). Their recommendations drew the following negative responses from the finance committee.

* The suggestion that the audit should be continuous was resisted on the grounds that it would contravene MCA 1882, ss. 26-7, which states: 'treasurer to make up accounts and then submit for audit'.
* The request that the elective auditors should have the power of surcharge, in line with a resolution passed at the conference of elective auditors held in Manchester in 1885, caused the finance committee to make the following observations: ratepayers already have the power of *certiorari*; only trained lawyers could judge what was illegal; Parliament contemplated an audit 'confined to the *bona fides* and arithmetic accuracy of the vouchers and accounts'.
* The suggestion that properties which had 'passed out of the hands of the corporation' (for example the gaol buildings had been handed over by Act of Parliament to central government) should not be taken as assets caused the finance committee to point out that there was no intention to treat them as assets; the accounts were simply an historical record of what the money had been spent on.
* The observation that there was too much bookkeeping drew the response that it was necessary in order to comply with statutory requirements.

The absence of any requirement for the elective auditor to be a professional became less important as time went by. The identified occupations of elective auditors, for the early period of this study, include - for Manchester 1838-1842, Birmingham 1839-42, Cardiff 1856-61 and Bradford 1867-9 - merchant, calico printer, manufacturer, surveyor, draper, stationer, agent, tortoiseshell combmaker, clerk, ship broker, grocer, actuary, provision merchant and painter. Gradually, however, it became more common for the position to be filled by practising accountants. Bristol was exceptional in that the elective auditors were professionals from the outset, with Robert Fletcher successful in the inaugural election held in 1836. His experience is a good example of the personal benefits that a municipal appointment might produce; the event being described as the first stage in 'a train of events which was to provide him personally with his biggest single professional job [investigation of Queen

Elizabeth's Hospital for Bristol Corporation] and within three years to elevate him to a position that in the modern idiom would be described as the local "establishment" accountant' (Cornwell, 1991: 78).

The unusual situation at Bristol - where the elective auditors were always professionals and no separate professional audit ever undertaken - produced some confusion. An audit analysis undertaken by Gunner of Croydon in 1902 listed Bristol amongst the towns which did not have a professional audit (*Financial Circular*, January 1902: 55). This drew the comment from Bristol's city accountant, J. Crompton, that the 'statement is incorrect and that for years past the Corporation of Bristol have appointed outside professional accountants to audit the accounts at a remuneration of 300 guineas per annum' (*Financial Circular*, February 1902: 82). Editorial comment makes it clear, however, that these people were elected not appointed (*ibid*). By 1914 the elective auditors were James Edward Grace and Gerald F. Todd who held office until 1926 when a local Act made provision for the firm of chartered accountants Grace, Derbyshire & Todd to be appointed instead as professional auditors.

At Birmingham, in 1856, E. Laundy was the first public accountant to be elected auditor; at Bradford, Thomas Thornton Empsall in 1869; and at Cardiff, Alfred Watkins Sargeant in 1881. From 1880 onwards we find the elective auditors in each of these three cities increasingly in possession of professional qualifications with the most common designation being 'chartered accountant'.

Elsewhere we find evidence consistent with the above. At Blackpool, prior to 1879, 'one of the elective auditors was a leading chartered accountant in the town' (BPP 1903, vii: minute 2582).[6] Similarly, it was possible to say, by 1886, that Huddersfield's elective auditors were usually accountants (*The Accountant*, 11 June 1886: 627); at Torquay in 1893 both elective auditors were professionals; while continuity is evident at Preston where Robert E. Smalley ACA of Moore & Smalley was elected auditors in replacement of W. F. Moore FCA who had held the post for many years. The fact that particular individuals sometimes held these 'elected' posts on an almost permanent basis, together with their possession of a professional qualification, is perhaps explicable in terms of a more widespread adoption of the practice, followed in Exeter, where each political party nominated 'old-established and respectable accountants' as auditors (*The Accountant*, 4 March 1893: 194).

The district audit

We have seen that the possibility of replacing the municipal audit by a district audit was explored by the 1874 Select Committee and that the case for change, put forward by the assistant secretary of the LGB, was successfully resisted by the town clerks consulted. The LGB therefore took the initiative and introduced a bill to Parliament in 1877 and, in the endeavour to make its proposals more palatable, the board accepted a government proposal to remove the power 'to disallow or surcharge any payment or expenditure which had been directed or approved by the council of the borough' (*The Accountant*, 22 November 1884: 4). The scheme was nevertheless defeated as a result of 'the strongest opposition from municipal authorities generally through the Municipal Corporations' Association' (*The Accountant*, 22 November 1884: 3).

From time to time, however, the case for the district audit was made by elective auditors, themselves, who felt that the absence of any 'power to surcharge items of illegal expenditure totally undermined their efforts' (Wells, 1887: 564). Brighton's elective auditor complained that 'the vouchers have been ticked-off mechanically [by the professional auditor], without the slightest reference to the legality of the items' (*ibid*). Specific transactions criticised by Wells included: an 'item of champagne supplied by a member of the corporation'; 'extras charged for by the borough solicitor for engrossing deeds, as out-of-pocket expenses. I think his salary sufficient to include these items'; fees paid to medical officers (in addition to their salary) for attending police-court examinations; the fact that the borough surveyor was under no obligation to account to anyone for the enormous sums expended in his department (Wells, 1887: 564-5). These complaints were echoed by Manchester's elective auditor who referred to 'hundreds of cases' of illegal or excessive expenditure (BPP 1903, vii: minute 2855), and the fact that 'in not one instance have they [the professional auditors] objected to an invoice; and they must have gone through something near one million invoices' over a period of twenty years (BPP 1903, vii: minute 2857).

The case for extending the district audit to municipalities, also made in the authoritative *Burdett's Official Intelligence*, was ridiculed by *The Accountant* leader writer who expressed incredulity at the idea that 'an audit by some barrister who has failed at his own business, and who, like the traditional shoe maker, turns accountant as a last resort, would be as good as an audit performed by a professional Accountant' (30 March, 1889: 158). E. O. Smith, city clerk of Birmingham, made a similar point in evidence presented to the 1903 Select Committee: 'I should not like to say anything disrespectful of them, but I think they are patronage appointments.[7] 'I believe Mr Long [head of the LGB] told me he was going to have barristers, but when I first knew them they were neither barristers nor accountants' (BPP 1903, vii: minute 750; see also *Financial Circular*, November 1897: 4). In a similar vein, the chartered accountant, J. Reay, commented that: 'It would be unreasonable to expect briefless barristers and other "misfits" with no commercial training to do justice to the audit of the accounts of such concerns' (letter to *Financial Circular*, March 1900: 72).

To meet these criticisms, the well known Manchester accountant Edwin Guthrie (his firm Thomas, Wade, Guthrie & Co. were appointed City auditors in 1884) put forward a proposal, to the annual general meeting of the County Councils' Association, 1892, that district auditors should be chartered accountants. According to Guthrie the change would produce the following further advantages: it would reduce the present delay in carrying out municipal audits - the existing service was heavily overstretched - and facilitate the transition to the 'continuous' (for example, monthly) audit (*The Accountant*, 2 April 1892: 286; 9 April 1892: 297-8). The 1903 Select Committee received a wealth of evidence in support of these ideas (BPP 1903, vii: Barrow, minutes 1558-60; Jeeves, minutes 1196-7, 1200; Murray, minutes 2317-8, 2389-91; Wilson, minutes 1122-3, 1170-2) and concluded: 'the fact that district auditors are not accountants seems to unfit them as a class for the continuous and complicated task of auditing the accounts of what are really great commercial businesses' (BPP 1903, vii: v).

A number of municipalities nevertheless made the decision to engage district auditors; the 1903 Select Committee's Report lists 4: Tunbridge Wells in 1890; Bournemouth 1892; Southend-on-Sea 1895 and Folkestone 1901 (BPP 1903, vii: Appendix B). This is cited by the LGB as evidence of the perceived comparative advantage of the district audit, but the true motivation was somewhat different. For example, the Plymouth Corporation raised a bill to request borrowing powers to enable a tramway to be built. Financial control had been poor, in the past, and the powers were granted subject to the inclusion of a requirement for the accounts to be the subject of a district audit as 'the only effective means of preventing, or at any rate, stopping at an early stage, the practice of overdrafts or other irregularities' (*Financial Circular*, June 1903: 157-8). Butterworth confirms that the Local Government Board audit was forced on Plymouth, but admits that the general experience under the Education Act 1902[8] is that 'we have not found them to be the bogies we previously imagined' (1908: 306).[9]

The 1903 Select Committee's Report listed four objections to the imposition of a district audit (BPP 1903, vii: minute 21): that sensible expenditure might be disallowed because it was technically illegal; the delay which the proposed change would cause in the issue of the accounts (see also Smith, minute 760; Jeeves, minutes 1196-7, 1200); the difficulty in mastering local Acts; and the irritation factor, arising from the power to make disallowances and levy surcharges, which might discourage good people from becoming members of town councils. The nit-picking legalistic nature of the district audit is underlined by the following extract from the *Councillor and Guardian*: 'The absurdities brought about by the district auditors' lack of discretionary power are notorious, and their decisions are frequently opposed to common-sense and to good and economical administration' and, whereas the LGB, while confirming the auditor's decision, nearly always remit the surcharge, 'the remission is usually accompanied by an intimation that there must be no repetition of the offence' (quoted in *The Accountant*, 23 November 1901: 1291).

The Permanent Secretary of the LGB, Sir Samuel Butler Provis, made a determined attempt to counter these allegations (BPP 1903, vii: minutes 22-28). Neither his arguments for the adoption of the district audit nor the Select Committee's recommendation for the introduction of a professional audit (BPP 1903, vii: 6) received Parliamentary approval. The apparent explanation is that a compromise solution was by this time already well developed.

The professional audit

The description 'professional audit' appears to have been developed in order to distinguish clearly this service from the 'amateur audit' undertaken for both municipalities and limited companies in the middle of the nineteenth century. The appointment of public accountants has been attributed to concern that the 'persons [previously] elected were not sufficiently qualified for the work' (Carter, 1904: xi), although the ability of municipal members and officials to exert control over individuals appointed and paid for by the corporation may well have been an additional important factor. The growth of the professional audit was naturally favoured by the emerging accounting profession, as illustrated by persistent condemnation of the alternatives in the columns of *The Accountant*.

The adoption of the professional audit also received support from municipal officials. The case was made both at annual meetings of the CTAI (see for example, *Proceedings*, 1894: 13) and in evidence presented by its President, William Bateson, to the 1903 Select Committee (BPP 1903, vii: minute 2607). The desired move also received enthusiastic support in *Financial Circular*, the official organ for the local authorities-based professional accounting body (see for example, Ashmole, 1901: 152). The first successful application to approve the appointment, by a corporation, of a professionally qualified auditor in addition to the elective auditor was contained in the Accrington Municipal Corporation Act, 1890. Municipal archives show, however, that such appointments were made, without recourse to legal formalities, at least four decades earlier.

We have seen that W. R. Kettle was first engaged to examine Birmingham Corporation's accounts in 1855. One of the city's clerks at that time was Howard S. Smith, who remained with them for some years but, in

1875, reappears as professional auditor of the Gas Committee. From 1880 the accounts of all departments were audited by firms of chartered accountants, and from 1889 Howard Smith & Slocombe had a monopoly of this work through to 1899 and 1904 when there were established an electricity works and a tramways respectively audited by the chartered accountants Sharpe, Parsons & Co and Charlton & Long. In 1934 the municipality took advantage of the new power (LGA 1933, s. 239) to discontinue the elective audit.

At Bradford, J. A. Heselton (a founder member of the ICAEW) was first engaged in 1873, continuing through, to the 1930's, in the form of successor firms J. A. Heselton, Son & Butterfield and W. T. Butterfield. From 1925 the appointment was made under a local statute which provided for the corporation's auditors to be members of either the ICAEW or the Society of Incorporated Accountants and Auditors and for the elective audit to be discontinued (s. 36).

David Roberts, who first describes himself as a chartered accountant when signing the accounts for 1883, was, as noted in chapter 4, initially appointed auditor at Cardiff in the late 1860's. He held this post through to the mid-1890's when the legitimacy of appointing professional auditors without statutory authority was raised. As mentioned earlier, a furore arose at this time concerning the level of fees payable to elective auditors and the extent of their powers to investigate the corporation's affairs. On 5 December 1895, Cardiff's finance committee resolved that the LGB should be contacted 'with a view of placing the whole subject of the audit of the borough accounts before them, and of seeking the board's advice as to the real state of affairs in respect thereto'. The decision to adopt this course is one illustration of a more general uncertainly concerning the application of regulations relating to municipal audit. The LGB's unhelpful (but correct) reply was that the matter was 'not within the board's jurisdiction' (Cardiff archives, minutes, 3 February 1896: 243). The Council therefore decided 'to strictly adhere to the provisions of the Municipal Corporation Act 1882, relating thereto (as interpreted by the Town Clerk), and that Mr David Roberts, senior, be employed as auditor to the Corporation as heretofore' (p. 244).

Other avenues were then explored. On 29 May 1896, the town clerk reported the results of recent meetings of the Municipal Corporations Association in London with reference to the position of elective auditors. It seems as though many town clerks continued to view the elective audit as unsatisfactory; the main concerns were that the council had no power to limit or control their work - which 'might take a whole year' - and that they 'knew practically nothing of figures' (minute 620). A number of town clerks favoured the appointment of professional auditors. However, the move to request a change in the law was defeated on the grounds that it might give rise to 'supervision by Government Auditors, or to give further powers to the LGB, and thus centralise in London the work of Municipal Corporations' (*ibid*).

Cardiff therefore worked on a local solution. The recommendation of the finance committee, on the grounds it would save a 'waste of £1,000 per year' (clearly an exaggerated estimate of the amount that the then present elective auditors Coleman and Giller might conceivably claim), was to encourage Messrs D. Roberts and his partner D. R. Roberts to seek election as auditors (*The Accountant*, 26 September 1896: 779). This solution, not surprisingly, received enthusiastic support from *The Accountant* (22 February 1896: 144).

In the election which ensued D. R. Roberts was successful but D. Roberts trailed in fourth place. The town council's decision to then continue with the appointment of David Roberts & Sons, as the professional auditors, on the grounds that it would be impossible for the elective auditors 'to personally undertake a complete audit for the whole of the corporation's accounts', drew criticism on the grounds that 'it would appear that little or no benefit will result to the ratepayers from the recent election' (*The Accountant*, 24 October 1896: 878). The council minutes show that on 15 January 1897 the finance committee recommended an increase in Roberts' remuneration from £150 to £300 to reflect the 'great' increase in work since the fee was last increased in 1891 (Cardiff archives, minutes, 15 January 1897: 283).

The new situation did not last for long. Criticisms made by David Roberts of the borough treasurer's accounts, in a report dated 13 October 1896, was followed by the treasurer circulating twelve other boroughs in order to discover details of their auditing arrangements. The upshot was a decision to advertise the post - the competitive audit - and applications were received from Alfred H. Thomas, D. Shepherd and G. Robertson. The decision made was to appoint, instead, Charles E. Dovey, a chartered accountant, at a remuneration of £300, with Thomas employed for the purpose of making-up the accounts ready for publication.[10]

Manchester's borough council, dissatisfied with existing arrangements, instructed its finance committee, in 1879, 'to consider and to report whether any, and if so, what alterations in the audit of the corporation accounts are desirable' (minute dated 3 December 1879: 38). At this time the procedure followed was to submit accounts, not only to the elective auditors, but also 'for the examination and sanction of an audit sub-committee before they are submitted to the general committee for approval; and such accounts only as are examined and approved are transmitted by the committee to the finance committee for payment' (minute dated 3 December 1879: 40). The enquiry conducted by the finance committee concluded that

> the only alteration in the present arrangements which appear to them to be either necessary or desirable, [is to] recommend that the appointment of a public accountant be authorised, with such remuneration as may be determined, to examine to the extent required and under the direction of the auditors the accounts of the Corporation. (*ibid*)

The rationale for making this recommendation was that the accounts of the corporation had become so voluminous that 'the labour involved in their examination, and the time for that purpose required is now more than in the opinion of your committee ought to be imposed upon them or required from the unpaid municipal auditors' (*ibid*).

Professional accountants had been engaged to audit Manchester's trading activities - gas and water - since 1874, but the above findings led to the appointment of Broome, Murray & Co., chartered accountants, as professional auditors of all the municipality's accounts, commencing 1881. In common with Cardiff, the 'competitive audit' had found favour with Manchester's officials, by 1909, when Halliday, Parson & Co., chartered accountants, were successful with a bid of £650, continuing in this position until 1914 when Kidsons, Taylor & Co. succeeded them at the same rate of remuneration.

Elsewhere, some early examples of professional appointments were at Salford, where a professional auditor was first called in, about 1866, 'to enquire into and investigate the particulars of default on the part of a former borough treasurer'. Writing some years later, the chartered accountant, T. Browning, confirmed that this led to his 'appointment as professional auditor' (*The Accountant*, 26 February 1887: 110). Another public (later chartered) accountant, F. R. Goddard, was first appointed by Newcastle Corporation in 1873 (Goddard, 1888: 653), and he soon became responsible for a monthly audit which, by 1888, took 281 days, with a planned increase to 324 days to accommodate modifications made to the arrangements between him and the corporation! Goddard's detailed audit programme, used for the purpose of the Newcastle audit, is reproduced with approval by Dicksee in his celebrated text entitled *Auditing* (1892: 94-103).

Professional auditors were appointed at West Ham in the late 1870's, following which, according to the leader writer for *Financial Circular*, 'the audit by elective auditors is simply a work of supererogation' (February 1897: 63). The chartered accountant, Charles E. Bradley, was appointed at Scarborough in 1892, while an investigation by Pritchard, Syers & Co., chartered accountants, of Carmarthen Corporation 'whose accounts are worst kept' led to their engagement on a more permanent basis (*Financial Circular*, 6 October 1894: 867). The need for these changes was also demonstrated at Birmingham where the elective auditor of that City admitted that 'all I do is to see that the Treasurer has obeyed the orders of the various committees' (minute 1762). In response to the question 'Do you think the system of auditing is worth anything?', he replied 'Not at all; I think that the accounts prepared by the Treasurer and his staff of clerks are perfectly kept, and they are gone over before we go over them by Messrs. Howard Smith & Slocombe, the auditors, and we simply check after them - it is simply a farce' (minute 1767). At the more general level, *The Accountant* observed, as early as 1892, 'signs that the audit of municipal accounts appears at length to be falling mostly into the hands of professional accountants' (5 March 1892: 202; see also 18 November 1899: 1120).

The popularity of the professional audit by 1914 is well illustrated by table 7.2. All 41 municipal corporations engaged professional auditors,[11] An elective audit was also undertaken at all corporations except Huddersfield and West Ham, but are stated as doing little or no work in three cases, at Blackpool, Darwen and Burton-on-Trent; in the first two cases because remuneration was banned by local acts. It is clear that a number of the authorities had also established their own internal audit sections by this time.

The fees paid to professional auditors were often fairly substantial, although it is impossible to assess their precise adequacy because of differences in the extent of the audit and the range of services supplied by the municipality. However, £100-200 per annum was the approximate 'going rate' for the young salaried professional accountant in public practice during this period, while the salaries of the chief accountants at the fifteen largest corporations ranged from £200-400. The idea that fees were attractive receives support from the experience at Cardiff, referred to above, and more general allegations of touting referred to in the columns of *The Accountant* in the scramble for municipal work during the 1890's.

The criticism that the professional audit was fundamentally flawed, because the person engaged was appointed by and reported to the borough council, was sometimes countered by the practice of limiting the period of office to a fixed number of years. This restriction would be effective, of course, only if re-appointment was banned, which seems rarely to have been the case. An alternative safeguard, given considerable prominence in evidence to the 1903 Select Committee, was for the appointment to be subject to the approval of the LGB (BPP 1903, vii: Grey, minutes 311-15, 326ff; Wilson, minutes 431-2, 515; Smith, minutes 710, 740, 742-5, 776-7; Bateson, minutes 2602-8, 2632-4). Indeed, the committee's abortive recommendation for the replacement of the elective audit by a professional audit contained this proviso.

Table 7.1: Audit fees

Borough	Year	Elective	Professional	Comments
Sunderland	1874	4 gns £20	£2	The higher rate paid t public accountant 'to do the additions'.
Accrington	1884	Nil	£25	
Barrow	1884	Nil	£105	
Bolton	1884	£50	£105	
Darwen	1884	£190	£2	
Bury	1884	£2	£80	
Burnley	1884	Nil	£50	Elective auditors 'do nothing'
Oldham	1884	Nil	£105	'Elective auditors hav not audited in reality for many years'
Preston	1884	£28	None	Elective auditors 'professional men'
Rochdale	1884	£50	None	
Southport	1884	Nil	None	
Blackburn	1884	Nil	£190	
Dover	1891	£10	£2	
Hanley	1891	10 gns	£2	
Maidstone	1891	4 gns	£2	
Stoke	1891	5 gns	£2	
Kidderminster	1891	£40	£2	
Wolverhampton	1891	£50	£2	
Manchester	1903	£3	£650	Chartered accountants
Leeds	1903	None	£300	Chartered accountants
Sheffield	1903	£3	£325	Accountant auditor (member of the "Society") provided with a staff of clerks

Notes

1 The figures given are per annum and apply to all municipal activities which vary considerably between towns.
2 No information available concerning whether or not these are appointed.
3 No information available concerning payment

Sources:

Select Committee on Boroughs, 1874, minutes 1388-9
The Accountant, 19 April 1884: 9
The Accountant, 30 May 1891: 406-7
Joint Select Committee on Municipal Trading, 1903, Appendix: 390-1

Table 7.2: Professional audit of municipal corporations, 1914[1]

Corporation	Population (1911 Census)	Frequency Of Audit	Trading Under-Taking[2]	Period Of Appointment	Remuneration Per Annum
Barrow	63,775	Quarterly	G,W,E,T M,A,C,B	1 year	£200
Blackpool	58,376	3 or 4 times during the year	G,E,T,M C,S,B	1 year (limited to 3 yrs)	£84
Bolton	180,851	Continuous (monthly)	G,W,E,T M,C.S,I	3 years	£300
Bradford	288,000	Quarterly	Q,T,G,E M,C.H	During the pleasure of council	£300
Burton-on-Trent	48,266	Annually	G,E,T	No limitation	£52.10.0
Bury	59,038	Monthly, continuous when going through annual accounts	G,E,T	Continuous	£100
Cambridge	55,812	Half-yearly	M	No definite term	£105
Cardiff	182,280	Half-yearly	E.T,E.L, W.A	No fixed term	£320
Carlisle	52,222	Yearly	G,W,B,E	1 year	£105
Chester	39,028	Continuous since 25 March last	M,T,E	5 years	£73.10.0
Darlington	55,631	Continuous	G&W,E&L.R, M,P.B,H&C	Until agreement determined by either party giving one month's notice in writing	£175
Darwen	40,344	General audit twice yearly. In addition the accounts are checked before presentation to the committees for payment each month	G,W,E,T,M MLH,SH,C	Re-appointment at present salary four years ago and subject to 3 months notice	£130
Derby	123,410	Yearly. The Corporation have their own audit staff for internal audit	W,E,T,M,C	At the pleasure of of council	£130
Devonport	81,678	Half-yearly and at any time the auditors think fit	G,W,E	1 year	£105
Dewsbury	53,351	From time to time at the discretion of the auditors	G,W,E,M	No fixed period	£75
Doncaster	30,516	Quarterly	G,W,E,T,M	At the pleasure of council	£75
Ealing	61,235	Half-yearly	E.L	From year to year	£52.10.50
Eastbourne	52,542	Continuous. About every 2 months for about 2 days each time; after the end of Sept about 10 days, and after the end of March a fortnight	E,MOS	Year to year	£105
Great Yarmouth	55,905	Continuous	E,T,P.G,P&P L.E	Year to year	£75
Grimsby	74,663	Continuous	E	3 years	£84
Halifax	101,553	At discretion of auditors	W,G,T,E,M	No fixed term	£200
Hornsey	84,592	Monthly examination of accounts paid & vouchers & of the accounts of moneys received, & a thorough audit at the	E	1 year	£63

		end of each year.			
Huddersfield	107,821	Continuous	W,E,T,M,B MLH,C	1 year	£183.15.0
Kingston-upon-Hull	278,024	Half-yearly	T,W,E,T&G	No fixed term	£250
Macclesfield	34,797	Half-yearly with annual reports	G,W	3 years (eligible for reappointment)	£65
Manchester	714,388	Continuous	E,G,M,T,W	5 years	£650
Rochdale	91,428	Continuous	G,W,E,T,CM	1 year	£180
Royal Lemington Spa	26,713	Half-yearly	W,PR&B,C	1 year	£60
Rotherham	62,483	Yearly	G,W,E,T,M B	General appointment subject to notice to determine	£250
Salford	231,380	Continuous	G,W,E,T,CM, C,B,MLH,HWC	3 years	£185 (by tend
St Helens	96,551	Continuous	G,W,E,T,M,C	2 years	£157.10.0
Smethwick	70,694	Not less frequently than each 3 months	G	3 months notice	£100
Southport	69,643	Continuous yearly audit	G,E,T,M	Permanent, but subject to revocation at the end of each financial year	£120
Stockton-on-Tees	61,958	Half-yearly	G,E,Q&WH,	1 year	£62.10.0
Wakefield	51,511	Continuous	Nil	1 year	£52.10.0
Walsall	92,115	General accounts, half-yearly;trading accounts quarterly	G,E,T	Subject to six months notice	£200
West Ham	1,253,450	Annual reports	E&T	1 year	£420
West Hartlepool	63,932	Half-yearly	T&E	Not specified	£78.15.0
Wigan	80,152	Continuous	T,G,E,W,M,	3 years	£100
Wimbledon	54,966	Monthly & yearly	E	Subject to 3 months notice	£131.5.0
York	82,282	Continuous	E,LR,RN,M	3 years	£125

Notes 1 The information is extracted from a survey undertaken by the City of Lincoln, circa 1914.

2

G	- Gas	W	- Water
E	- Electricity	T	- Tramways
M	- Markets	A	- Abattoirs
C	- Cemetery	T	- Tollbridge
B	- Baths	S	- Sea Water Works
C.S	- Cold Store	I	- Ice Making
C.H	- Conditioning House	E.T	- Electric Tramways
E.L	- Electric Lighting	W.A	- Waterworks Accounts
E&L.R	- Electricity & Light Railway Depts	P.B	- Public Baths
H&C	- Hospitals & Cemeteries	MLH	- Model Lodging Houses
SH	- Slaughterhouses	MOS	- Motor Omnibus Services
P.G	- Pleasure Gardens	P&P	- Pier & Pavilions
L.E	- Large Estates	T&G	- Telephones & Gas
CM	- Cattle Market	PR&B	- Pump room and Baths
HWC	- Houses for working classes	Q&WH	- Quay & warehouses
F	- Farm	RN	- River Navigation

Source: Cardiff Archives, Box 1757

Review and Conclusion

The differences between the audit requirements initially applying to municipal corporations compared with other local authorities may be explained on the grounds that, being self-governing and from 1835 democratically elected, municipal corporations were the sole concern of local ratepayers. The scrutiny of borough accounts by auditors elected by the ratepayers therefore had some appeal, in that these individuals had a vested interest in assessing the financial probity of local officials. Also, at a time when the level of borough activity was usually fairly modest and the method of accounting predominantly cash-based, the degree of technical expertise required was arguably insubstantial. Over the next sixty or so years the situation changed in many major respects. These included: the rising level of financial support provided by central government; the huge increase in the scale of operations undertaken by municipal corporations; and the growing complexity of their financial reporting procedures as the single cash statement, previously published, gave way to accruals-based accounts for each and every fund, producing financial reports generally upwards of 200 pages.

The outcome was a strenuously contested power struggle between vested interests, with the LGB keen to obtain a monopoly of local authority audits and the accounting profession determined to advance the interest of its members who were already making significant inroads, with the earliest identified appointment of a professional auditor occurring in 1852. The main media for advocating the adoption of the professional audit were the accounting journals, which missed no opportunity to air every sort of criticism of the elective audit and compare it unfavourably with the preferred alternative.

The matter was considered by government Select Committees in 1874 and 1900/3, where municipal officials giving evidence were first keen to block the aspirations of the LGB and, later, increasingly supportive of the introduction of the professional audit for reasons which have been discussed. Quite apart from the merits of the professional audit, however, its adoption might well have found favour among municipal officials simply because the great majority of them were also members of the Society of Accountants and Auditors or the ICAEW, and in almost every case 'they are the chief financial officers of the great municipalities' (BPP 1903, vii: minute 3071).

The 1903 Select Committee confirmed earlier opposition to any extension of the role of the district auditor, considering them unfit as a class for auditing the accounts of municipal trading concerns which are 'really great commercial businesses' (BPP 1903, vii: 6). Indeed, the Committee went further and recommended that the existing combination of district and elective audit should be abolished and replaced by a professional audit. It further recommended that the auditors should be members of the ICAEW or the Society of Accountants and Auditors, and that the appointment should be subject to the approval of the LGB (*ibid*).

It seems that the Select Committee reached the right conclusion. According to Carson Roberts, the doyen of district auditors during the early decades of the twentieth century, the enduring criticisms of the district audit - 'risk of irksome interference', the emphasis on cash accounting, lack of experience of trading accounts, and delay - were probably legitimate complaints in the late nineteenth century (1930: 192-5).

The Committee's recommendations were not implemented despite the following assessment attributed to the then Conservative Prime Minister, Mr Arthur Balfour:

> the Local Government Board having carefully considered the report of the Committee on Municipal Trading, had not found it possible to accept all the recommendations of the committee, and although the recommendations with regard to audit might be accepted with modifications, the government would not be able to deal with them that session. (Butterworth, 1908: 152)

We might surmise that the failure to legislate reflected opposition from the LGB, particularly as the only relevant legislative development, during 1903, was the introduction of an unsuccessful Bill - The Municipal Corporations Audit of Accounts Bill, 1903 (BPP 1903, iii: 425) - designed to extend the district audit to municipal corporations. There is also the suspicion of duplicity on the part of the Prime Minister, as he was a former President of the LGB and, under his Premiership, the application of the district audit to local authorities was significantly extended (Helmore, 1961: 62-5).

Municipal officials did not give up, and persistent initiatives included the following motion passed by the council of the Association of Municipal Corporations, 1919:

> that the government be asked to take the earliest opportunity in the interests of the economy and efficiency to secure the abolition of the present system of audit under the Municipal Corporations Act, and the substitution of a requirement that the accounts of all municipal corporations shall be audited by professional accountants, with proper provision as to qualifications of such auditors, publication of reports, and other matters. (*Financial Circular*, 1921: 169)

The relative merits of the elective/professional/district audit again received government attention, in 1932, when the Committee on Local Expenditure (Cd 4200) was appointed by a government keen to reduce national expenditure at a time when central government grants were a rapidly increasing proportion of municipal finance. The Committee recommended the replacement of the elective audit by the more 'efficient [district] audit' (quoted in Helmore, 1961: 94). The Minister of Health realised that direct imposition of the district audit by statute would cause 'controversy and difficulty', and the government instead decided to support a private Bill containing the compromise solution enacted as the Municipal Corporations (Audit) Act 1933 (Helmore: 95). This permitted municipal corporations to adopt, instead of the elective audit, either the district audit or a professional audit undertaken by members of the accounting bodies listed in a schedule to the Act.

As usual, in relation to British Company Law, the legislature had done little more than give recognition to market driven developments, with the position immediately prior to this change summed up by Carson Roberts as follows: 'the practical value of this [elective] audit is so small that audit by a firm of professional accountants has been substituted on local initiative in many of the more important cases' (1930: 191). The information presented in table 7.2 strongly suggests that this was an accurate assessment of the position.

The effect of adopting the district audit was that the onerous provisions of disallowance and surcharge applied. The professional auditor, by way of contrast, simply made, at the close of the audit, such 'observations and recommendations as he thinks necessary or expedient' (Jones, 1981: 12). Another difference was that whereas the district auditor reported to the Minister of Health as well as the borough council, the professional auditor in common with the elective auditor reported only to the latter.

The new Act was almost immediately replaced by LGA 1933. This consolidated the existing law, with the accounts and audit provisions relating to boroughs set out in ss. 120, 185, 237-40 and 244-8.

The system of elective audit therefore survived, but it continued to be the subject of judicial vitriol. In a 1937 case heard at the Devon Assizes, Mr Justice McNaughten addressed the defendant borough treasurer, who had fraudulently converted £3,000 to his own use, to the effect that 'without any difficulty at all, you could take money that belonged to the Council for your own purposes' and concluded 'The system of [elective] audit has been a farce' (*The Accountant*, 6 March 1937: 326).

The right to choose a professional audit proved increasingly popular. On 1 April 1974, at which date the municipal corporation was abolished by LGA 1972, 202 boroughs had moved over to the professional audit, while 119 had adopted the district audit and just 21 retained the elective audit.

NOTES

1 It will be noticed that the debate, which follows, makes no reference to the mayor's auditor. The simple explanation seems to be that no one took it seriously: 'in practice it may be stated that it is often the case that the exercise of powers by the mayor's auditor is limited to accepting office, and vacating it after twelve months service, with or without the added burden of writing his name on the accounts. Generally speaking, the whole scheme of audit by the mayor's auditor is a dead letter, though in rare cases a professional accountant, a member of the council, is appointed, and does his duty thoroughly' (Collins, 1908: 205-06).

2 *Certiorari* was initially developed as a remedy to enable a superior court to crush the actions of an inferior court. The concept was extended to enable various aspects of local authority expenditure to be challenged, on the grounds that the local authority could be treated as a 'court' because of the growing exercise of quasi-judicial functions (Jennings, 1935a: 422).

3 In a central government context, Funnell (1990) demonstrates the restrictive effect of the power of disallowance on the Commissariat's willingness to take sensible, put possibly unauthorised, initiatives during the Crimea War.

4 The following observation, made by the Select Committee on Boroughs 1874, suggests that the duties of the elective auditor were more onerous than was generally assumed to be the case: 'The duties of borough auditors extend only to the examination of accounts, with the vouchers and all papers connected therewith, including of course the orders for payment made by the town council, and certifying the accounts as correct' (BPP 1874, vii, iv).

5 It also appears that, on occasions, a town councillor would nominate a political opponent for the position of auditor in order to debar him from serving on the town council. The contest, if held, then became one to lose rather than win (BPP 1874, vii: minutes 1734-5).

6 This must mean that the individual became a chartered accountant when that designation was introduced in 1880.

7 These were discontinued in 1919, when an examination for entry was introduced (Davies, 1986: 29).

8 This made a borough's education account subject to the district audit.

9 By 1908 the following further town councils had obtained acts or provisional orders requiring their accounts to be subject to the district audit: Cheltenham, Merthyr Tydfil, Plymouth, Poole, Swindon (Butterworth, 1908: 143).

10 Not satisfied with this arrangement, Thomas, an incorporated accountant, submitted an offer to audit the 1898 accounts and prepare them for publication for an overall fee of £300. This proposal was rejected; Dovey again being appointed auditor at a fee of £300 and an offer from Thomas to prepare the accounts for £75 was accepted (Cardiff council minutes, 6 December 1897: 66; 17 January 1898: 251).

11 Special Parliamentary powers were obtained to authorise the appointment of professional auditors at 17 of the 41 corporations.

8

NATURE OF THE MUNICIPAL AUDIT - ISSUES

The desire to obtain control of the municipal audit gave rise to a power struggle between elective auditors, the LGB, municipal officers and professional accountants which was examined in the preceding chapter. In very broad terms, we saw that the elective audit initially reigned supreme. As time went by the government took steps to make certain of its activities subject to the district audit, while municipal officials increasingly made the voluntary decision to engage also professional auditors. From the 1890's municipalities began to obtain private statutes which allowed them to substitute the district audit or professional audit for the elective audit. This action was given general statutory approval in 1933. The nature of the audit changed dramatically, over time, reflecting differences in the expertise possessed by the individuals involved, the terms of their appointment and the fees which municipalities were willing and able to pay. These matters are explored further below.

Cost

The comparative cost of the various types of audit is likely to have been a factor in determining the arrangements made in particular towns. The Committee on Boroughs believed that 'considerable difficulty existed in obtaining competent persons having a practical knowledge of accounts to serve as auditors' (BPP 1874, vii: 4). We have seen that there were financial factors to explain this reluctance. The elective auditor had no right to remuneration for work performed on the borough fund. However, they were entitled to 'reasonable remuneration' for auditing the transactions of the district fund account under PHA 1848, s. 122, with the words 'not being less than two guineas per day' added ten years later (LGA 1858, s. 60 (3)).

It is presumably in exercise of the above powers that the elective auditors of Sunderland first received payment in 1851 (BPP 1874, vii: minute 1372). Twenty three years later a fee of four guineas was paid to one of its elective auditors and £20 to the other (a public accountant) for undertaking the additional duty of casting the accounts. An indication of the level of fees paid to elective and professional auditors over the next 30 years is given in table 7.1. We might reasonably view with some suspicion the comment, from the leader writer of *The Accountant*, that: 'it may be said with truth that the fees paid to professional accountants do not, in many cases, more than cover the bare cost of the work, the audit indeed being often more a matter of honour and credit than a matter of pecuniary benefit' (22 November 1884: 3). While it is likely that a local accountant, or firm of accountants, would have benefited from the high public profile associated with a municipal appointment, there is little concrete evidence that the late nineteenth-century professional accountant was any more willing voluntarily to accept work at below the market rate than would be the case today.

It is difficult to assess the adequacy of the fees paid to the professional accountants listed in table 7.1, however, because of differences in the amount of work involved depending upon the extent of the audit and the range of services supplied by the municipality. However, £1,000 per annum was the approximate 'going rate' for the salaried professional accountant, in public practice during this period, which suggests that the fees charged were often not insubstantial. This conclusion receives support from the columns of *The Accountant* during the 1890's when allegations of touting, in the desire to obtain a share of municipal work, were common.

The cost of the municipal audit became an issue at the borough of Darwen, in 1884, when it amounted to £190. 15s. 15d. The concern, expressed by Alderman Snape, was that the statutory right to remuneration at the rate of two guineas per day implied no limit whatsoever on total cost.[1] He therefore recommended the appointment of a sub-committee:

> with power to arrange with the elective auditors to be paid by fixed annual sum, or to make such other alteration as they might deem expedient for lessening the cost of auditing the municipal accounts; also to consider the desirability of obtaining a special power to employ a professional accountant to audit such accounts. (*The Accountant*, 19 April 1884: 9)

Similar sentiments were expressed by members at Kidderminster Corporation where a Mr Herring objected to elective auditors' fees amounting to £81. 6s. 4d. for 1890, and a Mr Perry is reported to have agreed that 'the charge made last year was preposterous, and the way in which the books were audited was not as satisfactory as could be desired. If they were to pay professional fees, he thought they ought to have the work done by chartered accountants' (*The Accountant*, 30 May 1891: 406). Further evidence of wide variations in the cost of the elective audit result from a survey carried out by W. Gunner, borough accountant, Croydon, in 1902, producing figures which ranged from 'the nominal sum of £2. 2s. to £315 per annum' (*Financial Circular*, January 1902: 55).

The range of fees paid to elective auditors is no doubt partly attributable to the extent of the audit work undertaken and this, in turn, would depend upon whether or not a professional audit was also undertaken. For example, a survey of 18 unnamed towns of roughly comparable size undertaken by the City of York in 1907 (*Financial Circular*, December 1907: 235) revealed the following:

* Of the ten boroughs which paid the professional auditor more than £100 per annum, eight paid the elective auditors less than £40 and one chose not to engage an elective auditor.

* Of the five boroughs which paid the elective auditors the highest fees (ranging from £60 to £236), three did not engage a professional auditor.

In terms of obtaining value for money, a further matter which needed to be considered by the borough was whether to establish its own audit department. *The Accountant* calculated, in 1884, that this would 'probably involve an expenditure of certainly not less than double the amount now paid' (18 October 1884: 4) but, in assessing the veracity of this statement, we must again remember that this journal was keen to highlight the comparative advantage of engaging a professional auditor. Liverpool is a well known early example of a corporation which set up its own audit department and saw no need to employ outside professionals. A compromise solution worked out at Sheffield was to employ, annually, an accountant/auditor (in 1903 he was an associate of the Society of Accountants and Auditors) who was provided with a staff of clerks paid by the corporation to conduct an internal audit (BPP 1903, vii: 390-1). The range of fees set out in table 7.2 demonstrate the fact that the professional audit continued to be a well paid appointment in 1914.

Extent of the Audit

MCA 1835, and successor statutes, made provision for the appointment of an elective auditor but contained no indication whatsoever of his powers or duties.[2] One might imagine from comments of contemporary writers concerning the meagre nature of the elective audit that in some corporations they did no more than add-up the totals of the published financial statement, but most would have gone further than this. In general, the minimum duty undertaken by the elective auditor and, where he was appointed, the professional auditor was to compare the figures in the accounts with the balances in the books. But it is quite possible that this was as far as many officials went, particularly in view of the fact that this 'mechanical audit' was not unknown in the private sector at this time (*The Accountant*, 13 October 1883: 8).[3] The more inquisitive, and thorough, auditor naturally went behind the books to examine some form of 'originating documentation', but we shall see that the municipal auditor often considered it sufficient to examine the 'orders for payment' certified by committee members and issued to the treasurer.

There were other factors affecting the amount of work undertaken by the auditor. The extent of investigation might vary from one department to another, reflecting doubt concerning the nature of the elective auditor's responsibility for the activities of trading departments. There was the further question whether the auditor possessed the power, not only to assess whether a payment was properly made, but whether the expenditure was legitimate and reasonable, and whether a proper allocation between capital and revenue had been made. Each of these matters is given some attention below.

The observation that the elective audit was 'a mere farce' was quite common (e. g. BPP 1874, vii: minute 1628). While Dicksee, writing in 1892, commented that 'non-professional auditors would pass over much detail, and are frequently content to merely cast the cash account submitted to the treasurer, considering such to be their sole duty' (1892: 93). The entire blame for this state of affairs should not be placed on the elective auditor, however, who sometimes faced considerable opposition from municipal officials when attempting to do a more thorough job. For example, in 1894, at Birmingham, a public meeting resolved that the elective auditor should be allowed access to all deeds, vouchers etc. According to borough officials, this led W. G. Floyd to request access, referring to suspicion of fraud, corruption and 'pickings', with land purchased at excessive prices and inflated salaries paid (Birmingham archive: minute 16679: 117-22). The town clerk and treasurer refused Floyd's request, claiming that it was sufficient for an elective auditor to see the 'order book', i. e. the treasurer's authorisation for payments signed by three members of council and the town clerk. The argument, that the order book should be regarded as the vouchers for the purpose of the audit, reflected their conviction that 'All that they [the elective auditors] are presumed to be able to check is the arithmetical accuracy of the Treasurer's accounts' (minute 16679: 130). Other justifications for non-disclosure put forward (minute 16679: 131-2) were:

* The audit might otherwise go on 'for ever' and give rise to a massive remuneration.

* Sensitive information might be made public by the elective auditor, for example the price paid by the municipality for land in circumstances where further land remained to be purchased.
* The accounts were subject to a professional audit.

The right of access became the subject of litigation in Thomas v Devonport Corporation (16 T.L.R.9, 1899). The elective auditor C. B. Courtneay-Thomas, a professional accountant, was refused access to the books, documents and vouchers of the Devonport Corporation, in 1894, when he attempted to carry out his responsibilities, 'as laid down by the late Mr F. R. Goddard, F. C. A., for the audit of the Newcastle-on-Tyne Corporation accounts, on page 94 of Mr. L. R. Dicksee F.C.A. 's work on auditing' (*The Accountant*, 11 August 1894: 692). Lord Russell concluded: if the audit of the accounts of local authorities is not to be absolutely ineffective, it is necessary that an auditor should not merely satisfy himself that vouchers, formal and regular, are produced for all items'. Indeed, he went as far as to suggest that the auditor should make a '"fair and reasonable examination of the accounts", and see whether there might not be amongst the payments made, payments which were not authorised or which were illegally paid' (*The Accountant*, 18 November 1899: 1119).

Floyd informed the town clerk of the court's decision, but it did not bring an immediate response. Further applications were made and eventually the town clerk 'wrote a polite letter saying that the finance committee had decided to submit the accounts I required' (BPP 1900, vii: minute 1747).

The question of whether the auditor had a duty to examine the transactions of trading undertakings received attention in Manchester, in 1883, when the elective auditor was refused access to the water and gas accounts on the grounds that these departments were audited by professional accountants, that this had proved a satisfactory practice for some years, and that it was not clear that MCA 1882 entitled them to look into these matters. When the matter was discussed by the town council, however, we see signs of a hidden agenda in the comment from one member that the elective auditor's priority was to obtain access to cigars etc. while criticising professional colleagues (*The Accountant*, 19 January 1884). The elective auditors' initiative was supported by *The Accountant* which argued that right of access followed from the fact that the accounts were kept by the treasurer. The elective auditor was eventually rewarded for his determination with access granted by a council minute dated 7 January 1885.

An example of elective auditors carrying out their duties in a thorough fashion is evident from the content of a report included with the abstract of accounts published by Macclesfield Borough Council for 1889. (Abstract of Accounts, 1889: 56). The elective auditors' report addresses the question of value for money,[4] draws attention to the inadequate system of internal control over stock, and criticises the high price charged for gas to the authority's public lighting department. The elective auditors recommend the extension of the gas undertaking to new householders in order to utilise spare capacity and make 'the homes of non-gas consumers both healthier and happier'.

The appropriate extent of the audit was the subject of careful questioning in evidence collected by the 1903 Select Committee. Manchester's elective auditor, S. Norbury Williams, considered that the function of the elective audit was to 'exercise a sort of oversight which the professional auditors could not profess to do owing to the exigencies of time' (minute 2832). Co-operation with the professional auditors was advocated on the basis that they would check the technical accounting details, with the elective auditor available to follow up complaints from ratepayers of possible corruption, illegality and extravagance (minutes 2843, 2893). Williams claims to have discovered many 'improper expenses ... passed over' by the professional auditor (minute 2839). Further:

> We have had professional auditors going through the accounts of Manchester Corporation for 20 years, and I believe I am correct in saying that, in not one instance have they objected to an invoice; and they must have gone through something near one million invoices. (minute 2857)

Williams was then cross examined concerning the percentage of transactions which should be vouched. Surprise is expressed at his willingness to sign a clean audit report despite the fact that only a small percentage of vouchers had been examined:

> do you think that it is what the rate-payers of Manchester understand [when reading your certificate]? - [Williams' reply] I think so; they know that one man, if he were engaged the whole of the year, could not go through the whole of our accounts. (BPP 1903, vii: minute 2957)

Further fierce questioning culminated in the following exchange: 'I ask, do you still say that was in your view the idea of Parliament, that an elective auditor will be doing his duty by examining a small percentage of the vouchers? - [Williams' reply] probably not' (minute 2964).

Birmingham's elective auditor, Floyd, was also invited to present evidence to the 1903 Select Committee where he was given a fairly rough ride. The essence of Floyd's evidence was that he believed that the elective auditor possessed insufficient powers to do an effective job and that municipal accounts should instead be made subject to a district audit. A specific criticism was that 'the different committees make up the accounts to appear exactly as it suits their own purposes', mainly by the misallocation of expenses between capital and revenue. An example of the motivation for this kind of behaviour is given: 'the electric department of the Corporation of Birmingham had made a profit, but they did not show it, because they thought the rate-payers would want their electric light cheaper' (minute 1738).

The above criticisms were not well received. Floyd's allegations were turned against him. The fact that he had signed a clean certificate gave rise to scathing comments and insults, with doubt cast on his honestly, suitability for the post of elective auditor, and professional standing. For example:

> [minute] 1911 Are you aware that Mr. Howard Smith [the professional auditor] has been President of the Society of Chartered Accountants? - [Floyd's reply] I do not know, I dare say he has.
>
> 1912 Have you ever been President of the Society of Accountants? - [Floyd's reply] No, I never have.
>
> 1913 Have you ever passed an accountant's examination; [Floyd's reply] I have not. There was no examination in my time.
>
> 1915 Do you wish to tell this Committee that the accounts of the gas committee of Birmingham over which he and his firm have been in every detail, and as to which he has put his own hand to a certificate certifying that they are correct, do you mean to tell me he did not know what he was about? - [Floyd's reply] Certainly not.

Year end versus continuous audit

A further important contemporary question was: At what stage in the financial year should the audit take place? The municipal corporations acts made it clear that the elective audit was to be a twice yearly event based on accounts made up to March and September; the wording of the statute which provided for the treasurer to prepare the accounts and then present them to the auditor implied an investigation *following* the end of the period under review. The period-end audit is the subject of criticism from the literature, at an early stage, with the following advantages claimed for the continuous audit: it reveals irregularities more quickly; reduces the likelihood of fraud due to constant supervision; and avoids delay in the publication of the accounts (*The Accountant* 18 October 1884: 4). The question then to be decided was whether this service could best be provided by an internal audit department or by engaging a professional firm (*ibid*).

Manchester's elective auditors, Joseph Scott and Francis R. Hollins, in a report submitted to the town council dated 12 August 1884, are critical of the professional audit, recently introduced to that town, which they describe as 'open to many objections' (minutes: 7 January 1885: 132). They instead advocate the establishment of an internal audit department under their own supervision. 'The cost of such a department would not much, if any, exceed the amount paid this year to professional auditors' (*ibid*). A special committee was appointed to look into this matter and reported 'that Liverpool is the only town where an internal continuous audit has been established, and, as stated in the appendix [to the report], the system is now under review and apparently has not given universal satisfaction' (2 September 1885: minute 489). Further 'the facts generally tend to show that a professional audit, following the expenditure as closely as possible, is perhaps as sound a method as any practicable. If the Auditors were appointed for a limited period of years ... their position would be as independent as it would appear to be possible to make it' (*ibid*).

Editorial comment in *The Accountant* continued to press the claim that 'the great balance of advantage lies in favour of a continuous audit' (9 April 1892: 298) and these sentiments receive support from the columns of *Financial Circular* (Carter, 1904), although it is fairly clear that this commitment is partly motivated by the scope it provided for emphasising the merits of a professional as compared with an elective audit. By the early years of the twentieth century, however, it does appear that an important motivation for the appointment of professional auditors was because they were able to 'make a continuous audit of the accounts' (Griffiths, 1904: x) although, according to the town clerk of the City of Leeds, a good many of the larger corporations had followed the example of Liverpool and established their own internal audit department (BPP 1903, vii: minute 1554; see also Butterworth, 1908: 306).

This development led, at Liverpool, to sensible co-operation between the internal audit department and the elective auditor (in this case a chartered accountant), with the latter giving 'comparatively small attention to the checking of vouchers and seeing that receipts are in order, but what they do is to make careful enquiries as to the apportionment of revenue and capital, as to the provision of sinking funds, and their audit is to that extent absolutely effective' (BPP 1903, vii: minute 1683).

The virtues of the continuous audit were lauded by the 1903 Select Committee: 'with a continuous, vigilant and thoroughly efficient system of inspection and audit, the surest guarantee to ratepayers against extravagance is to be found in the deterrent effect of public exposure, in addition to the existing legal remedies' (BPP 1903, vii: vi). It is perhaps this virtue, more than any other, which led the Committee to recommend the replacement of elective auditors - 'no complete or continuous audit is ever attempted by them' (BPP 1903, vii: v) - by professionals.

The audit report

It is sometimes possible to obtain an indication of the extent of the work undertaken, by auditors, by examining the wording of the audit report. Whether professional auditors made a report, and to whom, was dependant upon the terms of their appointment. Indeed, not even the elective auditors were subject to any statutory obligation to issue an audit certificate; the requirement was only that they should audit the accounts. We therefore find auditors, particularly in the early years, merely signing the accounts. Where reports were made, there is considerable variety in the wording used, and it is interesting and relevant to speculate upon the significance of these differences.

Table 8.1 lists examples of the range of audit reports attached to the accounts of Birmingham, Bradford, Bristol, Cardiff and Manchester by their elective and municipal auditors. In most cases the wordings listed were used for many years. A prominent feature is the positive and dogmatic nature of the assertions made, with 'audited [or 'examined] and found correct' the most common certification. One possible explanation for its use, particularly early on, was that the accounts were on a cash basis with the result that valuation problems did not need to be considered. Another is that the work was undertaken by amateurs unaware of the existence of matters of accounting principle which needed to be considered. Later on, one might be tempted to assume that the certification implied merely 'a mechanical audit' involving no more than a comparison of the figures reported with the balances in the books. A further factor which seems surprising, to us, is the absence of the qualifying phrase 'in our opinion', which accountants were required by law to include in reports on the accounts of registered companies from 1900 onwards. The only exception is at Bristol where the elective auditors, who were also chartered accountants, used this phrase from 1915 onwards.

It was sometimes the practice for elective auditors, and a requirement for professional auditors, to present a report to council or the department whose accounts were audited and, in some cases, these reports were bound with the published accounts thereby entering the public domain. The upheavals at Bradford in the early 1870's (see chapter 5) resulted in reports being made to the finance committee of the council by both the elective auditors and the professional auditor. The former reported that the accounts were found to be

Table 8.1: Typical audit reports

Year	Borough	Audit type	Fund	Report
1840	Manchester	Elective	Borough	We … have examined the accounts of receipts and expenditure of the borough … and have found the same correct.
1848	Bradford	Elective	Borough	… examined the accounts of receipts and expenditure … and have found the same correct.
1851	Birmingham	Elective	Borough	Examined and audited by us
1851	Bristol	Elective[1]	Borough	Audited and found correct.
1852	Bradford	Elective	Borough	… and declare and certify that we have examined the above accounts and find them correct.
1858	Cardiff	Elective	Borough	Examined and found correct.
1860	Manchester	Professional	Trading	Examined and found correct
1868	Cardiff	Elective	District	Correct
1875	Birmingham	Professional	Trading	Examined and found correct
1878	Bradford	Both	All	Audited and found correct.
1880	Manchester	Professional	Trading	Audited and found correct
1890	Manchester	Professional	All	Audited and found correct
1900	Bradford	Both	All	Audited and found correct.
1905	Birmingham	Professional	Trading	Examined and found correct
1906	Bristol	Professional	Trading	Audited
1910	Birmingham	Elective	Borough	I hereby certify that I have duly audited the accounts and receipts and payments … with the necessary vouchers and papers, and have found the same correct.
1915	Bristol	Elective	Borough	We have examined the accounts of the borough fund … and in our opinion the above balance sheet is properly drawn up so as to exhibit a true and correct view as shown by the books of the corporation.
1921	Bradford	Professional	All	Audited and found correct, as reported upon.

Note 1 Elective auditors were always professional accountants at Bristol.

'strictly correct, but the increased number of transactions has increased the time necessary for the audit', and that the new system is 'more rational and comprehensive'. The only criticism was that 'a few items of expenditure in the statements supplied to us would be more satisfactory if given in greater detail' (Report on 1873 accounts).

The municipality's professional auditor, J. A. Heselton - in a report addressed to the Mayor, Aldermen, and Burgesses - also goes into considerable detail concerning the operation of the newly installed accounting system, and describes how it enabled him to undertake a thorough audit involving a careful examination of 'the cash books with the vouchers rendered by the heads of the several departments'. The elective auditors' report for 1893 (one of them was an incorporated accountant) shows that close attention was paid to vouching transactions with original documentation, but makes it clear that they considered the allocation of income and expenditure between various departments to be outside the scope of their duties (Report on 1893 accounts).

At Bristol the elective auditors, both of whom were professional accountants, prepared what is described as a 'professional auditors' report to council'. This makes it clear that they had compared the accounts with the books and the books with the vouchers, also that they had examined departmental stock records and obtained certificates from the city engineer for the year end figures.

At Cardiff the auditors (elective and professional) merely signed the accounts from 1869 until 1910 when the professional auditor also addressed a report to the town council. This stated that the various departmental accounts 'have all been checked and vouched and the same are in order, and the published accounts convey a correct view of the City's financial operations according to the respective books of account'. Investments were compared with their certificates, cash in the hands of officials 'duly checked at the time,' and certificates obtained for stock values. The wording of the report, prepared for 1920 by the new professional auditor Gilbert D. Shepherd FCA (previously Charles E. Dovey FCA), was closely in line with the unenacted recommendation of the 1903 Select Committee, namely:

> I beg to certify -
>
> (a) that I have found the accounts in order and properly vouched.
>
> (b) that separate accounts for all trading undertakings have been kept, and that every charge which each ought to bear has been debited.
>
> (c) that in my opinion the accounts issued present a true and correct view of the transactions and results of trading for the year under review.

(d) that due provision has been made out of revenue for the repayment of loans, and that all known items of income and expenditure have been brought into account, and

(e) that I have verified the securities for the funds invested.

The work undertaken by William Aldred, professional auditor of the Manchester Waterworks accounts for 1879, enabled him to report the discovery of 'irregularities in the accounts of the chief clerk and cashier, who has purposely withheld from myself and previous auditors certain books in which discrepancies appear'. The professional auditors' report to the Manchester Town Council, for 1920, makes it clear that they had made the kinds of checks being carried out in Cardiff in 1910, also that 'we have satisfied ourselves as to the correctness of and authority for charges to capital account during the year'. The report also contains, unusually, observations concerning the adequacy of the renewals account (a duty also recommended by the 1903 Select Committee) and the profitability of a trading department, concluding that 'consideration of the charge for water to the public should, therefore, receive immediate attention'. It ends with the kind of tribute to the corporation's staff also found in other professional auditors' report.

> The bookkeeping of all departments has been well performed, and we are pleased to state that we have received willing assistance and the utmost courtesy from the officials and staff in the course of our audit.

NOTES

1 See discussion of this matter also in chapter 7.

2 MCA 1835 obliged the treasurer to submit to the auditors 'all the accounts, with the vouchers and papers relating thereto ... for the purpose of being examined and audited' (s. 93); MCA 1882 similarly stated that the treasurer 'be required to make up his accounts in each half year, submit them, with the necessary vouchers to the borough auditors, and they shall audit them' (s. 37(1).

3 Frederick Whinney - President of the ICAEW 1884-8 - pointed out, in evidence to the Companies Acts (Amendment) Committee 1895 (BPP 1895, lxxxviii, Appendix: 81), that this might be considered the extent of the auditor's obligation under the Companies Act 1879. This Act required a bank's auditors to report whether the financial statements exhibited 'a true and correct view of the state of the company's affairs *as shown by the books of the company*', (s. 7(6), authors' emphasis)

4 The fact that the value for money concept is by no means a recent phenomenon is also discussed by Coombs and Edwards, 1990.

9

COMPANIES AND CORPORATIONS - COMPARATIVE DEVELOPMENTS

Recent years have seen an upsurge of interest in the development of financial reporting practices which, perhaps, reflects the stage of accounting in its overall development. Prior to 1970 historical analysis focussed mainly on the achievement of a better understanding of the origin and gradual widespread adoption of DEB. This pre-occupation is not surprising in view of the fact that, for many centuries, it remained the major accounting innovation. But while Italian merchants are properly acknowledged as the 'creators' of DEB, Britain may be seen as the instigator of modern financial reporting practices. This 'British contribution' is thought to have its origin in the need to account for finance raised to build on the early fruits of the Industrial Revolution; more specifically, to finance development of the transportation network needed to move people and goods to their desired locations, and to exploit the technical innovations which increasingly required the replacement of small manufacturing units by large scale production.

The goods and services associated with economic and social developments in nineteenth-century Britain, however, were made available by a mixture of private and public provision. The registered company, created in 1844 and allowed to register with limited liability from 1855, was increasingly used as the vehicle for mobilising capital through public company promotions; a process given an early impetus by first and second generation entrepreneurs choosing to retire and/or release all or some of their capital investment by selling their businesses to public companies in the 1860's (Thomas, 1973: 122). We have already seen the enthusiasm with which town councillors embraced the opportunities available to extend their municipalities' scale of operations during the same time period, and these activities, in common with those undertaken by joint stock companies, required management, finance and investment. A fact which may be underlined by pointing out that municipal corporations, outside London, had total debts outstanding of £168.3 million, in 1899, equal to 27% of the then British National Debt and roughly equivalent to £8 billion in 1995 prices.

Accounting practice, in each case, developed against a background of regulations. For registered companies, in general, statutory accounting and audit requirements initially introduced in 1844 were repealed in 1856 and not re-introduced until 1900. During this period the only regulations were those contained in a company's articles of association, which were a matter for private negotiation between shareholders and managers. We have seen that requirements for accountability were introduced, for municipal corporations, by various statutes beginning in 1835, and it might be argued that soon after the government began to regulate more closely the degree of accountability required from limited companies, through provisions contained in the Companies Act 1929, the *broad framework* applicable to local authorities was already more or less complete with the issue, by the Board of Health, of the Accounts (Boroughs and Metropolitan Boroughs) Regulations 1930 (SR&O no. 30) and the passage of the Local Government (Audit) Act 1933.

A third category of 'business' organisation, relevant to any review of early financial reporting developments comprises what might be loosely described as public utility companies.[1] These companies, often created by private Act of Parliament (statutory companies), were established to supply the goods and services required to meet vital public needs, such as water, gas, electricity and transportation (railways, tramways and omnibuses). These were the subject of separate statutory provision.

It will be helpful, for the purposes of this chapter, to employ a terminology which distinguishes between the two private sector-based categories of business organisation. While they were (probably) all limited companies, some within each category were formed by private statute and some by registration under the Companies Acts. Moreover, while few of the non-public utility companies were the subject of regulation between 1856-1900, some minimal regulations were in force from the latter date. We will therefore use the term 'companies' to cover both groups, and the terms 'public utility companies' and 'non-regulated companies' to distinguish between the two constituent elements.

The purpose of this chapter is to add to our understanding of the nature of accounting change by comparing and contrasting the development of external reporting regulations and practices in non-regulated companies, public utility companies and municipal corporations. We identify, for each category of 'business' organisation, the procedures in use, between 1835-1935, and when changes occurred. We also consider the possible transfer of new practices between the three types of entity. The comparison is of particular interest in view of the fact that municipal corporations undertook trading activities,[2] in many cases directly comparable with corresponding private sector businesses, and in some cases in direct competition with those organisations. Also, municipal corporations were of a size comparable with some of the largest manufacturing companies. Not surprisingly, therefore, they were faced with similar accounting problems, and we will attempt to identify the sector responsible for developing solutions which, in due course, received more widespread support.

The chapter is structured as follows. Firstly, we examine recent developments in local authority accounting. This will provide us with an hypothesis which we then test by identifying the main financial reporting issues, faced between 1835-1935, and present out our findings concerning their adoption by each of the three categories of business entity. We then review our findings and present our conclusions.

Recent developments

The last twenty years has seen local authorities become more commercially oriented than they had been for some time and, as a reflection and reinforcement of this process, we have seen moves towards the adoption of commercial accounting procedures. New 'Accounts and Audit Regulations' (SI 1974 No 1169) were introduced in 1974 which replaced numerous earlier measures, notably including the 'Accounts (Boroughs and Metropolitan Boroughs) Regulations 1930'. The way in which this change was thought to redress the imbalance between commercial and local authority accounting was summarised as follows:

> For some years, the commercial world could have been forgiven for looking somewhat askance at the treasurers of the major cities or municipal authorities who were able to rush into print soon after the close of their municipal financial year, and present their accounts of stewardship of the public purse without any restrictions on accounting presentation imposed on them [by statute]. This contrasts with the lengthy and detailed provisions of the 1948 and 1967 Companies Acts on accounting matters. (*Local Government Chronicle*, 1974: 1214)

The Local Government Planning and Land Act 1980 introduced separate reporting for direct labour organizations (subsequently renamed direct service organizations), managed by local authorities, while LGA 1982 empowered the Secretary of State to issue detailed accounting regulations for local authorities generally. To achieve closer regulation of local authority accounting procedures, draft 'Accounts and Audit Regulations' were issued in 1985 as part of the consultation process, but these were withdrawn in exchange for a commitment to take action from the Chartered Institute of Public Finance and Accountancy and other interested parties (Innes, 1987: 13). This culminated in the issue of the voluntary 'Code of Practice on Local Authority Accounting' (1987, revised 1991). This includes the broad application of the 'true and fair' concept to local authorities under the requirement for the accounts to present fairly the financial position and transactions of the authority.

A further significant change (1987), also partly designed to counter the threat of further statutory prescription (Rogers, 1988: 14), was the application of Statements of Standard Accounting Practice to the published accounts of local authorities.[3] The implementation of capital accounting proposals - which is admittedly proving highly problematic - would eliminate an important difference between the financial reporting practices of companies and local authorities by incorporating a depreciation charge in the latter's accounts.

It may be argued that the above measures are based on the assumption that company accounting practices are in some sense superior, and it is therefore interesting to look back on an earlier period, when there was no statutory requirement for local authorities to adopt commercial accounting procedures, in order to discover where innovations first occurred.

Based on this work, one possible hypothesis, examined in this chapter, is that market pressures brought about the development and improvement of non-regulated company-based reporting practices, and that the new procedures were, in due course, adopted by corporations and public utilities as representing best practice.

Issues and findings

To examine the development of the external reporting practices of companies and municipal corporations, a number of areas require consideration. These include: the range of published reports; the method of presentation, including such matters as the desirability of requiring accounts to conform to a prescribed format; the amount of information disclosed, with the ability of users to assimilate data appearing to be the effective upper limit; the valuation methods adopted, since these will determine the extent to which reports portray underlying economic facts; the audit requirements designed to add credibility to information prepared by management for external consumption; and the steps taken to publicise results and circulate them to user groups. Individual aspects of these broad issues are now examined.

Financial reporting: cash versus accruals

Financial reports, in common with financial records, were initially cash-based. The use of accruals accounting by companies made sense from an early stage (see chapter 4), however, in view of the need to identify profits available for dividend and to provide investors with a basis for performance assessment. Towards the beginning of the period covered by this study, the use of accruals accounting was encouraged by the requirement to publish a balance sheet under the Joint Stock Companies Act 1844 (s. 43), while the model articles issued in 1856 refer to the need to keep the books upon the 'principle of double entry' and to publish 'a statement of the income and expenditure for the past year' (clauses 69-70). Presentation of a profit and loss account, to shareholders, was the common but by no means invariable practice before it became a statutory requirement in 1929, but even where a profit and loss account was not produced, the balance for the year was usually reported in the balance sheet.

We have seen, in chapter 5, that the continued use of cash flows as the basis for financial reporting by municipal corporations well after 1835, has a number of causes which include: the district auditor's preference for cash accounting; prevailing legislation; the objections of council members; the merit of simplicity; the dislike of estimates of assets and liabilities; and the need to avoid delay.

We have seen, however, that much progress had been made as time went by. For example, the President of the CTAI drew attention to the fact that some municipal corporations produced income and expenditure accounts by 1889 (*Proceedings*, 1890: 5), while the 1907 Departmental Committee reported that it was the common practice within larger authorities by that time (BPP 1907, xxxvii: para. 25). These observations are consistent with our own findings, presented in chapter 5. Further encouragement for the move towards accruals accounting was provided by the 1907 Departmental Committee which recommended use of the income and expenditure basis by all local authorities except the 'Overseers of the Poor, and a few classes of small authorities [which] are of such a character' that the cash basis remained appropriate (BPP 1907, xxxvii: para. 79(c)).

We can therefore see that both DEB and accruals accounting developed, first, within the private sector and were not widely adopted by municipal corporations until the late nineteenth century. These changes therefore occurred during a time period consistent with Jones' conclusion that 'trading undertakings in competition with the private sector must reject "receipts and payments" in order to be able to produce "profit and loss"' (1986: 156). However, we must emphasise that the move towards accruals accounting was in train from at least 1850 (table 5.2), and probably earlier, and chapter 5 has shown that the development of trading undertakings merely speeded up its rate of adoption.

The balance sheet

Some British companies and firms were preparing balance sheets (usually called balance accounts or stock accounts) and, indeed, profit and loss accounts, in the seventeenth century (Littleton, 1933: 130-2; Yamey, 1959: 537-41; Baladouni, 1986: 27) and, quite possibly, much earlier. The 1844 requirement for registered companies to present a balance sheet to shareholders attending the annual general meeting,[4] together with all other accounting requirements, was made optional in 1856 for reasons which possibly include: the poor quality of financial statements prepared under the Act; the absence of suitably qualified personnel to do the job; the difficulty of enforcing the regulations; the lack of need for such data since companies largely remained family concerns; and the contemporary political philosophy of *laissez faire*. In response to market pressures, however, the evidence suggests that articles of association filed during the second half of the nineteenth century usually obliged the directors to present shareholders attending the annual general meeting with a balance sheet and, less often, also what might broadly be described as a profit and loss appropriation account (Edwards and Webb, 1985: 183-5). The legal obligation to present a balance sheet and a profit and loss account to shareholders attending the annual general meeting became requirements in 1900 and 1928 respectively.

We have seen that, for municipal corporations, MCA 1835 (and other statutes) seemed to imply the need to publish only a cash statement and, for some time, this broad format was used for the purpose of the abstract. Our study has shown that the publication of a balance sheet, to provide a stewardship record of assets and liabilities, progressed steadily during the second half of the nineteenth century; with Birmingham publishing this information from 1852. A further important impetus for this process seems to have been provided by the CTAI's recommendation (1889) that a revenue account, capital account and balance sheet should be prepared for each fund account. Given that the CTAI was a relatively small body at this time, we might imagine that the recommendation reflected prevailing practice at the Institute members' authorities.

The broad direction of expertise transfer seems clear enough - from companies to municipal corporations, with balance sheets probably adopted by the latter as they increasingly took on the responsibility for providing trading services, and in recognition of their potential for displaying a clearer indication of the financial position and obligations of non-trading operations.

Standardisation

This topic, often referred to as 'uniformity' in the nineteenth century, aroused great interest. The Joint Stock Companies Bill 1856 made initial provision for registered companies to publish a standardised balance sheet, but it emerged from the Parliamentary process as a model which companies could, but rarely did, choose to incorporate in their articles of association, and it was not until 1981 that their use became a statutory requirement for registered companies in general.

Standardised formats were introduced for public utility companies starting with the railways in 1868, followed by gas in 1871 and electricity in 1882. It is likely that these actions caused standardisation to become an important issue within local authorities which operated trading organisations. Under the Electric Lighting Act 1882, electricity undertakings (whether operated by companies or local authorities) were required to prepare and publish accounts in a form prescribed by the Board of Trade (s. 9). Such forms, first issued in 1893, consisted of a capital account, a revenue account, a net revenue account, a sinking fund account, a reserve fund account and a general balance sheet (Stevens, 1899: 51). One may surmise that these broad formats (and possibly those contained in the Gas Works Clauses Act 1871, Schedule B, which strictly applied only to companies) formed the basis for financial reporting by trading undertakings in general.

We have seen, in chapter 5, that a gradual consensus developed concerning the range of reports to be published, their presentation and content. Nevertheless much variety remained at the time the 1907 Departmental Committee met. It was, once again, the local authority-based professional accounting association, the IMTA, which led the endeavour to improve standards, commencing with a suggested form of tramway accounts in 1905, issued in conjunction with the Municipal Tramways Association. We also saw, in chapter 5, that the IMTA prepared the standard forms of accounts reproduced as an appendix to the 1907 Departmental Committee's Report. In the absence of government action, however, the IMTA continued to take the initiative and issued standard forms of accounts 1913, developing these further in 1938 and 1955.

It can therefore be seen that standardisation occurred, first in public utilities, second in the municipal corporations, finally moving on to the (initially) non-regulated companies. A possible explanation for local authority leadership in the move towards uniformity is that arguments used to resist the standardisation of non-regulated company accounts - such as the need to give directors a free hand and to conceal information from competitors - simply did not apply. Moreover, because there was public money involved, the case for regulation and additional disclosure was seen as that much stronger.

Depreciation accounting

The appropriate accounting treatment of fixed assets has received more attention, over the years, than any other single financial reporting issue, save possibly secret reserves and inflation accounting. Although an exaggeration compared with what are today seen as problem areas in accounting, Pixley neatly summed up the perceived contemporary significance of the problem as follows: 'if the construction of the profit and loss account could be carried out without reference to this difficult but interesting subject [depreciation], accountancy might certainly be described as one of the exact sciences' (1908: 199). There are much earlier examples of depreciation being charged in the accounts, but the practice became more common during the industrial revolution and received serious attention from managers of railway companies who, having made enormous investments in the 1830's and 1840's, perceived a possible need to make provision for ultimate replacement.

The appropriate accounting treatment of fixed assets in company accounts was seen to be linked with the question of capital maintenance, and very different views were held by businessmen, lawyers and accountants, dictated by their background and current priorities. Problems with charging depreciation were seen to be its calculation and negative impact on levels of reported and divisible profit; while its inclusion seemed to be required to produce a fairer measure of reported profit and to earmark for retention funds required to finance replacement. The wide range of opinions expressed in the high quality debate, which ensued, was reflected by massive diversity and inconsistency in financial reporting practice (Edwards, 1986a). For example, the entire omission of a depreciation charge on the grounds that assets were maintained in good working order, the inclusion of round sum charges depending upon the level of profit and often treated as an appropriation of profit remained not uncommon practices even in the 1930's (Edwards, 1980: 21-8). It was the result of a series of 'regulations' commencing with Recommendation on Accounting Principles 9, issued by the ICAEW in 1945, and culminating in Statement of Standard Accounting Practice 12, issued by the Accounting Standards Committee in 1978, that the inclusion of a charge for assets possessing a finite useful life became widely accepted.[5]

We have seen that similar issues arose in the case of municipal corporations, but that their resolution was complicated by the need to account for loan repayments. In laying down the requirement that such repayments should be charged in the revenue account, central government's basic objective was to encourage fiscal integrity; to ensure that councillors considered carefully the financial implications of their expenditure plans, and that the generation which benefited from the provision of a particular service also paid for it (see chapter 6). Only when municipal corporations became heavily involved with trading activities, in the latter decades of the nineteenth century, did the possible need for an annual depreciation charge become an important issue. At that stage, probably because the power to borrow money was tied to the obligation to use it for approved capital expenditure, the question of loan repayment and depreciation became intermingled and confused. One persuasive line of argument put forward - in effect a rationalisation of existing practice - was as follows: because the loan period was often intended to match the life of the fixed asset, the write off of loan repayments against revenue could reasonably be regarded as a surrogate for the annual depreciation charge.

We have seen, in chapter 6, that numerous writers, sometimes with their background mainly in the private sector, were unconvinced that this was an adequate solution. The result was a debate about whether a depreciation fund should also be built up, producing a double charge, and even a reserve fund as well, giving rise to a treble charge. We also saw, in chapter 6, that a further outcome was the maintenance, by numerous corporations, of funds for one or more of the following: depreciation; renewals; reserves; contingencies; and repairs.

The impact on the level of the rates of making additional charges and the possible subsidisation by one generation of services enjoyed by another has been considered by Jones. He concludes that, in contrast with the receipts and payments versus income and expenditure debate, the practice widely used within local government survived because 'charging depreciation in addition to the loan repayments could not be afforded' (1986: 157). This was clearly an important factor, but a practical justification for the selected 'solution' was that, increasingly, the level of loan repayment required by statute was at least equal to the conventional depreciation charge. The 1907 Departmental Committee's conclusion - namely that debt repayment may properly be regarded as the provision for depreciation, unless the loan repayment period was excessive, in which case some further provision might be necessary - summed up fairly well the conclusions reached by that time (BPP 1907, xxxvii: para. 79(l)).

In this area, therefore, we have a good example of different priorities giving rise to the continued use of different methods. Depreciation accounting was adopted by companies and discussed at length by local authorities but, in the main, rejected on the grounds that it was not relevant to their needs.[6]

The double account system

This system of financial reporting appears to have been developed by canal companies and railway companies, and its first known full-scale application was at the London and Birmingham Railway Company in 1838 (Edwards 1985: 30). The system was soon widely adopted by railway companies, and its use became a statutory requirement for both these and certain public utility companies when standardised procedures were introduced between 1868-82. The method was adopted voluntarily by other companies which incurred a similar pattern of expenditure (docks, mines, quarries and shipping companies), i. e. a heavy initial outlay required to establish a substantial infrastructure followed by the need to finance only operating activity and replacements as they fell due. Public utility companies required by law to use the double account system disappeared as a result of nationalisation by the immediate post-Second World War Labour Government. Water escaped this move towards state ownership (most of the water supply was anyway already in the hands of local authorities), and a small number of water companies continued to prepare financial statements conforming broadly to the double account format until required to apply the provisions of Statement of Standard Accounting Practice 12, 'Accounting for Depreciation', in the late 1970's.[7]

We have seen that the double account system was well suited to the circumstances of local authorities; it was a stewardship oriented report, which required a rigid distinction to be made between capital and revenue expenditure, and fixed assets to be stated at their original cost. Its use might have been further enhanced by the backgrounds of the accountants working for local authorities at the time. A number of the founder members of the CTAI had industrial or commercial accounting experience. John Henry Bailey had worked for the Lancashire and Yorkshire Railway Company; T. A. Mercer had been employed by the Furness Gas and Water Company; William Cooper had been in the iron trade; Charles Moss had his own accounting practice; and J. E. Bryan started his career in a bank (Poynton, 1960: 9-14). Moreover, in many instances the utility services provided by local authorities were acquired from private companies which would already be using the double account system.[8] There would therefore be a natural inclination to assess the benefits of using this accounting method for the purpose of preparing the acquiring local authority's entire published accounts.

The widespread adoption of the double account system by local authorities was quite possibly also reinforced by the fact that public utility companies, offering the services also supplied by municipal corporations, usually employed that system. The skeleton form of accounts attached to the 1907 Departmental Committee's Report used this format, as did the specimen forms of accounts issued by the IMTA in 1905, 1913 and 1938. The basic principles were enshrined in statute law by the Accounts (Boroughs and Metropolitan Boroughs) Regulations 1930.

The evidence therefore suggests that the double account system, devised by public utility companies, proved eminently suitable for municipal corporations and its use was accordingly transferred to that sector.[9]

Public information

An important factor impinging on the usefulness of accounting reports concerns the steps taken to make the data available to interested parties. The Joint Stock Companies Act 1844 contained extensive provisions in this direction. The directors were required to circulate an audited balance sheet to shareholders prior to the annual general meeting, to present it to the annual general meeting, and to file the document with the registrar of companies. There were also requirements for the directors' reports to be read out at that meeting, and for the shareholders to have the right to inspect, over a 6 week period spanning the date of the annual general meeting, the company's books of accounts and balance sheets and to take extracts therefrom.[10] In 1900, forty four years after the abandonment of these provisions, the requirement to present an audited balance sheet to shareholders was revived. From 1907 the balance sheet again had to be filed with the registrar. The 1929 Companies Act contained requirements for this information to be circulated to members prior to the annual general meeting, and for a profit and loss account to be presented to shareholders attending that event.

Public utility companies were, as usual, subject to special rules. Those incorporated as statutory companies were usually subject to the provisions of the Companies Clauses Act 1845, which included requirements for the company's books and balance sheet to be open to inspection by shareholders around the date of the annual general meeting (s. 117). Turning to particular categories of company, the Railway Clauses Consolidation Act 1845 obliged companies to file an audited annual abstract of receipts and expenditure with the clerk of the peace where it was available for public inspection (s. 107), while the Regulation of Railways Act 1868 provided for half yearly accounts to be returned to the Board of Trade and supplied, on application, to shareholders and debenture holders (s. 4).

The need for Parliament to be informed of the application of public monies, and concern about possible extravagance, resulted in occasional returns of receipts and expenditure being required from overseers of the poor as early as the eighteenth century. And we have seen that, from 1836, municipal corporations were placed under an obligation to make an *annual* return containing this information. As noted above, the treasurer was obliged to make available for inspection by ratepayers 'a full abstract of his accounts', and for this abstract to be delivered to them 'on payment of a reasonable price for each copy' (MCA 1835, s. 93). Ratepayers also had the right to inspect both the books of accounts and the minutes of council meetings, although the amount of financial information these contained varied considerably from one authority to another.

We can therefore see that municipal corporations have been under a continuous obligation to publish financial information since the date of their creation in 1835. This principle was extended to the newly created registered company in 1844 but suspended, twelve years later, for nearly half a century. It is possible that the less precise financial reporting obligations, imposed on municipal corporations, supplied the degree of flexibility needed to make their initial implementation a practical proposition and, at the same time, provided scope for the development of financial reporting practices to meet changing circumstances as time went by.

Consolidated accounts

The first known British example of a consolidated balance sheet was published by the Pearson & Knowles Coal & Iron Co. Ltd in 1910 (Edwards, 1991). However, it was the publication by Nobel Industries (the forerunner of ICI Plc) of a combined statement of assets and liabilities of companies within the group, together with Sir Gilbert Garnsey's lecture in the same year (1922), which focussed attention on the importance of this subject and brought about an upsurge of experimentation with different methods of group accounting in Great Britain. It was in 1948 that the publication of a consolidated balance sheet became a statutory requirement.

Turning to municipal corporations, legislation required the maintenance of separate accounts to record transactions through the borough fund and through the district fund, and when municipal corporations began to undertake trading activities in the second half of the nineteenth century, these activities were often also separately recorded. These developments gave rise to the need for a form of financial statement to summarise the financial position of the various operations, and we have seen (chapter 5, table 5.2) that it was the practice of some municipal corporations to publish an 'aggregate balance sheet', in rudimentary form, commencing in the 1850's. The procedures employed included the cancellation of inter-fund indebtedness - a basic feature of the consolidation process.

The move towards the widespread publication of the aggregate balance sheet received encouragement from the CTAI in 1889 and, in due course, its preparation was given legal recognition by the Accounts (Boroughs and Metropolitan Boroughs) Regulations 1930.

Preparation of the aggregate balance sheet did not oblige borough treasurers to face the difficult technical issues associated with the preparation of consolidated accounts, such as the calculation of goodwill, minority interest and distributable profit. These issues simply did not arise. But it must be remembered that many of the companies that pioneered the use of 'consolidated' accounts, including Nobel Industries (Edwards and Webb, 1984: 39), chose initially not to tackle these problems and instead simply produced a combined statements of the group's assets and liabilities, which is about as near as you can get to an aggregate balance sheet. In adopting this course of action, it seems likely that such companies were utilising the scheme developed by municipal corporations. The 'change agent' at Nobel Industries may well have been its secretary, Sir Josiah Stamp. He was a stern critic of secretive accounting practices during the 1920's and, as a distinguished economist and former civil servant, he would have been familiar with the accounting practices employed by local authorities.[11]

Audit

The accounts of registered companies were made the subject of annual audit in 1844 and again in 1900 following repeal of the earlier provision in 1856. The Companies Clauses Consolidation Act 1845 anticipated the appointment of two auditors from among the body of shareholders. Particular categories of company were made subject to audit, including railways (1867) as a result of revelations concerning the failure of Watson Overend & Co. (a firm of railway contractors which placed a lot of railway paper on the market), and banks (1879) as a result of the publication of 'imaginary balance sheets' by the City of Glasgow Bank. In 1948 the requirement was introduced for the auditor to be a professional, although most quoted companies already had professional auditors at the time the statutory audit was re-introduced in 1900.

We have seen that, since 1835, the accounts of municipal corporations had at various times been the subject of one or more of four different types of audit; a government audit, an elective audit, the Mayor's audit, and a professional audit. It has been pointed out that there was a certain logic behind the concept of elective auditors, introduced by MCA 1835, namely that they were appointed by and responsible to individuals - the ratepayers - who had a direct interest in ensuring that municipal affairs were properly conducted. Moreover, they might be seen as the equivalent of the amateur/shareholder audit which was soon to become (temporarily) common amongst registered companies (Parker, 1986: 23-39).

We have seen, in chapter 7, that the question whether the elective audit should be replaced by the district audit and/or a professional audit was a controversial topic which aroused strong emotions, beginning in about the 1870's. Accountants working in the private sector were keen to obtain a share of this work, whilst the LGB, which gradually extended the district audit to many areas of local government, was keen to bring the entire activities of municipal corporations within its ambit. The elective audit survived for a variety of reasons which include the view that it worked fairly well, that there were judicial avenues that could be explored in the event of grievance, that the government audit would be an unwarranted intrusion into the actions of democratically elected local officials, that the elective auditor was often a professional, and that municipal corporations were always free to a appoint professional auditors in addition to the elective auditor and increasingly adopted this course of action. Eventually, in 1933, the Municipal Corporations (Audit) Act permitted boroughs, subject to the elective audit, to adopt instead either the district audit or a 'professional audit' undertaken by members of professional accounting bodies listed in a schedule to the Act.

The evidence therefore suggests that the amateur audit, initially common amongst registered companies, recommended for statutory companies and prescribed for municipal corporations, was superseded by the professional audit, first amongst companies and later - to a large extent - in municipal corporations. Within local authorities, the government audit at one time covered the vast bulk of their expenditure, but went into retreat (Coombs and Edwards, 1990) and was effectively abolished, in 1982, with the establishment of the Audit Commission which may appoint either a district auditor (employed by the Commission) or a firm of professional accountants to do the job.

Details and diagrams

A comparison of the published accounts of a large nineteenth-century non-regulated company with those of a contemporary municipal corporation would show immense differences. The company's accounts usually consisted of a brief director's report, dealing with overall business developments, a balance sheet, and occasionally what might broadly be described as a profit and loss appropriation account. Balance sheets were presented in horizontal format, with approximately a half-dozen entries on each side fairly typical. The use of what came to be described as 'omnibus headings' - an extended narrative describing a number of assets or liabilities covered by a single financial total - was commonplace. The format did not change substantially until 1948, though the number of headings increased following the introduction of a statutory requirement, in 1929, to show certain items separately. The use of diagrams to represent performance is a post-Second World War development which seems to have received some impetus from experimentation with different methods of employee reporting during the 1970's.

The accounts of nineteenth-century municipal corporations, by way of contrast, contained an immense amount of detail. The decision to show receipts and payments (and later income and expenditure) in considerable minutia quite possibly reflected the stewardship orientation which is a fundamental feature of charge and discharge accounting. In the context of accountability for public money, the desire to present to ratepayers the full facts is entirely understandable. Moreover, the possible use of published information by competitors produced a constraint on company disclosures which did not apply to municipal corporations. The legal obligation to provide cash flow data continued when authorities applied commercial accounting principles to trading and non-trading activities. Detail in both cash-based and accruals-based accounts remained a prominent feature and, with separate sets of accounts prepared for each fund, voluminous financial reports well in excess of 200 pages, and sometimes much more, were common.

The finding that local authorities made early use of a wide range of diagrams to portray facts and performance, at first surprising, is less so when one becomes aware of the vast quantity of financial information which ratepayers otherwise had to assimilate. The use of diagrams in the form of pie charts, bar charts and graphs was sufficiently well established at Sheffield, by 1912, to be the subject of a short book published by its city accountant (Allen, 1912). Diagrams are used to make historical comparisons covering periods of up to 60 years and, although Sheffield may have been the exception rather than the rule, at this stage, their use became more common. For example, in 1926 Cardiff published graphs setting out changes, over the period 1914-1926, in the rate levied for various purposes and loans raised and outstanding (*Financial Circular*, February 1927: 80-1); in 1930 Manchester published graphs setting out, for the period 1914-30 key statistics relating to water, and for 1919-30 the various sources of rate fund income.

The practice of publishing historical summaries covering a ten or twenty year period was by no means unusual even at the turn of the century. For example, from 1890 Manchester published a detailed year by year summary of 'the amount of gross profits, and the mode of its appropriation; also the amount of borrowed money owing, and the excess of assets &c. from the year 1862 to the present date'. Bristol provided similar information in relation to its electricity undertaking from 1894 while, on a more modest scale, Bradford published comparative figures for income on the 'city fund' and 'police pension fund' from 1894.

The difference in financial reporting practice between companies and corporations is therefore perfectly understandable. The information published by non-regulated companies was already highly summarised and could be easily assimilated.[12] As published corporate reports became more extensive in the post-Second World War period, and the range of potential users arguably included certain less financially sophisticated groupings, the advantages of using some form of visual aid became more apparent. The ratepayer might be expected to have been, on average, even less financially aware than the company shareholder. Added to this the fact that published financial information was enormously detailed, the early decision to publish graphs, bar charts etc. can be more easily understood.

This is not to suggest that the abstracts were by any means always models of lucidity. Towards to end of the time period covered by this study, Lamb points out that there was little uniformity in the accounts of municipal corporations, except for those of the trading undertakings which were in many cases 'based upon the statutory returns' (1925: 358). However, he does go on to point out that the overall presentation was logical and neatly represented in the aggregate balance sheet. Criticisms of municipal corporations' financial reporting practices, particularly in relation to their length, nevertheless continued up to the date of their abolition (Bucknall, 1973: 1243).

Review, analysis and conclusion

Given the time span of this study, and the breadth of the subject matter, attention has necessarily been confined to a survey of major accounting developments within companies and municipal corporations. However, enough has been done to demonstrate important differences and similarities between the accounting and audit practices of each category of entity over a 100 year period. How can this be explained?

Today we hear much about agency theory and market forces as the most efficient mechanism for bringing about accounting change, with companies providing the information required to reassure shareholders and creditors and keep down the cost of capital. This led us to postulate that the accounting practices of municipal corporations may have initially lagged behind and subsequently adopted, whole-scale, practices developed within the private sector. This has not turned out to be the case. The weakness in the theory partly follows from the fact that the financial reporting objectives of companies and municipal corporations, and the environmental conditions within which they operated, differed a great deal during the time span of this study.

The considerable detail provided early on in the financial statements published by municipal corporations, and experimentation with graphical presentation, is indicative of the stewardship orientation of such reports, the desire to inform the financially illiterate and even to boast of financial prowess. Other areas where municipal corporations seem to have been 'ahead' of the general run of companies - aggregated accounts and standardization - were the consequence of size and the nature of their activities.

By way of contrast, the importance of profit to commercial organisations may be seen as the reason why companies embraced, at an early stage, DEB, the profit and loss account and the balance sheet. Indeed, it was not until the late nineteenth century, and the rapid development of trading activities, that accruals accounting became the 'norm' amongst municipal corporations, although we have seen that moves in that direction were already well underway. The double account system is also seen to have had its origin within the private sector, albeit among what have been described as public utility companies, while one of the most persistent and vexing accounting problems, namely the appropriate valuation of fixed assets, led to a heated debate about the possible inclusion of a depreciation charge in local authority accounts, and the eventual decision that it was not necessarily appropriate to their requirements. Similarly, in relation to auditing, different approaches were initially deemed desirable, though the increased involvement of municipal corporations in trading activities reinforced an already developing conviction that commercially trained accountants were probably better equipped to audit their affairs.

The above findings suggest that companies and municipal corporations displayed a common interest in a wide range of accounting issues, and that, on various occasions, one or the other was at a different point along a developmental path. Whether or not that path led towards an improvement of procedures is a matter of debate, however, since it is by no means clear that the accounting practices used by companies were, at any point in time, in any respect superior to those employed by municipal corporations, or vice versa.

The broad sequence of accounting change has been similar for companies and corporations, though there have been significant differences in emphasis. Accounting requirements were introduced for municipal corporations in 1835 and registered companies in 1844. There is some evidence to suggest that the poor quality of company accounts published under the 1844 Act was the reason for transferring the requirements to an optional appendix in 1856. This did not happen in the case of municipal corporations, where regulations were anyway minimal, and the form and content of their published accounts the subject of increasing criticism by the beginning of the fourth quarter of the nineteenth century. Since then, in both sectors, the tendency has been for the introduction of new regulations to re-enforce improvements in existing practice; an important difference is that the local authority oriented professional accounting body was the main source of new regulations in relation to municipal corporations, whereas private sector companies had to rely on statute law for guidance until well into the twentieth century. Furthermore, the development of accounting practice amongst municipal corporations has not been crisis driven - e. g. none have never gone bankrupt in Great Britain - and so it was left to borough councillors and borough officials in conjunction with the accounting profession to develop new procedures.

NOTES

1 In many European countries such services have traditionally been supplied entirely by the State, whereas in Britain they have moved between the private and governmental sector, often depending on contemporary political dogma. Public utilities were initially provided by companies but increasingly by local authorities which either started from scratch or, more usually, took over a local company. Immediately following the second world war, gas, electricity and railways were reorganised as nationalised industries, leaving only a few water companies within the private sector. Recently we have seen gas, electricity and water transferred into private ownership, with consideration currently being given to the privatisation of British Rail.

2 Trading services were also supplied by local boards of health in larger towns not possessing borough status. In due course (1894) these became the urban district councils. This left some trading undertakings run by rural district councils.

3 The Statement of Recommended Practice entitled 'The Application of Accounting Standards to Local Authorities in England and Wales' is, however, selective - four Standards then extant (SSAP's 3, 8, 22 and 23) were deemed inapplicable to local authorities and certain others were adopted only in part - producing the suggestion from some quarters that an important priority when choosing material for inclusion was to minimise the need for change.

4 This reference will be used for convenience, although it was not until 1900 that the Companies Act indicated that the general meeting should be held once a year. Earlier references to 'each ordinary meeting' and 'once at least in every year' are indicative of the fact that nineteenth-century meetings were sometimes held half yearly.

5 In recent years, however, we have seen an increasing tendency to revalue but not depreciate appreciating fixed assets. While this ploy has the attraction of improving gearing without spoiling earnings per share, the

explanations for non-depreciation given have been criticised as amounting to a contravention of existing regulations (Hanson, 1989: 54).

6 As with the other 'Issues' discussed in this chapter, broad generalisations are unavoidable. Wide variety in the adoption of depreciation accounting practices by private sector companies remained the subject of strong criticism well into the twentieth century (Leake, 1923, Introduction), with public utility companies least convinced of the need to make a charge (Edwards, 1986b). Whereas, as noted in chapter 6, some municipal corporations *did* charge depreciation.

7 The accounts of the Lee Valley Water Company, for example, were prepared up to the mid-1970's firmly in accordance with double account principles. A separate capital account was maintained and the major fixed assets (Properties, Reservoirs, Wells, Borings and Mains) were renewed and repaired out of a contingency fund. The accounts for 1979 followed a typical commercial presentation, and a note to the accounts referred to the full adoption of depreciation accounting with effect from 1 April 1978.

8 In response of a circular from Cardiff Corporation, just six out of 64 boroughs supplying gas reported that these undertakings had *not* been acquired from private companies (Cardiff archive, box 503).

9 The 1955 standard forms marked a break with tradition, however, by combining capital and revenue items within the balance sheet but, where relevant, incorporating a subsidiary statement giving a break-down of items into capital and revenue.

10 These provisions could be modified by the company's deed of settlement or, later, articles of association.

11 However, Bywater (1986: 262-3) suggests that Stamp's familiarity with consolidated accounts dates from his study of the combined balance sheets of Kodak Ltd (1900/1) when helping to prepare a tax case against the company.

12 The message conveyed, however, could be some distance removed from the underlying economic reality due to the use of secret reserves, obscure and misleading terminology, excessive summarisation, 'omnibus' headings, diverse accounting methods and a group structure to conceal performance by operating through subsidiaries (Marriner, 1980b).

10

CONCLUDING COMMENTS

The main findings from this research are summarised in chapter 9, which also compares and contrasts the development of accountability within municipal corporations and private sector companies. In this concluding chapter we make some further comments concerning the nature and cause of accounting change within municipal corporations.

Regulation

The early 1830's, in Great Britain, marked the end of an era when local affairs had been left to the local people, unfettered by intervention from central government. In 1834 the Poor Law Amendment Act made the administration of poor relief the subject of central control in the endeavour to combat spiralling expenditure. A year later MCA 1835 tackled corruption within the boroughs by establishing a framework designed to make town councils more accountable to local ratepayers. The framework included a franchise, more democratic than that contained in the Reform Act of 1832, and the requirement for the town council to account to both the ratepayers and Parliament for resources entrusted to it. It was intended that the stewardship of the members should be monitored and the credibility of the published abstract of accounts enhanced by an audit carried out by the ratepayers' representatives.

Parker (1990) has explained the accounting regulation of certain categories of large private sector companies during the nineteenth century (the remainder were unregulated 1856-1900) - public utilities, railways and financial institutions - on the grounds of monopoly, privileges granted by the State and the need to guarantee financial security. One can see certain parallels between the development of regulations in these areas and the obligations imposed on municipal corporations. In particular, the State 'created' the boroughs in the same way that they were directly responsible for authorising the formation of statutory companies, which most of Parker's 'regulated companies' were. Statutory accountability to Parliament may therefore be seen as a 'quid pro quo' for the granting of monopoly powers, with the obligation to account to ratepayers also dictated by the stewardship requirement for public officials to explain the application of money entrusted to their use.

From 1860 onwards the nature of municipal corporations began to change dramatically. Whereas, previously, they were mainly concerned with administering the provision of local services such as policing, sanitation, lighting and street improvements, they now began to provide a range of trading services and other amenities (particularly housing and education) to meet the growing aspirations of a more prosperous society. These developments rendered existing statutory regulations and prevailing reporting practices inadequate in a number of respects. In particular, cash accounting, still based on charge and discharge in some quarters, was deficient because it did not enable the performance of trading organisations to be measured. One might have expected the introduction of further statutory regulations, at this stage, with monopoly powers in the supply of trading services justifying the kind of requirements introduced for Parker's 'regulated companies'. With one exception - the introduction of specimen formats for electric lighting undertakings[1] - this did not happen

This does not mean that the government did not monitor and control, to some extent, the activities of municipal corporations. Their progress was monitored through the local taxation returns, while control was exerted through: loan regulations; and by the extension of the district audit to those activities which increasingly came to benefit from central government grants.

Overall, however, governmental requirements cannot explain the development of municipal financial reporting practice since, fundamentally, they did not amount to very much more in 1935 than they had one hundred years earlier.[2]

Market forces

The mechanism of market forces has been used, in some quarters, to explain the process of accounting change in the British private sector. It is tempting to assume that progress was made in a similar manner within municipal corporations, particularly in view of the fact that they managed substantial trading undertakings. Also there are similarities in the organisational structures of corporations and companies which make such an explanation plausible. In the private sector, shareholders provide the finance and directors make broad policy decisions, in turn employing middle managers to give these policy decisions practical effect. In the case of municipal corporations, the ratepayers elected the town council which was responsible for managing the corporation's affairs and appointing officers to give its decisions practical effect. For each type of entity auditors were appointed by the 'shareholders' to examine and report on the published accounts.

There are further similarities between the organisational structure of these entities. Where the principals - the ratepayer or shareholder - were dissatisfied with performance, they could remove their agents (town councillors and directors) at the next election or general meeting. However, there are also important differences. Ratepayers do not own shares which produce dividends and, possibly, capital growth, although one might argue that equivalent benefits are 'value for money' in the form of civic amenities made available. Moreover, where municipal corporations undertook trading activities, the benefit for local inhabitants was either lower prices than would have been charged by a private sector-based company or profits which could be used to develop the local infrastructure without imposing a charge on the rates. But ratepayers cannot realise their 'investment' and, if they believed that the rate is being better spent elsewhere, they were obliged to move to the new location in order to obtain the perceived benefits. This is, of course, an extreme measure and, although not impossible, is much more difficult than simply selling securities. Against this disadvantage might be balanced the fact that it was easier to change the town council than a board of directors, in the sense that there was a readily available alternative.

A further difference between companies and corporations is that council members did not necessarily possess management expertise, were part-time, and unpaid. Moreover, the fact that the municipal officers were professionals possibly meant that they were capable of exerting a larger measure of influence on a corporation's development than management below board level on the future of a private sector company. We have seen that the municipal officers were certainly forceful characters; they were also highly paid and, presumably, well placed in local society (see table 10.1).[3] The possible outcome was a very different relationship between municipal officers and elected members compared with management and the board of directors. Arguably, a significant degree of power sometimes lay outside the elected members in the case of municipal corporations, and in the hands of officials who were not a part of the principal agent relationship.

We have examined a great deal of material, during the course of this study, and the absence of demands from ratepayers for additional or improved financial information has been a noticeable feature. This finding is consistent with the Downsian model, accepted by Jones, that the rational voter will not seek out information because 'the probability of a single vote in itself making a difference is very small indeed' (1992: 127). It may also be that there was information overload, exacerbated by haphazard forms of presentation until towards the end of the nineteenth century when more attention was paid to

Table 10.1: Salaries of officials at the sixteen largest municipal corporations, in terms of population, in 1891.

Borough	Population	Town Clerk	Surveyor/ Engineer	Accountant
		£	£	£
Liverpool	613463	1,600	1,199[1]	650
Manchester	484937	1,750	1,000	850[2]
Birmingham	400774[4]	2,000	1,000	1,000[3]
Leeds	363799	1,500	800	700
Sheffield	327433	1,250	800	600
Nottingham	245000	1,900	800	500
Salford	242509	1,000	700	264
Bradford	240515	1,500	550	850
Bristol	229361	1,000	750[1]	850
Hull	218833	1,200	500	300
West Ham	200000	1,140[5]	1,200	320
Newcastle	160983	6	6	6
Oldham	146716	700	450	200
Portsmouth	141253	700	400	none
Sunderland	140000	1,150	400	400
Cardiff	131741	800	700	700[3]

Notes

1. As well as employing surveyors, Liverpool engaged two engineers and Bristol one engineer, each paid £850.
2. Manchester, in addition, employed a full time City Treasurer paid £1,000.
3. This is the salary of the City Treasurer who also undertook the accounting work.
4. This figure is for 1881.
5. Out of this the town clerk paid his staff.
6. Information not provided.

Source: Cardiff Archive, Box 532.

these matters. Ratepayers were naturally interested in the amount of the rate, and we certainly have evidence of town councils shelving plans to acquire trading organisations in the face of strong opposition. But we find little or no use made of accounting information to strengthen the ratepayers' case. So why was there a continuous movement towards the publication of more and better financial information? We will make some suggestions after referring to developments, mainly market driven, concerning the second main feature of accountability within municipal corporations, namely the elective audit.

We have seen that the elective audit came under attack, but survived, although this may be attributed partly to the lack of agreement about whether it should be replaced by the professional or district audit. The LGB made a strong case for taking over this work at the beginning of the twentieth century, but the growing commercial activities of municipal corporations raised justifiable doubts about the suitability of an intensely legalistic audit, usually performed by barristers without any commercial training. In their resistance to change, borough councillors were possibly supported by the growing 'municipal interest' in Parliament, i. e. MPs returned by boroughs where they had received their political training and where they had become convinced that policy decisions and administration were the prerogative of the democratically elected borough council rather than a government appointed auditor.

The continuation of the elective audit is also partly attributable to the fact that the post was, in many respects, an anachronistic irrelevance. By the 1930's the elective auditor was not the independent minded amateur striving to control local excesses; he was often either professionally qualified, himself, or served municipal corporations which chose also to engage the services of a professional accountant or the district auditor and, therefore, redundant.

Public duty

This study has shown massive innovation regarding accounting practice over the period 1835-1935, but this cannot be attributed to legislation either in terms of accounting requirements, which were minimal, or audit requirements, which were generally ineffective. However, regulations were permissive rather than restrictive and this provided *scope* for the development of a comprehensive framework of accountability during the one hundred years covered by this study. We have seen little evidence of the ratepayer, as principal, actively demanding change, but it would still be possible to argue that the town council, as agents, were successfully anticipating increases in user needs.

It is of course also likely that accounting innovation was required, internally, in order to provide members, as top management, with better information for decision making purposes. And in this respect the role of the trading undertakings was important, not in the sense that the move over to income and expenditure accounting would not otherwise have occurred (it was already underway), but because it helped speed up the rate of progress.

This acceleration occurred because, although the trading activities were not necessarily expected to make a profit, the town council needed to be informed of the surplus made available in relief of the rates or deficit requiring subsidisation from the rates in accordance with the town council's policy decision; also to discharge the reporting obligations sometimes laid down in the local Act which established the trading undertaking. While profit was not even a consideration in relation to non-trading activities, there was again the need to measure outstanding liabilities in order to ensure a sound basis for setting the rate. A balance sheet was needed, in each case, to provide a stewardship record of the assets belonging to the corporation. We might therefore conclude that financial information, having been prepared for each committee, was simply aggregated and made available to the public because it was readily available and involved very little by way of additional cost.

This may be part of the explanation but we find more persuasive the idea that members embraced enthusiastically the practice of full disclosure to signal the success of the corporation, and the town council, over the previous twelve months. Municipal corporations expanded rapidly, during the second half of the nineteenth century, reflecting the application of socialist principles and associated with the concept of 'civic pride', spurred on by a determination to outperform the neighbouring authority. We see no reason why these ideals should not also explain the efforts made to improve internal accounting practices which democratically elected officials were willing to make public. In this context, the publication of valuation statements, at Cardiff and Manchester, were unsuccessful experiments designed to report the corporations achievements in an even more favourable light. The use of comparative tables and graphs would emphasise achievements over time in a format which could be more easily understood by the ratepayer.

Mechanism of change

The cause of accounting change remains problematic, but the mechanism of change has been clearly demonstrated in this study. Innovation occurred, initially, at the level of the corporation, where an important contribution was made, beginning in the 1850's, by professional accountants. These were brought in, by the members, for such reasons as the investigation of irregularities, improvement of the system of record keeping, to prepare accounts, and to audit accounts. In the role of auditor, which became more widespread as time went by, they were appointed by and responsible to the town council, though their report was often also made public.

The members favoured the appointment of professional accountants for the following reasons: they could provide technical services which the elective auditor might not be able to supply and certainly could not be expected to supply; they undertook an audit of the officials on behalf of the members; they remained under the control of the members; and their appointment helped counter proposals for the extension of the district audit to municipal corporations. The development of trading departments made the appointment of professional auditors, expert in techniques developed in the private sector, increasingly desirable.

The growth in size of the municipal corporation also gave rise to the need for a more substantial internal accounting function. Whereas in 1835 the financial affairs would be conducted entirely by the treasurer; often a bank manager or lawyer who provided the service free of charge, by the 1890's the larger municipal corporations either had a full time accountant or full time treasurer, and often both. These were assisted by a growing array of clerks, bookkeepers and cashiers, with the IMTA providing training for student members. The development of the internal accounting function was reinforced by the professionalisation of local authority accounting, and it becoming a subject for criticism where a corporation's financial officials were unqualified. We have seen that these officials, particularly the treasurers, were sometimes instrumental in modernising a municipality's reporting practices. The more radical treasurers were those who had been recruited from outside and, when evaluating alternative schemes, it was common practice to survey the experience of other boroughs. This study has therefore shown that the members (often possessing knowledge of private sector accounting developments) and the officials (knowledgeable of accounting developments at other local authorities), often working in conjunction with the professional auditor, were the foundation stones for accounting change within municipal corporations.

The role of the local authority-based professional accounting bodies - the CTAI/IMTA - was to encourage the further development and, most importantly, standardisation of reporting practices commencing in 1889. Their willingness to take the leadership in such matters, in the endeavour to strengthen their own position and that of their members, has been shown to contrast starkly with the behaviour of other professional accounting bodies, operating mainly in the private sector. For example, a degree of responsibility for the form and content of published accounts was not accepted until the

ICAEW began to issue its series of *Recommendations on Accounting Principles* in the 1940's.

The contribution of the CTAI/IMTA was recognised by the Departmental Committee on the Accounts of Local Authorities, 1907, which drew attention to the fact that over the years there had 'sprung up variations of every kind and degree of importance, not merely in method but in principle' (BPP 1907, xxxvii: para. 20), but goes on to note that:

> in recent years efforts have been made, with some degree of success, by the various associations of members of authorities and their financial officers, both to raise the standard of efficiency in the keeping of the accounts and to secure a general uniformity in their presentation. (*ibid*)

The general development of accounting practice in municipal corporations may therefore be summarised as follows: innovations occurred at the level of individual corporations; some of these innovations were copied by other local authorities (with particular corporations acknowledged as at the forefront of accounting change at particular points in time); while standardization was encouraged by the professional accounting bodies. This process went far beyond the minimum statutory framework of accountability, established in 1835, which was expanded only to a small extent over the next 100 years.

NOTES

1 The forms, issued by the Board of Trade under the Electric Lighting Act 1882, s. 9, consisted of: details of loans authorised etc.; a capital account; a revenue account; a net revenue account; a sinking fund account; a reserve fund account; the general balance sheet.

2 The few extensions to accounting requirements introduced by 1935 lagged well behind the development of accounting practice.

3 A further indication of salary levels, of professionals, in the late nineteenth century is that the two partners in the firm Sully & Allott were entitled to £600 and £300 respectively in 1865 (Sully, 1951: 2).

References

Allen, Sidney E. (1912) *The Diagramatic Presentment of the Accounts of Local Authorities*, London: Gee.

Ashmole, W. H. (1901) 'The government audit of municipal accounts', *Financial Circular*, August.

Baladouni, Vahe (1986) 'Financial reporting in the early years of the East India Company', *Accounting Historians Journal*, Spring.

Baxter, W. T. (1983) 'Accounting roots and their lingering influence', in *Selected Papers from the Charles Waldo Haskins Accounting History Seminars*, edited by James F. Gaertner, The Academy of Accounting Historians.

Bird, Peter (1973) *Accountability: Standards in Financial Reporting*, Haymarket Publishing.

Bradley, Charles E. (1893) 'Corporation accounts', *The Accountant*, 16 September 1893.

Briggs, A. S. A. (1952) *History of Birmingham. Borough and City 1865-1938*, Oxford: Oxford University Press.

Bucknall, Bert (1973) 'Abstract reflections', *Local Government Chronicle*, 23 November.

Bunce, John Thackray (1878) *History of the Corporation of Birmingham: With a Sketch of the Earlier Government of the Town*, Vol. 1, Birmingham: Cornish Brothers.

Burdett, Henry C. (1890) *Burdett's Official Intelligence for 1889*, London: Spottiswoode.

Burdon, E. J. (1986) 'The antecedents of the district auditor', in *Watchdogs' Tales, the District Audit Service - the First 138 Years*, edited by R. U. Davies, HMSO.

Butterworth, George R. (1908) 'The audit of the accounts of municipal corporations', *Proceedings*.

Bywater, M. F. (1984) 'Edwin Guthrie, accountant', in *Dictionary of Business Biography*, Vol. 2 (D-G) edited by David J. Jeremy, London: Butterworths.

Bywater, M. F. (1986) 'Josiah Charles Stamp, statistician and railway company chairman', in *Dictionary of Business Biography*, Vol. 5 (S-Z) edited by David J. Jeremy, London: Butterworths.

Carson Roberts, A. (1930) *Local Administration. Finance and Accounts*, London: Harrison.

Carter, F. (1904) 'The professional auditor', *Supplement to the Financial Circular*.

Chua, W. F. (1986) 'Radical developments in accounting thought', *The Accounting Review*, October.

CIPFA Manual of Local Authority Accounting, 1987.

Clare, T. H. (1902) 'Municipal accounts', *The Accountant*, 25 January.

Collins, A. (1908) *The Organisation and Audit of Local Authority Accounts*, London: Gee.

Collins, W., D. Keenan and I Lapsley (1991), *Local Authority Financial Reporting* (The Institute of Chartered Accountants of Scotland and The Chartered Institute of Public Finance and Accountancy).

Contributed (1910) 'Municipal methods of bookkeeping: the question of the debtors' and creditors' ledgers', *The Accountant*, 14 May 1910.

Cooke, S. (1887) 'Municipal accounts', *The Accountant*, 19 March.

Coombs, H. M. and J. R. Edwards (1990) 'The evolution of the district audit', *Financial Accountability and Management*, Autumn.

Coombs, Hugh M. and John Richard Edwards (1991) *Local Authority Accounting Methods: The Early Debate, 1884-1908*, New York: Garland.

Cornwell, S. V. P. (1991) *Curtis, Jenkins, Cornwell & Co. : A Study in Professional Origins 1816-1966*, New York: Garland.

Cottrell, P. I. (1984) 'David Chadwick (1821-1895), company promoter', in *Dictionary of Business Biography*, Vol. 1 (A-C) edited by David J. Jeremy, London: Butterworths.

Cudworth, William (1881) *Historical Notes on the Bradford Corporation*, Bradford: Thomas Brear.

Dalrymple, James (1905) 'Glasgow corporation tramways', *The Accountant*, 4 March.

Davenport-Hines, R. P. T. (1985) 'Sir John Sutherland Harmood-Banner, accountant and steel manufacturer', in *Dictionary of Business Biography*, Vol. 2 (D-G) edited by David J. Jeremy, London: Butterworths.

Davies, R. U. (1986) 'The district auditors' society', in *Watchdogs' Tales, the District Audit Service - the First 138 Years* edited by R. U. Davies, HMSO.

Dicksee, Lawrence R. (1892) *Auditing*, London: Gee. (Reprinted by Arno Press, New York, 1976)

Dicksee, Lawrence, R. (1907) 'Depreciation: with special reference to the accounts of local authorities', *The Accountant*, 13 April.

Dring, T. A. (1899) 'Uniformity of municipal accounts', *Financial Circular*, February.

Edwards, John Richard (1980) *Company Legislation and Changing Patterns of Disclosure in British Company Accounts, 1900-1940*, London: The Institute of Chartered Accountants in England and Wales.

Edwards, John Richard (1985) 'The origins and evolution of the double account system: an example of accounting innovation', *Abacus*, March.

Edwards, John Richard (ed.) (1986a) *Reporting Fixed Assets in Nineteenth-century Company Accounts*, New York & London: Garland Publishing.

Edwards, John Richard (1986b) 'Depreciation and fixed asset valuation in railway company accounts to 1911', *Accounting and Business Research*, Summer.

Edwards, John Richard (1989) *A History of Financial Accounting*, London & New York: Routledge.

Edwards, John Richard (1991) 'The process of accounting innovation; the publication of consolidated accounts in Britain in 1910, *Accounting Historians Journal*, Fall.

Edwards, John Richard and K. M. Webb (1984) 'The development of group accounting in the United Kingdom to 1933', *Accounting Historians Journal*, Spring.

Edwards, John Richard and K. M. Webb (1985) 'Use of Table A by companies registering under the Companies Act 1862', *Accounting and Business Research*, Summer.

Falkus, Malcolm (1977) 'The development of municipal trading in the nineteenth century', *Business History*.

Financial Circular passim.

FIS - *Financial Information Service*, The Institute of Municipal Treasurers and Accountants, 1972.

Forster, J. W. (1907) 'Sinking funds and their relation to depreciation funds', *Proceedings*.

France, R. Sharpe (1952) 'Mr. Treasurer - Lancashire before 1835', *Local Government Finance*, July.

Friedman, L. M (1985) 'On regulation and legal process' in *Regulatory Policy and the Social Sciences* edited by R. G. Noll, Berkeley: University of California Press.

Funnell, Warwick N. (1990) 'Pathological responses to accounting controls: the British Commissariat in the Crimea 1854-1856', *Critical Perspectives on Accounting*.

Goddard F. R (1888) Report to the finance committee of Newcastle-upon-Tyne corporation, *The Accountant* 13 October.

Goldberg, Louis (1957) 'Jeremy Bentham, critic of accounting method', *Accounting Research*, July.

Greatrex, Jas. Cobden (1897) '"Income and expenditure and the district auditor"', *Financial Circular*, February.

Griffiths, A. (1904) 'The elective auditors', *Supplement to the Financial Circular*, 1904.

Guthrie, Edwin (1886) 'Corporation accounts' *The Accountant*, 30 October; 6 November.

Hammond, J. L. (1935) 'The social background 1835-1935', in Laski *et al.*

Hanson, J. D. (1989) 'Developments in Financial Reporting over the Last 20 Years', in *Financial Reporting 1988-89, A Survey of UK Published Accounts* edited by D. J. Tonkin and L. C. L. Skerratt, London: Institute of Chartered Accountants in England and Wales.

Harris, Fred E. (1893) 'Municipal accounts', *The Accountant*, 11 November.

Harris, Fred E. (1903) 'Municipal accounts - balance sheets', *Financial Circular*, August.

Harvey, Charles E. and Jon Press (1988) *Studies in the Business History of Bristol*, Bristol: Bristol Academic Press.

Helmore, Leonard Mervyn (1961) *The District Auditor*, London: MacDonald & Evans. (Reprinted by Garland Publishing, New York & London, 1990)

Hopper, Trevor (1986) 'Private sector problems posing as public sector solutions', *Public Finance and Accountancy*, 3 October 1986.

Hopwood, A. M. Page and S. Turley (1990) *Understanding Accounting in a Changing Environment*, London: Prentice Hall/ICAEW.

Hughes, William R. (1889) *Birmingham Faces and Places*, Vol. 1, Birmingham: Hammond & Co.

Hume, L. J. (1970) 'The development of industrial accounting: Bentham's contribution', *Journal of Accounting Research*, Spring.

IMTA (1908) *Income Tax and Depreciation. Correspondence with the Inland Revenue, Proceedings.*

Innes, Peter (1987) 'A look at the accounts code in practice', *Public Finance and Accountancy*, 9 January.

Institute of Municipal Treasurers and Accountants (1913) *Standard Form of Accounts for Eleven of the Main Local Authority Non-trading Accounts.*

Institute of Municipal Treasurers and Accountants (1938) *The Standard Form of Abstract of Accounts.*

Institute of Municipal Treasurers and Accountants (1955) *The Form of Published Accounts.*

Jennings, W. Ivor (1935a) 'Central control', in Laski *et al.*

Jennings, W. Ivor (1935b) 'The municipal revolution', in Laski *et al.*

Jeremy, David J. (ed.) (1984-6) *Dictionary of Business Biography*, London: Butterworths.

Jones, Haydn (1985) *Accounting, Costing and Cost Estimation, Welsh Industry: 1700-1830*, Cardiff: University of Wales Press.

Jones, J. T. (1940) *History of the Corporation of Birmingham*, Vol. 5, Pt 1, Birmingham: Cornish Brothers.

Jones, Reginald (1981) *Local Government Audit Law*, HMSO.

Jones, Rowan H. (1985a) 'Accounting in English local government from the Middle Ages to c. 1835', *Accounting and Business Research*, Summer.

Jones, Rowan H. (1985b) 'Accruals accounting in local government; some historical context to continuing controversies', *Financial Accountability and Management*, Winter.

Jones, Rowan H. (1986) 'The financial control function of local government accounting', PhD thesis, University of Birmingham.

Jones, Rowan H. (1989) 'On local government accounting history: the case of central establishment charges', *Financial Accountability and Management*, Summer.

Jones, Rowan H. (1991) Review of H. M. Coombs and J. R. Edwards (1990) *Accountability of Local Authorities in England and Wales 1831-1935*, New York & London: Garland, in *The Accounting Historian's Journal*, June 1991.

Jones, Rowan H. (1992) *The History of the Financial Control Function of Local Government Accounting in the United Kingdom*, New York & London: Garland Publishing.

Jones, Rowan H. and Maurice Pendlebury (1982) 'Uniformity, v. flexibility in the published accounts of local Authorities: the UK Problem and some European Solutions', *Accounting and Business Research*, Spring.

King, Alderman (1888) 'Corporation gas works accounts', *The Accountant*, 4 August.

Lamb, Norman E. (1925) 'A comparison of commercial accounts with municipal accounts', *The Accountant*, 29 August and 5 September.

Laski, Harold J., W. Ivor Jennings and William A. Robson (eds) (1935) *A Century of Municipal Progress 1835-1935*, London: Allen & Unwin, 1935. (Reprinted by Greenwood Press, Westport, Connecticut, 1978)

Leake, P. D. (1923) *Depreciation and Wasting Assets, and their Treatment in Computing Annual Profit and Loss*, 4th edn, London: Gee.

Lee, G. A. (1986) *Modern Financial Accounting*, 4th edn, Wokingham: Van Nostrand Reinhold.

Lee, Geoffrey A. (1977) 'The coming of age of double entry: The Giovanni Farolfi Ledger of 1299-1300', *Accounting Historians Journal*, Fall.

Leftwich, R. (1983) 'Accounting information in private markets: evidence from private lending agreements', *Accounting Review*, January.

Littleton, A. C. (1933) *Accounting Evolution to 1900*, New York: American Institute Publishing Co. (Reprinted by The University of Alabama Press, Alabama, 1981)

Livock, D. M. (1965) 'The accounts of the corporation of Bristol 1532-1835', *Journal of Accounting Research*, Spring.

Local Government Chronicle, *passim*.

MacMillan, Lord, and other lawyers (1934) *Local Government Law and Administration in England and Wales*, Vol. 1, London: Butterworth.

Marriner, Sheila (1980b) 'Company financial statements as source material for business historians', *Business History*, July.

Marriner, Sheila (1980a) 'The Ministry of Munitions 1915 - government accounting procedures', *Accounting and Business Research*, special accounting history issue.

Matheson, Ewing (1984) *The Depreciation of Factories*, London: E & F Spon.

McCall, J. H. (1930) *Municipal Book-keeping*, 3rd edn, London: Pitman.

Miller, R. F. (1905) 'Discussion on municipal accounts', *Financial Circular*, January.

Murray, Adam (1888) 'Corporation gas works accounts, depreciation and sinking fund', *The Accountant*, 18 August.

Murray, Alexander (1903) 'The Glasgow corporation accounts, with special reference to depreciation and sinking Funds', *The Accountant*, 13 June.

Napier, Christopher (1991) 'Aristocratic accounting on the Bute estate in Glamorgan 1814-1880, *Accounting and Business Research*, Spring.

Newman, Sir George (1935) 'The health of the people', in Laski *et al.*

Noke, Christopher (1981) 'Accounting for bailiffship in thirteenth-century England', *Accounting and Business Research*, Spring.

Page, Sir Harry (1985) *Local Authority Borrowing. Past, Present and Future.*, London: George Allen & Unwin.

Parker, R. H. (ed) (1980a) *British Accountants: A Biographical Sourcebook*, New York: Arno Press.

Parker, R. H. (1980b) 'The want of uniformity in accounts: a nineteenth-century debate', in *Essays in Honour of Trevor R. Johnson* edited by D. M. Emanuel and I. C. Stewart, Auckland: Department of Accountancy, University of Auckland and The New Zealand Society of Accountants.

Parker, R. H. (1986) *The Development of the Accountancy Profession in Britain to the Early Twentieth Century*, The Academy of Accounting Historians.

Parker, R. H. (1990) 'Regulating British corporate financial reporting in the late nineteenth century', *Accounting, Business and Financial History*, October.

Payne, P. L. (1967) 'The emergence of the large scale company in Great Britain 1870-1914', *Economic History Review*.

Peasnell, K (1978) 'Statement of accounting theory and accounting acceptance', *Accounting and Business Research*, Summer.

Pixley, Francis, W. (1908) *Accountancy*, London: Pitman.

Pocock, Bernard G. (1910) 'Bookkeeping and modern methods of accountancy', *The Accountant*, 6 August 1910.

Poynton, T. L. (1960) *The Institute of Municipal Treasurers and Accountants. A Short History 1885-1960.*

Proceedings of the Annual Meeting of the Corporate Treasurers' and Accountants' Institute, 1886-1900.

Proceedings of the Annual Meeting of the Institute of Municipal Treasurers and Accountants, 1901 onwards.

Ralph, Elizabeth (1953) 'Mr. Treasurer - Bristol before 1835', *Local Government Finance*, March.

Ralph, Elizabeth (1973) *Government of Bristol 1373-1973*, Bristol: Corporation of Bristol.

Robson, William A. (1930) *The Law Relating to Local Government Audit*, Sweet & Maxwell.

Rogers, Mike. (1988) 'Accounting developments', *Public Finance and Accountancy*, 8 April.

Smellie, K. B. (1968) *A History of Local Government*, 4th edn, Allen & Unwin, 1968.

Sowerby, T. (1985) *The History of the Chartered Institute of Public Finance and Accountancy*, London: CIPFA.

Stacey, Nicholas A. H. (1954) *English Accountancy 1800-1954*, London: Gee.

Staff of the County Record Office (1952) 'Mr Treasurer - Middlesex - before 1889', *Local Government Finance*, December.

Stevens, H. M (1899) 'Corporation electricity works accounts', *Proceedings*.

Sully, Alfred Victor (1951) *Towards the Centenary. Notes on the Origin and History of an Accountancy Practice. J & A W Sully and Co*, London.

Sutcliffe, Robert (1927) 'The good and bad features of some abstracts of accounts', *Local Government Finance*.

Swainson, George (1886) 'Presidential address', *Proceedings*.

Swainson, George (1889) 'Uniformity in the form of abstracts of accounts', in *Proceedings*.

Swainson, George (1893) 'Municipal accounts', *The Accountant*, 4 November.

Swainson, George (1894) 'Municipal accounts', *The Accountant*, 7 July.

Swainson, George (1895) 'Municipal capital accounts: should assets of value be depreciated as the loans are paid off?', *Proceedings*.

Swainson, George (1898) 'The Treasurers' Institute and *The Accountant*' *The Accountant*, 19 February.

Swainson, George (1901) 'The evolution of municipal balance sheets', *The Accountant*, 22 June.

The Accountant, passim.

Thomas, W. A. (1973) *The Provincial Stock Exchanges*, London: Frank Cass.

Tinker, A. B. Merino and M. Neimark (1982) 'The normative origins of positive theory and accounting thought', *Accounting, Organisations and Society.*

Towers, A. (1901) 'Depreciation of electricity works and plant', *Proceedings.*

Waller, P. J. (1983) *Town, City and Nation: England, 1850-1914*, Oxford.

Watts, Ross, L. (1977) 'Corporate financial statements, a product of the market and political process', *Australian Journal of Management*, April.

Watts, Ross, L., and Jerold L. Zimmerman (1979) 'The demand for and supply of accounting theories: the market for excuses', *Accounting Review*, April.

Watts, Ross, L., and Jerold L. Zimmerman (1986) *Positive Accounting Theory*, Prentice-Hall.

Wells, Ebenezer (1887) 'Brighton Borough auditor's report', *The Accountant*, 8 October.

Whitehead, S. (1931) *Municipal Accounting Systems*, 2nd edn, London: Pitman.

Williams, L. R. (1904) 'Depreciation, sinking funds and reserves', *Financial Circular*, December.

Wilson, John F. (1991) *Lighting the Town. A Study of Management in the North West Gas Industry 1805-1880*, London: Paul Chapman Publishing.

Wing, William (1903) 'Municipal profits', *The Accountant*, 24 January.

Woodcock, Audrey M. (1954) 'Mr. Treasurer - Leicester before 1835', *Local Government Finance*, September.

Woodhouse, Lister (1893a) 'Municipal accounts', *The Accountant*, 21 October.

Woodhouse, Lister (1893b) 'Municipal accounts', *The Accountant*, 18 November.

Woodhouse, Lister (1894) 'A borough treasurer's abstract of accounts', *The Accountant*, 12 May.

Yamey, B. S. (1960) 'The development of company accounting conventions', *Three Banks Review*, September.

Yamey, B. S. (1956) Introduction to *Studies in the History of Accounting*, edited by A. C. Littleton and B. S. Yamey, London: Sweet & Maxwell.

Yamey, B. S. (1959) 'Some seventeenth and eighteenth-century double entry ledgers', *Accounting Review*, October.

Yamey, B. S. (1982) 'Two seventeenth-century accounting statements', *Accounting and Business Research*, Spring.

Acts of Parliament

1597	Poor Relief Act, 39 Eliz. 1, c. 3
1601	Poor Relief Act, 43 Eliz. 1, c. 2
1738	County Rate Act 1739, 12 Geo. 2, c. 29
1744	Poor (Overseer's Accounts) Act, 17 Geo. 2, c. 38
1776	Poor Law (Returns) Act, 16 Geo. 3, c. 40
1782	'Gilbert's' Relief of the Poor Act, 22 Geo. 3, c. 83
1810	Poor (Overseers Accounts) Act, 50 Geo. 3, c. 49
1831	'Hobhouse's' Parish (Audit) Act, 1&2 Will. 4, c. 64
1834	Poor Law Amendment Act, 4&5 Will. 4, c. 76
1835	Municipal Corporations Act, 5&6 Will. 4, c. 76
1844	Joint Stock Companies Act, 7&8 Vict., c. 110
1845	Companies Clauses Act, 8&9 Vict., c. 16
1845	Railway Clauses Consolidation Act, 8&9 Vict., c. 20
1847	Commissioners Clauses Act 10&11 Vict., c. 15
1847	Poor Laws Administration Act 1847, 10&11 Vict., c. 109
1848	Poor Law Audit Act, 11&12 Vict., c. 91
1849	Poor Law Amendment Act, 12&13 Vict., c. 103
1854	Bradford Waterworks Act, 17&18 Vict., c. 129.
1856	Companies Act, 19&20 Vict., c. 47
1858	Bradford Corporation Act 1858, 21&22 Vict., c. 76
1858	Local Government Act, 21&22 Vict., c. 98
1868	Regulation of Railways Act, 31&32 Vict., c. 119
1870	Tramways Act, 33&34 Vict., c. 78
1871	Bradford Corporation Gas and Improvement Act, 34&35 Vict., c. 94
1871	Gas Works Clauses Act, 34&35 Vict., c. 41
1871	Local Government Board Act 1871, 34&35 Vict., c. 70
1872	Public Health Act, 35&36 Vict., c. 79
1875	Public Health Act, 38&39 Vict., c. 55
1879	Companies Act, 42&43 Vict., c. 76
1879	District Auditors Act, 42&43 Vict., c. 6
1882	Electric Lighting Act, 45&46 Vict., c. 56
1882	Municipal Corporations Act, 45&46 Vict., c. 50
1887	Local Authorities (Expenses) Act, 50&51 Vict., c. 72
1888	Local Government Act, 51&52 Vict., c. 41
1890	Accrington Municipal Corporation Act, 53&54 Vict., c. 63
1894	Local Government Act, 56&57 Vict., c. 73
1899	London Government Act, 62&63 Vict., c. 14

1900 Companies Act, 63&64 Vict., c. 48
1902 Education Act, 2 Edw. 7, c. 42
1902 Metropolis Water Act, 2 Edw. 7, c. 41
1919 Ministry of Health Act 1919, 9&10 Geo. 5, c. 21
1925 Bristol Corporation Act, 15&16 Geo. 5
1929 Companies Act, 19&20 Geo. 5, c. 23
1933 Municipal Corporations (Audit) Act, 23&24 Geo. 5, c. 28
1933 Local Government Act, 23&24 Geo. 5, c. 51
1948 Companies Act, 11&12 Geo. 6, c. 38
1967 Companies Act, c. 81
1980 Local Government Planning and Land Act, c. 65

Government Reports, Abstracts and Returns to Parliament

1715 Select Committee on Poor Rates within the Cities of London and Westminster, BPP 1715, xviii, 392
1833 Select Committee on Municipal Corporations Report, Minutes of Evidence, etc., BPP 1833, xiii, 1
1834 Royal Commission on the Poor Laws Report, Minutes of Evidence, etc., BPP 1834, xxvii-xx, xxxiv-xxxix
1835/9 Royal Commission on Municipal Corporations Report, Minutes of Evidence, etc., BPP 1835, xxiii-xxvi; BPP 1837/8, xxxv; BPP 1839, xviii
1867 General Order of Accounts dated 14 January 1867, issued by the Poor Law Board, BPP 1867, xxxiv, 51. Circular letter dated 22 January 1967, sent by the Poor Law Board with the foregoing Order, BPP 1867, xxxiv.
1870 Appendix to Report on Local Taxation, BPP 1870, lv
1874 Select Committee on Boroughs (Auditors and Assessors) Report, Minutes of Evidence, etc., BPP 1874, vii, 1
1881 General Order issued by the Local Government Board under the Public Health Act 1875, s. 245 and the District Auditors Act 1879, s. 3, BPP 1881, xlvi.
1884/5 Statistical Abstracts for the UK, BPP 1884-85, lxxxii, i
1889 Circular letter dated 29 March, sent by the LGB to County Councils, BPP 1889, xxxv: 441
1895 Joint Stock Companies, Departmental Committee Report, etc., BPP 1895, lxxxviii, 151
1900/3 Joint Select Committee on Municipal Trading Report, Minutes of Evidence, etc., BPP 1900, vii, 1

	and BPP 1903, vii, 1
1906	Local Taxation Returns 1904-5, BPP 1906, ci
1907	Departmental Committee on the Accounts of Local Authorities Report, Minutes of Evidence, etc., BPP 1907, xxxvii, 577
1909	Returns by Municipal Corporations of Reproductive Undertakings BPP 1909, xc, 1
1909	Statistical Abstracts for the UK, BPP 1909, Cd 4805, c, 1
1909	Royal Commission on the Poor Law Report, Minutes of Evidence, etc., BPP 1909, xxxvii-xxxix, BPP 1910, lv, Part II, 1
1930	The Accounts (Borough and Metropolitan Borough) Regulations 1930, SR&O 1930, No. 30 made by Minister of Health.
1932/3	Annual Report of the Ministry of Health, 1932-33, Cmd 4372
1937/8	Statistical Abstracts for the UK, 1937-38, cmd, 5627, xxvii, i

INDEX

The names of towns and cities in this index indicate references to the activities of the relevant borough, city or corporation